Gary Wood
Sept. '68

THE FORMATION OF CHRISTENDOM

The Formation of
CHRISTENDOM

>>

by CHRISTOPHER DAWSON

SHEED AND WARD : NEW YORK

PUBLISHER'S NOTE

The material in this book has been somewhat expanded from the
Harvard lectures. In the lectures themselves, Mr. Dawson sometimes used a few paragraphs from earlier books. This accounts for
a few passages which the reader may feel that he has met before.

AUTHOR'S NOTE

As the first occupant of the Charles Chauncey Stillman Chair of Roman Catholic Studies at Harvard, from 1958 to 1962, I chose as my theme CHRISTENDOM. The lectures fell naturally into three groups—The Formation of Christendom, The Dividing of Christendom, The Return to Christian Unity.

The second group, covering the period from the Reformation to the French Revolution, were published in 1965 in the book *The Dividing of Christendom*. The present book contains all the lectures of the first group, dealing with the formation of Christendom, from its origins in the Judeo-Christian tradition through the rise and the decline of the medieval unity.

CONTENTS

AUTHOR'S NOTE   *vii*

Part One: Introductory

I. INTRODUCTION TO THIS STUDY   *3*

II. CHRISTIANITY AND THE HISTORY OF CULTURE   *17*

III. THE NATURE OF CULTURE   *30*

IV. THE GROWTH AND DIFFUSION OF CULTURE   *49*

Acts of Apos 1 - 7

Part Two: Beginnings of Christian Culture

V. THE CHRISTIAN AND JEWISH IDEA OF
REVELATION   *67*

VI. THE COMING OF THE KINGDOM   *83*

VII. CHRISTIANITY AND THE GREEK WORLD   *101*

VIII. THE CHRISTIAN EMPIRE   *116*

IX. THE INFLUENCE OF LITURGY AND
THEOLOGY ON THE DEVELOPMENT OF
BYZANTINE CULTURE   *136*

X. THE CHURCH AND THE CONVERSION OF
THE BARBARIANS   *154*

Part Three: Formation of Medieval Christendom: Its Rise and Decline

XI.   THE FOUNDATION OF EUROPE: THE MONKS
       OF THE WEST   165
XII.   THE CAROLINGIAN AGE   178
XIII. FEUDAL EUROPE AND THE AGE OF
       ANARCHY   190
XIV.   THE PAPACY AND MEDIEVAL EUROPE   201
XV.   THE UNITY OF WESTERN CHRISTENDOM   214
XVI.   THE ACHIEVEMENT OF MEDIEVAL
       THOUGHT   229
XVII. EAST AND WEST IN THE MIDDLE AGES   251
XVIII. THE DECLINE OF THE MEDIEVAL UNITY   266

Epilogue

XIX.   THE CATHOLIC IDEA OF A UNIVERSAL
       SPIRITUAL SOCIETY   283
       INDEX   299

Part One: Introductory

I. INTRODUCTION TO
THIS STUDY

This Chair is a very recent foundation and hitherto the study of Roman Catholicism has not had any place in the curriculum of the Harvard Divinity School. It is easy to understand the historical reasons for this. Harvard College was one of the original institutions of this Commonwealth, and so from its foundation down to the Revolution it was essentially a Protestant institution, closely bound up with the established Church of Massachusetts and with the tradition of Puritan and Calvinist theology.

When the Divinity School was founded early in the nineteenth century, it reflected the religious changes that had passed over New England since the Revolution and found their intellectual expression in the Unitarian movement, which had its origin and center here at Boston at the end of the eighteenth century. This was essentially a liberal movement which sought to widen and liberalize theological studies, but of course its liberalism did not extend as far as Catholicism. It is true that William Ellery Channing, who was perhaps the leading influence on the Divinity School in its early days, was an advocate of Catholicity, but his conception of "Catholic Christianity" (to use his own expression) was further from historical Catholicism than even the Calvinist orthodoxy against which he reacted.

In the course of the nineteenth century the bond between the Divinity School and the Unitarian Church was gradually relaxed until in President Eliot's day it became a purely nonsectarian

3

school for the historical and scientific study of religion. Thus there was no longer any reason to exclude the study of that form of Christianity which occupies the foremost place in space, time and membership. At that time, however, such a development was inconceivable. If you read President Eliot's address on the Religion of the Fathers, which he delivered in 1909 to the Summer School of Theology here, you will see that he had very little interest in Christianity as an historical reality, or in theological study, but looked rather to the identification of religion and culture by an increasing ethical concern with social progress and public health, so that the doctor and the sanitary inspector would take the place of the priest or the bishop as the bearers and representatives of a new order.

I am far from wishing to depreciate the importance of the cultural issue—it is just the subject I am most concerned with. But I am sure that this is not the right approach. If it were so, the Divinity School ought to close and we should all betake ourselves to the School of Medicine or the School of Public Health.

Theology must be mistress in its own house. For it is an autonomous field of study which cannot be reduced to a department of social ethics, any more than the Church itself can be reduced to a philanthropic association. Since Eliot's day there has been a widespread recognition of this and a genuine movement of return towards theology and a new understanding of the meaning of the Church. This movement is common to Protestants and Catholics, and it is no doubt largely responsible for the development of the Ecumenical Movement and the growing interest in the problem of Christian reunion: a movement and an interest which are destined to become still greater in the years ahead. It is impossible to go very far with these questions without some study of Catholicism. For the existence of the Catholic Church is one of the great objective realities of history. It is impossible to write the history of Christianity without it, and it is equally impossible to understand the history of our own civilization, since Catholicism has been one of the greatest culture-forming forces in history and has left its mark on many of the characteristic institutions of Western civilization.

This cultural predominance is due above all to the fact that it was the Catholic Church that was responsible for the conversion of Northern Europe to Christianity and that it was from the Church that the Northern peoples received the elements of the new civilization which they continued to develop during the following centuries under Catholic influence. But on the other hand, it must be recognized that during the last four hundred years, ever since the Reformation, it has become increasingly difficult to realize the religious values of this common cultural inheritance. The fact that Catholicism was so deeply involved in the history and culture of the European past became a source of antagonism rather than unity, since the Protestants, and especially the Calvinists and the Puritans in England and America, had come to look on the whole Christian past for a thousand years as a dark age of religious superstition and idolatry, of a cultural barbarism out of which the reformed Churches were emerging.

Thus there arose a strong cultural antagonism as well as a religious opposition between the two halves of divided Christendom. More and more, religious differences became merged with political and national divisions, so that Catholics and Protestants no longer spoke the same language or belonged to the same social world. This tendency for religious and cultural divisions to become fused with one another was no new phenomenon in Christian history. The great schisms of the ancient Church tended again and again to follow the lines of race, language and nationality. The schism, for example, between Catholicism and Monophysitism was part of a general rift between East and West, between the Roman Byzantine Empire and its Syrian and Egyptian subjects. So too the schism between the Catholic West and the Orthodox

East in the Middle Ages was the outcome of a growing cultural and social alienation between the subjects of the Byzantine Empire and the new peoples of the West.

In such religious changes as these, the element of individual responsibility is small, sometimes infinitesimal. Granted all that the Fathers of the third and fourth centuries and all the later theologians say about schism and heresy being the greatest of evils, granted that in every actual schism and heresy some men must be individually responsible, the fact remains that the ordinary man and woman had hardly any part in this guilt. Emperors, kings and bishops made decisions, and their subjects often did not so much as know that a decision had been taken. They were carried away bodily in a kind of socio-religious landslide which changed their ecclesiastical relations with the rest of the Christian world without changing their own beliefs or traditions.

This was also true, to a greater degree than we are inclined to admit, with the changes that followed the Reformation. The new ecclesiastical map of Europe was the work not of the Reformers but of the politicians and soldiers, and the outcome of the conflict was to draw a fairly sharp line of cultural division between the Protestant North and the Catholic South. And it was against this background of European cultural division that the prevailing patterns of religion in the New World were formed. Protestant North America and Catholic South America were two different worlds which had as little to do with one another as possible. The possibility, therefore, would have been inconceivable of any fruitful religious discussion between a Harvard professor and a professor of the University of San Marcos in Peru in the seventeenth century, in spite of the fact that their educational systems shared a number of common features.

It was not until the nineteenth century that this state of separation and noncommunication came to an end, above all in the United States, which in the age of the great migrations became a melting pot of peoples and a meeting place of religions. Nowhere are the results of this process more remarkable than in New England. For it was here that the American Protestant tradition was most highly developed, dominated the culture and institutions of the region most strongly. Yet it was also the region that was most exposed to the tide of immigration which brought to Boston and the other maritime towns a new population almost entirely Catholic. As one of the historians of the movement writes, "By 1850 New England was the home of two peoples, each of whom possessed its own manner of living, its own standards of conduct and an intense hostility towards the other."[1]

In the course of the following century this cultural dualism has been gradually overcome. The two peoples have become one people sharing a common American culture. But the process of assimilation had stopped short at the church door. The social juxtaposition of the two sections of the population has not produced any close religious or spiritual contact between them. The gulf remains very wide—wider perhaps than in the Old World.

Such a situation was natural enough in the nineteenth century, when the religious difference corresponded with a division of classes; the Protestant tradition still retaining its political and social dominance, whereas the immigrants and their children were regarded as outsiders not yet fully assimilated to the American way of life. But today this is no longer the case. The great immigration of the nineteenth century has become as much a part of American history as the coming of the original colonists, and the American Catholics are an integral part of the American nation. This situation, which has arisen from the meeting of different religions within a common culture, is a distinctive American phenomenon. During the same period, however, there was another type of meeting—the encounter between Catholicism and Protestantism that occurred during the nineteenth century in England. It is a situation of which I have intimate personal knowledge and

[1] M. L. Hansen, *The Immigrant in American History* (Magnolia, Mass.; Peter Smith, 1942), p. 110.

which has had a direct influence on my own religious life. I am
referring, of course, to the Oxford Movement, which has brought
Catholics and Protestants together in a peculiarly intimate way for
120 years—a kind of civil war which divided friends, families and
schools of thought for generations but which nevertheless was
often accompanied by a considerable measure of personal understanding and sympathy.

This movement was from the beginning a distinctively Anglican movement. It arose in the very heart of the Establishment—
in those closely guarded clerical corporations which were the Oxford colleges in the days before the University Reform; and it
developed out of the attempt of the Oxford theologians of the
early nineteenth century to study and understand the nature of
Catholicism. Thus, whereas in New England the encounter of the
two religious traditions was due to an external invasion by Catholic immigrants of a Protestant population, in England it was the
result of an internal change—an intellectual revolution within the
Protestant tradition itself. It was, of course, a very small-scale
movement which began in the Common Room of an Oxford College and gradually spread to affect the University and to a limited
extent the clergy and the educated laity of the Church of England.
Nevertheless, it had very far-reaching effects on English religion,
on both sides of the religious frontier. On the one hand it transformed the spirit of the Church of England, by introducing new
liturgical ideals and new theological standards, especially in patristic studies; on the other, it influenced English Catholicism
through a continuous succession of converts—Newman and Faber,
Ward, Manning and Robert Wilberforce, Lord Ripon and Lord
Bute, Coventry Patmore and Gerard Manley Hopkins, a stream
which has continued to flow down to our own day, producing men
like Ronald Knox in our own time.

The great and perhaps unique importance of this movement is
not, in my opinion, to be found in its intellectual achievement, although in the case of Newman it produced an original religious

thinker of outstanding merit. It is rather the intimacy of social contact that it produced between Catholics and Protestants for the first time since the Reformation. This operated in two different ways—first by division within a family, so that Newman had a Unitarian brother and an Anglican brother-in-law, and the Wilberforces were divided between one influential Anglican bishop and two Catholic brothers—Robert, the friend of Manning, and Henry, the friend of Newman. Most surprising of all was the division of the Stanley family, where the elder brother became a Mohammedan, the younger brother a Catholic bishop, and the sister was the mother of Bertrand Russell. Secondly, and this was perhaps more important, was the division between friends—the fact that Manning had been the intimate friend of Gladstone; Newman retained his personal friendship with Keble, Pusey and Dean Church; W. G. Ward was the friend of Tennyson and Dean Stanley and many other eminent Victorians. Thus although the social gulf between Protestants and Catholics in England continued throughout the nineteenth century, it had already broken down on the higher intellectual and social levels, so that a bridge had been built over the gulf which can never be broken down. I think —I speak of the matter as an interested party—that this movement marks a turning point in Western religious history during the last 130 years, and it is all the more significant because it was the work of a very small minority whose influence has worked like a leaven on the surrounding masses.

The situation in America is, of course, essentially different. Here it has been a question of the impact on one another of two great masses of population with different religious traditions. It has not been a question of intellectual and religious contact, for these two groups have ignored each other's existence on the religious level. The result, however, has been similar or parallel. For in both cases there has been a meeting of long-separated religions within the same culture: in the one case by a process of religious discovery or rediscovery, and in the other by the sheer force of circumstances which has driven two different populations together to form a new social unity. In both cases the dominant traditions of culture were Protestant, with much in common, since they shared the same linguistic tradition and to some extent the same religious literature, especially the English version of the Bible. But on the Catholic side there were considerable differences between England and America. In the United States, and especially in New England, the predominant influence has always been Irish, and the case of a convert like Orestes Brownson was very exceptional. In England, on the other hand, the Catholic Revival has always been predominantly English and the influence of the Irish immigrants was secondary, though far from unimportant.

Thus it would seem that the American and English expressions in this matter are complementary and we can learn a good deal from one another. In comparison with America the English development has been a very small affair, but it represents just the element lacking here—the continuous century-long dialogue of Catholic and Protestant on a relatively high level of culture. But from the sociological point of view it is the American development that is the most important, owing to the magnitude of the forces involved and to the fact that the culture in which they operate is still mobile and plastic. Thus the co-existence of these two different religious traditions within a common society has become one of the characteristic features of modern American culture and must be accepted as the starting point of our inquiry.

It must be admitted that from the religious point of view this pluralist type of society involves serious disadvantages. It tends to make religion a matter of secondary importance. It means that man's first duty is not religious but political. We do not ask whether a man is a good Christian or a good Catholic, but whether he is a good citizen or a good American. If he is this, his religion is a matter that concerns only himself—and there is even a danger that it may be treated as a private hobby, so that a man's church membership will mean no more than his membership of a golf club.

On the other hand, a pluralistic society of this kind has certain compensating advantages for religion. It lays a greater weight of spiritual responsibility on the individual Christian. He can no longer afford to take his religion for granted. If he is to stand firm amid the shifting sands of democratic opinion, he must know where he stands and what he stands for, and since he is in constant contact with other forms of Christianity, he must know where they stand too—where they agree and where they differ and how far it is possible or necessary to co-operate with them in defense of their common interests and common spiritual values.

All this involves a considerable intellectual as well as a moral effort, an effort which it is difficult for us to make at the present day when the whole tendency of modern popular education and public opinion is concentrating our attention on the problems of our modern secular democratic and technological culture which force themselves on our attention, through the thousand brazen tongues of organized publicity. No doubt here at Harvard we are in an exceptionally favorable position. This school is an oasis of theological culture in a secularized world, and it possesses a tradition of theological study that reaches back to the very beginnings of American history. Nevertheless, in the past this tradition of study, however widely it was conceived, did not include the study of Catholicism. In the past it was easy to study Christian theology and the history of Christianity with no more than a passing glance at the history of Catholicism, which remained an alien world.

This was the case not only here in America but in Europe also, so that one of the most learned Protestant scholars of my youth— Adolf Harnack—singles it out as one of the outstanding defects in the German system of higher education: "I am convinced," he wrote, "from constant experience of the fact that the students who leave our schools have the most disconnected and absurd ideas about ecclesiastical history. Some of them know something about Gnosticism, or about other curious, and for them worthless, details. But of the Catholic Church, the greatest religious and political creation known to history, they know absolutely nothing, and they indulge in its regard in wholly trivial, vague, and often directly nonsensical notions. How her greatest institutions originated, what they mean in the life of the Church, how easily they may be misconceived, and why they function so surely and so impressively: all this, according to my experience, is for them, apart from a few exceptions, a *terra incognita*."[2] The present generation has seen a great change in this respect, as the foundation of this Chair proves. For such a foundation would have been inconceivable a hundred or even fifty years ago. Only a hundred and thirty years ago a New Englander wrote that the foundation of a Catholic Church in Boston was as astonishing as the foundation of a Protestant chapel in the Vatican would be! But the result of generations of neglect still remains, and those of you who are to become ministers must expect to find the state of ignorance which Harnack describes still prevailing among the great majority of the laity.

Therefore in coming to the study of Catholicism, I think we should approach it, in Harnack's phrase, as *terra incognita*—an unknown spiritual continent that we have to explore. For whatever we may think of the truth of Catholic doctrine or the worth of Catholic spiritual values, there can be no question but that they represent a very considerable slice of history and spiritual experience. If we are ignorant of it, we cannot claim to be fully educated.

If, however, we intend to explore this unknown continent, we shall need the help of a number of different disciplines. A purely theological approach is not enough, though it is this that calls for the greatest effort of understanding. But we must also study it as historians, since of all the forms of Christianity, Catholicism is the one that is most deeply committed to history; finally and above

2 *Aus Wissenschaft und Leben* (Giessen, 1911), Vol. I, p. 97.

all, as students of culture who seek to comprehend an unfamiliar
way of religious life. For when Protestants and Catholics meet,
the first thing that strikes them about one another is not a different set of theological dogmas but a different pattern of religious
life. Even where we use the same words (and we do use the same
words—Church and Sacrament, Faith, Grace, and Redemption),
they are built into a different structure of religious institutions and
practices, produce different social and intellectual results.

Mutual understanding of these differences in culture between
Catholics and Protestants is one of the most necessary preliminary
tasks that has to be undertaken to prepare the way for Christian
unity. Its pursuit, however, is a most difficult study because it involves so many factors that are not really religious at all. Every
culture is a complex phenomenon, and it is only too easy to mistake a political or material factor for a religious or spiritual one.
All through history we are confronted with the spectacle of political or social conflicts masquerading as religious, and it is this confusion of motives that imparts so much social bitterness to many
apparently religious controversies. But it would be a great mistake
to conclude that all cultural differences are irrelevant from the
religious point of view. For religious faith must have some effect
on human behavior, even if it has much less effect than religious
people demand or expect. In some cases, especially perhaps in
modern America, the demand is mainly for a higher standard of
behavior. But in the past and in other parts of the world, religion
has made much more explicit demands of human life—as, for example, with the Jews, who required that every detail of human
life should be regulated and fenced round by religious laws.

Now Catholicism has always had this kind of external impact
on culture. It has been a highly institutionalized and socialized
form of religion and has expressed its beliefs and aims through
every material and spiritual channel available. This, of course, has
been one of the main criticisms of Catholicism in the past, both
at the time of the Reformation and still more in the eighteenth

century. Religious and social reformers alike objected to Catholicism as being too extravagant. It took too many working days away for the celebration of feasts, locked up too much capital in unproductive forms of expenditure.[3] But whatever view we may take about these objections, there is no doubt that this Catholic tendency to express itself outwardly in institutions and culture is an advantage to the historian and the student of culture because it gives them a great mass of material evidence to study.

It has always been the tendency of Catholicism to incarnate itself in culture. In every age and in every people we find Catholicism expressing itself in new forms and institutions which are typical of the particular culture. At first sight, this seems inconsistent with the authoritarian discipline and the centralized unity of the Catholic Church. But in fact this is not the case. For the forms of Christianity that are most conservative and least amenable to cultural change are the smaller dissident denominations such as the Russian Old Believers or some of the religious groups that are to be found in this country, such as the Schwenckfeldians or the Dunkers.

But in the case of Catholicism, each successive age of the Church manifests a different aspect of Catholicism and, one may say, a different form of Catholic culture. As I see it, there have been six of these ages, each lasting three or four centuries with the exception of the sixth, which is still in process. There is (1) the Early Christian period, from the beginning to the Peace of the Church; (2) the Patristic period, from the conversion of the Roman Empire to the rise of Islam; (3) the age which saw the formation of Western Christendom and the predominance of the Byzantine culture in the East, from 600 to 1000; (4) the Great Age of Medieval Culture, which lasted from the movement of ecclesiastical reform in the eleventh century to the Renaissance and the Reformation; and (5) the age of Divided Christendom—the age of the Counter-Reformation—the Baroque culture from the Council of Trent to

[3] Cf. C. W. Eliot on Cathedrals.

the French Revolution. Finally there is (6) the Modern Age, of which we do not know the duration or the end.

Each of these ages has its own distinctive character and expresses a different facet of Christian culture. Yet none of them is final, so that we cannot say that a particular period, like the fourth or the thirteenth century, is the complete expression of Catholicism. Still less can we make our own age the standard of judgment, as though the achievements of the past ages were only valuable in so far as they contribute something to the modern world. As Ranke said in reply to the Hegelian philosophers of history, *"Jeder epoche ist unmittelbar zu Gott."* "Every age stands in immediate relation to God."

This is the familiar problem of historical relativism about which so much has been written in recent years. The position of the Catholic, however, is different from that of the secular historian in as much as he is spiritually committed to each and all of the cultures of the past in so far as they are Christian, since he believes in the persistence of a spiritual tradition which preserves its identity through all the changes of history and culture.

This view, however, of the multiplicity of Christian culture does not necessarily involve an evolutionary theory of religious development. The course of this development is rather to be explained as St. Augustine describes it in his thesis of the Two Cities, as due to the continual conflict between two opposing spiritual and social principles. Every age is an age of crisis for the Christian Church. In every age the Church has to face a new historical situation whose problems cannot be solved in the same way as in the past. The crisis can be met only by creative spiritual action, and in so far as the Church is successful, she creates a new way of life, since it is bound up with the particular situation which confronted her at that particular period.

Today it is clear enough to everyone, Catholic and non-Catholic, Christian and non-Christian, that we are living in an age of crisis. It is perhaps dangerous to attempt to define the nature of this crisis too precisely, since the issues are so complex and far-reaching. Nevertheless it is, I think, possible to say that in this country and in this century we have reached a decisive point in the movement towards Christian unity. As I have been saying, during the three centuries from the Reformation to the nineteenth century, Catholicism and Protestantism have stood over against one another in hostile camps, each pledged to the other's destruction. Each of the nations of Europe and the new peoples of America took one side or the other, and hounded out any member of their own society who made a different choice, so that every Catholic in a Protestant country and every Protestant in a Catholic country was regarded as a potential traitor and a public enemy.

But today in America we find a totally different situation. Within one society all the different forms of religion and irreligion coexist and share a common culture. There is no longer any exclusive dominion of one form of Christianity, not even an exclusive dualism of Catholic and Protestant, but a spectrum in which every shade of religious belief is represented. Churches and rites which in the past and in the Old World existed in such isolation that they were hardly conscious of one another's existence have been brought face to face with one another here and jostle one another in the streets of the modern Babylon. In some respects we are reminded of the situation at Rome and Alexandria in the first centuries of Christianity. The situation is painful in as much as it exposes the scandal of Christian disunity in its full dimensions. Yet at the same time it offers an opportunity such as has never existed in the world before for Christians to meet and understand one another. Without such an understanding there can be no hope for a return to Christian unity. But it is not enough for Christians to meet one another in an atmosphere of good will. What is most necessary is an understanding in depth, and this cannot be achieved without a serious and persistent effort of study and research.

II. CHRISTIANITY
AND THE HISTORY OF CULTURE

The history of Christianity is the history of a divine intervention in history, and we cannot study it apart from the history of culture in the widest sense of the word. For the word of God was first revealed to the people of Israel and became embodied in a law and a society. Secondly, the word of God became Incarnate in a particular person at a particular moment of history, and thirdly, this process of human redemption was carried on in the life of the Church which was the new Israel—the universal community which was the bearer of divine revelation and the organ by which man participated in the new life of the Incarnate Word.

Thus Christianity has entered into the stream of human history and the process of human culture. It has become culturally creative, for it has changed human life and there is nothing in human thought and action which has not been subjected to its influence, while at the same time it has suffered from the limitations and vicissitudes that are inseparable from temporal existence.

Now there are those who reject this mingling of religion and history, or Christianity and culture, since they believe that religion is concerned with God rather than man, and with the absolute and eternal rather than the historical and the transitory. We certainly need to recognize how important this aspect of religion is and how man has a natural sense of divine transcendence. And we know from the history of religious thought that we do actually find religious men of this kind—men who seek to transcend human nature by the flight of the Alone to the Alone, in the words of the Neo-Platonist philosopher, and who find the essence of religion in the contemplation of pure being or of that which is beyond being.

But this is not Christianity. Although Christianity does not deny the religious value of contemplation or mystical experience, its essential nature is different. It is a religion of Revelation, Incarnation and Communion; a religion which unites the human and the divine and sees in history the manifestation of the divine purpose towards the human race.

It is impossible to understand Christianity without studying the history of Christianity. And this, as I see it, involves a good deal more than the study of ecclesiastical history in the traditional sense. It involves the study of two different processes which act simultaneously on mankind in the course of time. On the one hand, there is the process of culture formation and change which is the subject of anthropology, history and the allied disciplines; and on the other there is the process of revelation and the action of divine grace which has created a spiritual society and a sacred history, though it can be studied only as a part of theology and in theological terms.

In Christian culture these two processes come together in an organic unity, so that its study requires the close co-operation of Theology and History. It is obvious that this is a difficult task, but it is a very necessary one, since there is no other way of studying Christianity as a living force in the world of men and it is of the essence of Christianity that it is such a force and not an abstract ideology or system of ideas. Thus the history of Christian culture differs in nature from *Church History*. The latter has been for centuries a highly specialized study, which stands somewhat outside historical categories. There is a sense in which the Church as a theological concept stands outside and above history. But during recent centuries Church History has been regarded as equivalent to ecclesiastical history—a kind of special subject which lies outside the margin of political history. From this point of view Church History is something only to be found in societies and periods which distinguish clearly between Church and State or between Religion and Politics. It therefore tends to become a somewhat arbitrary and artificial subject, since the history of the modern churches is conditioned and limited by the history of the state to which in a sense they belong. And where there is a complete separation of Church and State, as in the United States in the nineteenth century, Church History becomes emptied of significant content, as one sees in the (typical) nineteenth-century, twelve-volume *American Church History Series*. It has no scientific unity, so that finally it is held together only by the corporate traditions of the particular sect.

Church History can, of course, be studied scientifically from the sociological angle as Ernst Troeltsch did in his famous book, but this leads to theological difficulties.

The study of Christian Culture, on the other hand, does not involve this dualism, since the concept of culture is a unity which embraces both Church and State. Culture is a universal phenomenon which can be made the subject of scientific study, and since every historic culture has its religious aspect, Christian culture is not exceptional in this respect, but is comparable to the other cultures which are associated with a particular religion, the culture of India, for example, or the culture or cultures of the Moslem peoples. The distinctive institution of Christian culture, a Church of its nature independent of the political society is irrelevant to the comparative scientific study of cultures.

On the other hand, we cannot ignore the great difficulties which affect the higher study of religion today and the change of intellectual climate which has become increasingly unfavorable to the study of the relations between religion and culture in the modern world and the modern university. For theology has long since lost its position as a dominant faculty in the university and as an integral part of the general educational curriculum. It continues to exist on sufferance only as a specialized ecclesiastical study designed for the clergy.

Consequently the student in a modern university may be totally ignorant of religion, so that he requires a very elementary type of instruction, whereas the theological student has no need of elementary studies, since he already takes for granted (however unjustifiably) the validity of some particular form of Christian theology. This is a very unfortunate state of affairs, for it creates a gap between university studies and theological or ecclesiastical studies which it is nobody's business to fill. There is, as I see it, a no-man's-land between the university and the theological school.

It is clear that in this situation there is no longer any common religious tradition. One can no longer take for granted any common principles or truths that are generally accepted. We have to allow for the existence of four or five fundamentally different points of view in religious matters, secular and Christian, Protestant and Catholic. And there is a wide difference in the secularist camp between the liberal humanists and the dogmatic materialists. And again in the case of the Protestants, there is a division between the liberal Protestants, who represent the old humanist Unitarian tradition, and the neo-orthodox, who seek to revive the traditions of the Reformers and the Puritan theologians. So wide is this gap that it is difficult to find anything, above all in regard to natural theology and the nature of religion, on which these two agree.

In these circumstances the only remaining approach that is common to all potential students is the phenomenological approach, which is both social and psychological. On the one hand, everyone is agreed that Christianity and Catholicism are momentous sociological and historical facts which have had a profound influence on human history; while on the other, religion is a psychological phenomenon which is almost universal and common to all cultures and periods, so that it is impossible to question its subjective human importance. Moreover, in spite of the almost infinite diversity of religious phenomena, there are certain elements that are common to them all and which may be regarded as essentially religious. Such are worship and prayer and such also is the rite of sacrifice.

Worship implies the existence of some power other than man which men venerate as greater than themselves, while prayer and sacrifice imply the existence of a twofold relation by which man establishes some channel of communication with the higher power. This unknown power which man instinctively and naturally worships is habitually known as God or the Gods; in fact, the phenomenological definition would be: "God is what man worships, and what man worships is God."

It may be objected that this notion of worship tells us nothing about the real nature of the object of worship. Indeed we know from the study of comparative religion that man is capable of worshipping almost anything from the highest to the lowest, and it has been the great task of philosophy to purify man's concept of the divine and to liberate the mind from the service of idols— from the worship of all that is not God. And this process is in some respects parallel to the work of revelation, which has also consisted in the purification of man's natural religious instincts by the elimination of false objects of worship and the redirection of the human mind towards God, the one ultimate and absolute transcendent reality.

To modern man the word "God" means far more than this, for it has come to us enriched by the content of the Jewish and Christian revelations, so that it has acquired moral and personal values which have become almost inseparable from the word. But even apart from this religious tradition, the word has also acquired a philosophical meaning and has been enriched by centuries of philosophical tradition.

For Western religion and theology represent a synthesis of two different traditions, the Hebraic tradition of religious revelation, which is represented by the Bible, and the Hellenic tradition of metaphysical or natural theology, which has been accepted by the Christian Fathers and theologians as a kind of rational propaedeutic or foundation for theology in general. Nevertheless, this philosophic tradition was by no means lacking in religious content, a content supplied by the aesthetic or mystical contemplation which was characteristic of it. On the one hand, Greek philosophy contemplated the universe as a visible order which was the reflection or creation of a spiritual principle—the divine logos; on the other, it saw the spiritual world as an ascending order or hierarchy of intelligible forms which culminated in absolute good and absolute unity, so that for the Stoic and Neo-Platonist the intellectual disciplines of science and philosophy found their final end in a religious act of contemplation which resembles that of the mystic.

This Hellenic theology was readily adopted by the Christian theologians, as we see in St. Augustine's early writings, in the Greek Fathers, and in the works that pass under the name of Dionysius the Areopagite. There has been a somewhat similar development of philosophic theology in modern times during the seventeenth and eighteenth centuries, the product of deism and rationalism. But this modern movement tended to lose its religious character as soon as it became separated from the Christian tradition, and it soon ceased to show any trace of those contemplative or mystical tendencies which characterized the older Hellenic tradition. Consequently in modern times the historical alliance between natural theology and the theology of revelation has been broken, except in the case of Thomism, which has held fast to the old tradition.

Modern Protestant theology, especially the school of Karl Barth, has utterly rejected as false and worthless any rational or philosophical theology and has refused to admit the existence of any form of genuine religious knowledge except that contained in biblical revelation and apprehended by divine faith. If, however, we accept the Barthian principle, the complete nonexistence of any natural channel of understanding between God and Man, it is difficult to see how such an act of faith can be elicited except from those who already possess some kind of faith. The God who spoke to Abraham was not a totally unknown being. He was one who was accepted or taken for granted as the God of his fathers.

There is, however, nothing in natural theology, or the philosophic idea of God, which contradicts or excludes the idea of Revelation. For once granted the existence of a divine transcendent being who is the object of human veneration and prayer, it is very conceivable that such a being should intervene in human life by manifesting his will to man or by establishing some channel of communication. The difficulty of this belief lies not in its abstract possibility or probability but in the apparent impossibility of man understanding the divine purpose or mode of operation. For it is obvious that if man were to possess the power of influencing the behavior of insects by scientific means, the insect would be incapable of understanding what was happening, and that it could only be explained from the human standpoint. The difference, however, between God and the rational animal is far greater than that between man and the insect world, and it is inconceivable that the human intelligence can understand the process of divine revelation, even though he is the recipient of it. God is not only the giver of revelation, he must also create the vehicle for its transmission and the faculty for its reception.

The Christian takes for granted the idea of a *word* that is in some sense common to God and Man, but this is a truth of faith, which is unattainable by human reason. It involves what the Greek theologians term a divine "economy"—an adaptation of divine truth to the means of human understanding, whether by inspired Scripture, as in the case of the Hebrew prophets, by a historical dispensation, as with the history of the Chosen People, or above all by the central mystery of the Incarnation by which the Word of God is embodied in a historical Person who is both human and divine. This marks a new beginning in the history of the human race—a new creation by which humanity is raised to a higher spiritual level which transcends the natural life and the rational knowledge of the human animal.

It is true that man can make a rational study of this higher dispensation and of the content of revelation—the study which is traditionally known as theological science. But the function of rational enquiry is strictly limited in this study, since the data on which it rests are the truths of faith which transcend the sphere of reason. On the other hand the extension of revelation and the life of the Incarnate Word in the Church creates, as it were, an intermediate zone between God and Man which is "supernatural" in the language of the theologians but which is nevertheless as accessible to experience and rational study as the rest of human history. This penetration of a divine language into the world of human discourse is a conception which is difficult for the modern secular intelligence to understand or assimilate, but it is an essential part of the Christian's view of history and no less, or hardly less, of the Jew's and the Moslem's. Indeed to some extent it is a feature of all the great world religions; even those like Hinduism which seem at first sight to be based on metaphysical theories and speculations.

Those religions which are, or claim to be, founded on pure reason have never had any deep influence on the spiritual life of humanity or on human history. The Natural Religion or Deism of the eighteenth-century philosophers, the Positivist Religion of Humanity in the nineteenth century, or the more recent attempts to construct a purely ethical religion are of some interest for the light that they throw on contemporary culture, but they have all failed completely in the religious field as attempts to provide a human substitute for the historic religions which have required faith in a divine revelation.

For genuine religion, even in its simplest and most elementary forms, goes deeper than reason. It reaches the deepest level of the human soul and consciousness. For there is in human nature a hunger and a thirst for the transcendent and the divine which cannot be satisfied with anything less than God, and since the knowledge of God exceeds the measure of human reason, the student of religion is brought up, at the very outset of his study, against a fundamental difficulty which seems insurmountable. As St. Anselm wrote, "This is the inaccessible light, yet it is even closer to the soul than the soul itself. It cannot be grasped, yet it is most intimately present. . . ."

This paradox has been understood and fully accepted by the great Christian thinkers of the past, like St. Augustine, for example, St. Gregory Nazianzen or St. Anselm. Indeed all naturally religious minds, even without Christianity or any revealed religion, recognize the divine being as a mystery which transcends human intelligence and is inaccessible to reason and yet at the same time as a reality which is mysteriously present to the human soul—an all-embracing reality "in which we live and move and have our being."

But this is not to say that the knowledge of God is purely intuitive and that reason is unable to affirm the truth of God's existence. Human thought has always been conscious of the need for a first cause or an absolute principle of being in order to explain the existence of the natural world or of contingent being. A world of pure becoming, without beginning or end, without cause or ground, would be a chaos in which the mind itself could not exist. Thus man is conscious of the existence of a principle of unity and order in the universe, and he could not introduce this principle into the world of reason, of science and philosophy, if he was himself merely an irrational product of a world of disorder—a flying spark in chaos.

This conception of the universe as an intelligible order has inspired the whole development of Western science, alike in classical antiquity and in modern times; and in the formative period of modern science from Galileo to Newton the belief in God as first cause and creator of the order of nature, as well as the supreme governor and lawgiver of the moral world, formed an essential part of the scientific *Weltanschauung*. No doubt these beliefs became rationalized and anthropomorphized by the philosophic vulgarizations of Deism and the theological vulgarizations of Christian theologians, like Paley. Nevertheless, as Professor Whitehead pointed out in his *Science and the Modern World*, the achievements of modern science are hardly conceivable without this theological preparation which established a link between the subjective order of human reason and an objective rational order in the universe which derives its origin and guarantee from its divine creator.

The secularization of modern science and of the civilization which is its creation is due in part to the fact that the natural theology of the eighteenth century was discredited by its superficial character, but even more to the effects of the specialization which has made the modern scientist a technologist rather than a "natural philosopher." A technological civilization like our own has a natural tendency to secularism, since it extends the limits of social control so far as to make man a prisoner within an artificial world of his own creation.

In the past, especially in the peasant cultures, man was immediately dependent on nature and his life was intimately bound up with the natural cycle of the seasons, of seed time and harvest, and this dependence on powers which lay outside his own control made him familiar with the conceptions of mystery and divine providence. Today mystery has been banished from man's daily life. If things go wrong, he looks for help to the government or to science rather than to God and religion. No doubt this has freed mankind from the burden of superstition and irrational fear, but it has also left man at the mercy of his own inventions and has substituted the omnipotence of that man-made monster, the bureaucratic, technocratic state—the New Leviathan—for the mystery of nature and the power of God. When these new powers are developed to their full extent by the social organization of the mass media of communication and by scientific methods of psychological control, the secular state becomes almost automatically totalitarian, so that no room is left for man's spiritual freedom.

Nevertheless the essential nature of the human situation has not been changed by the advent of science and technology. Modern man may deify these things and set up a religion of "Scientific Humanism" which offers the utopian prospect of unlimited progress. But all such constructions are inevitably fragile, since they are dependent on human will and passion as well as intelligence, and we have seen in our own generation how the irrational element in human nature may prove stronger than scientific intelligence, so that it perverts all the resources of technological civilization to lower and destructive ends.

Human nature always retains its spiritual character—its bond with the transcendent and the divine. If it were to lose this, it must lose itself and become the servant of lower powers, so that secular civilization, as Nietzsche saw, inevitably leads to nihilism and to self-destruction. If we look at the world today in isolation from the past and the future, the forces of secularism may seem triumphant. This, however, is but a moment in the life of humanity, and it does not possess the promise of stability and permanence. The lesson of history suggests that there are enduring traditions which may become temporarily obscured, but which retain their underlying strength and reassert themselves sooner or later. Such is the case with the tradition of Christian culture today. It has not disappeared, but it has undergone a great loss of social influence and intellectual prestige owing to the social changes of the last two centuries which have transformed the educational systems as well as the political and economic order.

This temporary diminution of the religious element in our culture greatly increases the difficulty of our task. It makes all theological study uphill work—swimming against the current of our age. In many cases it amounts to a real occultation of the divine, a loss of that spontaneous sense of religious values which has been a normal part of human experience in the past. It may even seem as though God has turned his face away from our civilization and has left the world in spiritual darkness.

But we know not only from our faith as Christians, but from the dispassionate study of the history of human culture, that this is a transitory and exceptional state of things. Sooner or later the tide is bound to turn and man will recover his sense of spiritual values and his interest in ultimate realities. Indeed, I believe that this is already happening and that the present century is witnessing the reawakening of the religious consciousness. That is only a private opinion, for no one is able to know where his own generation is going. The great spiritual changes that alter the course of history have their origin below the level of consciousness and are not fully manifest until their fruit is ripe. We shall see in the course of these studies how often this has been the case, both for good and evil.

In studying this process of the waxing and waning of Christian culture through successive ages of history, we are studying a natural process which follows the normal processes of culture formation and change. But we are also studying a theological mystery —the life of Christ in history—the progressive penetration of humanity by divine revelation, the extension of the Incarnation in the life of the Church. This is the aspect of Catholic doctrine which is being more fully worked out by the theologians of our own day than ever before, and it is important that we should gain a general idea of it before embarking on a study of Catholic culture. It is stated very simply and concisely in the late Cardinal Suhard's pastoral letter on *The Church Today*.[1] It has been developed more fully by a whole series of modern writers like Karl Adam, Henri de Lubac and Yves Congar, but the theological foundations were established by the theologians of the Catholic

[1] Published in English as a paperback by the Fides Press.

revival in the nineteenth century like J. Adam Moehler and M. Scheeben. If we study this idea or complex of ideas, it will take us very deep into theology but at the same time, I think, will throw a new light on Christian culture and on the Christian view of the meaning of history.

III. THE NATURE OF CULTURE

The study of Christian Culture is of unique importance, first, because it is necessary for the understanding of our own past and our own traditional form of culture, and secondly, because of the exceptional wealth of material that is available for study. We not only possess an unparalleled wealth of religious documents dealing with the development of Christianity for nineteen centuries, we also have a continuous historical tradition through which these documents can be situated in place and time to a degree that hardly exists in the case of other great cultures. In India, for example, we have also a great wealth of religious writings, but we often have not, at present, detailed knowledge of the past history of Indian cultures. In other cases we have a full historical tradition, but there are gaps in the religious records, so that our knowledge of Christian culture is both deeper and wider than that of the other contemporary world cultures.

Above all owing to the progressive expansion of Christian culture, first by the conversion of the Roman and Roman-Byzantine empires, secondly by the conversion of Northern and Western Europe, and thirdly by its extension to the New World and its association with the progress of world exploration and scientific discovery, it has acquired a universal world-wide extension such as no other civilization has ever possessed. It is true that the full development of these world tendencies has been post-Christian rather than Christian, but the modern ideological world movements—the Enlightenment, Liberalism, Democracy and Socialism are none of them comprehensible without a knowledge of the Christian culture which underlies them all. It is a very complex field of study.

This historical culture of Christendom lies midway between the modern transformation of Western culture into world civilization, which is the characteristic phenomenon of the present age, and the early forms of Christian cultures which grew up in the Mediterranean world and in Western Europe more than fifteen centuries ago.

But before we attempt to trace the history of this development or those developments, we must first go back to the beginnings and study the nature of culture and the process of cultural evolution and change.

Culture is the name which has been given to man's social inheritance—to all that men have learnt from the past by the process of imitation, education and learning and to all that they hand on in like manner to their descendants and successors. And this involves all that man has and is. For if it were possible to separate an individual altogether from his culture and his social inheritance, he would be an idiot, living in a private world of formless feelings, but lower than the beasts, since he would no longer possess the guidance of instinct which is the basis of animal behavior. Hence any human society, however primitive or barbarous, is a culture, and it is the cultural process or tradition that creates the society. Even very simple and primitive people can recognize intuitively the diversity of cultures and the importance for each people of its own way of life. Miss Ruth Benedict quotes a striking instance of this from a conversation she had with a Californian Indian. "In the beginning," he said, "God gave to every people a cup, a cup a day, and from this cup they drank their life. They all dipped in the same water, but their cups were different. Our cup is broken now. It has passed away."[1]

And in the same way no society can become so advanced that it transcends culture. For a civilization is also a culture which follows the same laws of growth and development as a primitive culture, although it may have become incomparably larger and more com-

[1] *Patterns of Culture* (Boston, Houghton), p. 33.

plex. Thus the distinction between culture and civilization is somewhat arbitrary. I myself follow the tradition which defines civilization as the stage of higher culture which is associated with the growth of cities and the use of writing—the form of culture which first appeared in Mesopotamia and Egypt some five thousand years ago and which has gradually spread, until it has come to embrace the whole inhabited world. Thus civilization is a comparatively recent phenomenon despite the enormous changes that it has produced in human life, and in man's natural environment. If our knowledge of the past continues to advance as it has done in the last hundred years, we may be eventually able to write the History of Civilization as we write that of a state or a nation today. Five, or even ten, thousand years are only a moment in the life of nature. Yet the whole course of human civilization and all its works are only a matter of a few thousand years. And it is a continuous process which is still in the course of development, so that when we study the growth of civilization, we are living witnesses of the greatest of all the works of creation.

How was this miracle achieved? How did it come about that man alone among the countless forms of life that have existed on this planet has been able to separate himself from the other animals, to change his ways of life and finally to transform the world in which he lives? We do not know exactly how and when man came into existence. But we do know that humanity is vastly older than civilization: that its beginnings go back to a remote geological period and that even in those remote ages human nature differed from that of the other animals and the social foundations were already being laid on which eventually civilization would be constructed.

It is not merely that man is a social animal, for as Aristotle, the father of anthropology, recognized, other animals—bees, for example—are social also. It is, as Aristotle says, that man, unlike other animals, is endowed with the gift of speech. And it is the faculty of speech which distinguishes human communities from animal societies, communities which are not ruled entirely by instinct but possess wider possibilities of communication and understanding and social co-operation.

In the beginning was the word. Language is the gateway to the human world, which is also a moral world, since, as Aristotle again says, "the word shows what is advantageous or harmful and likewise what is just and unjust. For this is peculiar to man, as compared with the other animals, that he alone has a sense of good and bad, of just and unjust, and the rest. And the community of these things makes the household and the city." Language is far older than civilization. Its origins go back to the beginnings of human culture and consequently to the origins of humanity itself. But we do not know when this all-important event took place, and the history of language affords no clue. For there is no such thing as a primitive language and no evidence of any intermediate stage that prepares the way for the emergence of the higher forms of speech. The assumption of the early ethnologists that the lower we go in the scale of culture the poorer language becomes, so that savages have small vocabularies and little grammar, has not been justified by modern research. On the contrary, the languages of backward peoples, like their forms of social organization, all show a remarkable degree of development and complexity.

No doubt it is possible and even probable that manlike creatures existed on earth for ages before the development of language. Indeed many anthropologists believe that language emerged only in the last stages of the Pleistocene age, and that the makers of the hand axes of the earlier paleolithic industries did not possess the faculty of speech. But in that case they were not men in the full sense of the word, and we must place the advent of *homo sapiens* relatively late in the archeological record. The fact that it is possible to teach apes to ride bicycles, but impossible to teach them to talk, suggests that it is the use of language rather than the use of tools which is the essential characteristic of humanity. The word, not the sword or the spade, is the power that has created human culture. The invention of language was the first step in the process that has led to civilization, and none of man's subsequent inventions—agriculture and the domestication of animals, the use of metals and the discovery of writing, the building of the city and the state—important as these have been, can be compared with this archetype and source of all cultural activity.

Without language it would have been impossible for man to free himself from the domination of instinct which determines the unchanging life of non-human existence. For it is only by language that he can pass on the memory of past experience to future generations and thus form the accumulation of knowledge which is the condition of culture. Language is the organ of social tradition and the means of social communication, and these are the two main factors which make human culture possible.

A culture is a common way of life by which man adjusts himself to his natural environment and his economic needs. It is conditioned by the same fundamental factors as those which condition the development of an animal species—the interrelation of organism, environment and function. But the mere differentiation of societies by these factors is not a sufficient explanation of culture. It was the coming of language that added a new dimension to society and imparted a new, specifically human, character to all its elements. Language enlarges the physical inheritance of the blood by a spiritual inheritance of memory and tradition which makes the community conscious of its existence in the past, of its historic continuity and experience, by which it is possible to generalize individual inventions and transmit acquired techniques. Finally and above all, it enables man to think, to create a new world of imagination and reason. This intelligible or psychological world is no less important for culture than the outer world of social and economic activity. Each influences the other, and the culture represents the whole complex of life and thought—ways of behavior, forms of belief, standards of value, techniques and symbols and institutions—which constitutes the life of the community.

Thus there is no reason to suppose that the simplest and most primitive forms of culture and the earliest forms of language were limited to material and utilitarian ends. Matter and utility are abstract concepts, and to primitive man a prayer or a magical formula may be more "useful" and is certainly more powerful than a digging stick or a hut shelter. From its origins human culture has always been purposive and dynamic. But since language lies at the root of culture, this dynamism is embodied in the power of the word no less than in work and war. The more primitive the level of culture, the greater seems to be the importance that man attaches to *names*. The giving of names and the knowledge of names seem to primitive peoples to involve an element of power or control over the thing named, and are closely analogous to the symbolic forms of ritual and art which are similar expressions of the dynamic character of primitive culture, as we can see most clearly in the cave paintings of the later paleolithic period which express the dynamism of primitive culture with extraordinary force and immediacy. Art, gesture, and language are all closely related to one another as forms of symbolic communication, but of the three, language is far the most important, since it interpenetrates the whole of culture and there is nothing in culture which is not reflected in it. Culture and language are inseparable aspects of the same process, so that it is impossible to regard one of them as existing without the other. Moreover, they resemble one another in being organized systems which possess a certain unity of form. A language is not a mere collection of words, it is, as Sapir says, "a self-contained, creative, symbolic organization" which may be compared to a mathematical system.

In the same way a culture is not a mere collection of "culture-traits"—customs, habits, institutions and beliefs—it is an organized system of social life and behavior with its own laws and principles of development which are distinct from the external biological, geographical and ecological forces that condition its existence. Thus a culture and its language taken together form an autonomous world of meaning and existence which is indeed the only world of which the individual is conscious. It is man-made in the sense that it is the product of man's creativity and his power of symbolic communication. But the individual is not aware of this, since both culture and language are unconscious processes in which men are immersed from their earliest infancy and on which this earliest social and intellectual activity is based.

Man lives within this many colored and patterned web which his culture and history created as the bee lives in its hive and the coral-building polyp on its reef. But while all insect societies and all animal societies of the same species are always the same and maintain their form unchanged from age to age, all cultures are different and possess powers of expansion and change, of adaptation and assimilation, which do not exist in other forms of life.

This new principle of dynamic change which is peculiar to human culture is, of course, inseparable from the gift of language without which the evolution of culture is impossible. No doubt when we look at such a distinctive and highly differentiated form of culture as that of ancient Egypt or eighteenth-century China, and see how it has kept its identity and its special institutions and traditions intact for thousands of years, it is easy to conclude that these are closed worlds which are immune to change and external influence. But this immunity is always relative. Even the more stable and static cultures are constantly changing, and the more advanced they are the greater is their power of assimilation and receptivity. For a culture, unlike an animal way of life, is an open system—open not only to new knowledge and new ways of behavior but also to other cultures, if a bridge of communication and social contact can be established between them.

This is made possible, above all, by the fact that the individual is not bound to his culture, as an animal is bound to its way of life, by instinct and innate habit. Culture and language are acquired by social communication, so that the culture of the individual depends not on birth but on education, and individuals can be transferred from one culture to another by a process of re-education and social adaptation. Even when a culture attempts to shut itself off from its neighbors by a deliberate policy of exclusion and isolation, like Japan in the seventeenth and eighteenth centuries, or Soviet Russia today or yesterday, there are always individuals who for one reason or another seek, or are compelled, to break through the barriers, as prisoners or hostages, mercenaries or traders, missionaries or renegades, and such individuals may become the agents of cultural diffusion and change. A captive enslaved in a barbarian raid like St. Patrick may become the starting point of a movement of religious and cultural change which transforms the whole culture.

Thus the human world is a world divided into a multiplicity of different cultures which are separate but not incapable of communication. All of them, from the highest civilization to the lowest form of barbarism, possess certain common elements: language, religion and ritual, morality, art, technology, social organization and law and custom, education or enculturation; and in many cases this element of cultural parallelism is so clear that the observer is inclined to translate the forms of an alien culture into terms of the culture with which he is familiar.

Thanks to this basic similarity, it is comparatively easy for a conquering people or class to unite different cultures within a common political structure based on tribute or servitude, and this may be the starting point of a process of cultural diffusion and fusion which ultimately produces a new culture. And if this culture is sufficiently advanced for man to be conscious of the process of change, as was the case with the World Empires of antiquity, the idea of a common civilization begins to emerge: that is to say, a standard norm of culture which can be applied to a number of different societies which are not necessarily uniform but which all possess a certain degree of cultural communication. From this it is only a step to the conception of *"the civilized world,"* a world which is regarded as coextensive both with social and geographical reality, "the inhabited world" or *oecumene* of the Hellenistic Greeks, the *orbis terrarum* of the Romans, or "All that is under Heaven" of the Chinese. Thus for thousands of years, man in East and West has seen the world and humanity in this unitary but limited way; as a circle of light surrounded by a rim of darkness, an island of civilization in a sea of barbarism.

But in the beginning, every people must have regarded itself in this way and every culture must have appeared to be the only right way of life for reasonable men to follow. This is suggested by the frequency with which tribal or national names are identical with the word for "men," as though anyone outside the community of common speech and culture was not fully human. Indeed the original development of distinct languages involves a high degree of cultural isolation, since they could never have come into existence if their speakers had not lived in separate worlds of thought and culture without regular intercourse with other societies. Thus the language community is the most fundamental of all human groups, language the most fundamental element of culture. As the use of language distinguishes man from the other animals, so it is the formation and use of a particular language which distinguishes one culture from another.

This, it is true, is no longer the case when we come to these higher forms of culture which we call civilization. For here we may find examples of common cultures with different languages, as, in the case of Breton, Provençal and Basque, which are still spoken by minorities who share the common heritage of French culture. Nevertheless these linguistic differences correspond to ancient cultural divisions and point back to an age in which Breton and Provençal and Basque had a separate cultural existence. On the other hand, a change of language is invariably accompanied or preceded by a change of culture, so that the disappearance of the old native languages of Southern Europe before the advance of Latin is a conclusive proof of the importance of the cultural changes which took place under the Roman Empire. In the same way minor linguistic phenomena, like the borrowing of words and names, are valuable as evidence of cultural influence and diffusion, as for example the Turkish loan words in Russian or the considerable Arabic element in modern Spanish.

Of all the elements of culture, language is the most susceptible to exact scientific study. It is far easier to trace the exact distribution of languages and the relationship between them than the relations between institutions or forms of social behavior. And thus while the study of culture is still in its infancy and still subject to infantile disorders, the study of language has long established its status and its methodology. Indeed the study of language has always been the standard humanist science and provides a pattern for the other, younger social sciences.

In contrast to language, the study of physical anthropology and the concept of race have comparatively little relation to culture, though they have often exercised a very deleterious influence on its study. No doubt in remote prehistoric ages the segregation which was the condition of racial differentiation was equally a condition of cultural differentiation, but this period is so remote that we can say nothing about its cultural characteristics. In any case, culture follows its own path of development, which is independent of physical race. We find some Negroes who belong to the Islamic culture and others who share the same cultures as the Anglo-Americans or the Portuguese Brazilians, while even the autochthonous cultures of Negro Africa contain elements derived from non-Negro sources. It is true that the consciousness of common blood, whether this is real or fictitious, has a most important influence on social and cultural unity, but this is a comparatively short-term factor and the resultant unity is tribal or national, not racial. Indeed a nation of mixed racial stock may possess a stronger consciousness of unity and a greater measure of cultural heredity than one of relatively pure racial stock.

Unfortunately in modern times there has been a tendency to exaggerate the racial element in nationality and to attribute the most highly valued elements in the tradition of a culture to the innate characteristics of a supposedly superior race, and this is perhaps the greatest single factor making for mutual intolerance and antagonism between nations and civilizations. In reality a culture has far more resemblance to a language than it has to a race. As a language is a particular way of communication created by a group of men inhabiting a common area to express its common needs and ideas, so a culture is a particular way of behavior developed by a group of men to enable them to live successfully in their particular circumstances and environment. Language is, of course, itself only a part of culture, but it is the aspect of culture which is most sharply defined and most clearly separate from non-cultural elements. Culture as a whole is far more difficult to grasp, since it involves many different factors, so that a highly developed culture is perhaps the most complex phenomenon that it is possible to study. Even in the case of the simplest known or conceivable culture there are at least four of these factors without which it cannot exist.

There are: (1) the sociological factor, or the principle of social organization; (2) the geographical or ecological factor—the adaptation of culture to its physical environment; (3) the economic factor —the relation between man's "way of life" and the way in which he "gains his living"; and (4) the moral factor—the regulation of human life in conformity with some system of values and standards of behavior.

The first of these factors is so fundamental that many anthropologists have treated it as the sole or predominant subject of their study. For unless we understand the structure of a society and the nature of the social unit we have no concrete basis for the study of culture. Culture and society are interdependent aspects of a single reality, neither of which can exist without the other. In Aristotelian terms every culture is the form of a society and every society is the matter of a culture. No doubt it is possible to conceive of societies without culture: indeed we know that such societies actually exist, but these are animal or insect societies and no human society can exist without cultural form. And the same is true of the family, which is the ultimate social unit. The biological family exists among animals and can attain a comparatively stable form. But the human family is a cultural as well as a biological unit, since it is the center of an organized system of social relations and the basis of an elaborate cultural superstructure.

Throughout human history, from the lowest forms of primitive barbarism to the most advanced types of civilization, the family has retained its importance as the foundation of society and the organ of cultural continuity. In primitive societies its importance is even greater than in modern times, since their life is spent in smaller groups which are organized to a greater or lesser extent by the principle of kinship. In these little societies the family is the center of the social order. It is fenced round internally with an elaborate code of marriage restrictions and regulations and it ramifies outward into a succession of kindreds, until the widest socio-political unit that they know—the tribe or the people—is often regarded as a sort of super-kindred which traces its origin to a mythical common ancester. Thus some of the most primitive societies known to us, notably the natives of Central Australia, possess an extraordinarily complex system of kinship and social organization.

This emphasis on the family and the bond of kinship is also to be found in primitive religion. For the family in the past was not only a link between the present and the past; it was also a bond between man and the spiritual world. The cult of the dead and the worship or veneration of sacred ancestors have had an extraordinarily wide and deep influence on human culture. This is still alive today in the family worship of orthodox Hinduism and in Confucian China, and it extends backwards in time to the very origins of culture. Our knowledge of prehistoric man is largely derived from the evidence of tombs and burials, all of which possess a religious significance and which in some cases, as in the Megalithic monuments of Western Europe, remain an impressive witness to the power of the prehistoric religion that created them.

Existing primitive peoples show a similar preoccupation with the cult of the dead or the divine ancestors. An outstanding example is the totemic cult of the Australian, which is bound up on the one hand with the pattern of his social organization and on the other with the sacred world of the divine ancestors, so that the traditional Australian culture is centered in the consciousness of a sacred community which envelops man and nature, the present and the past, in timeless ceremonial patterns expressed in the tribal rites and dances.

Of course the family and kinship are not the only forms of social organization even in the most primitive societies. The factor of place or physical environment and that of work or economic function also influence the structure of society and the form of culture from the beginning. The most elementary form of society known to us, the "band" of hunters or food gatherers, which must have existed even in paleolithic times, owes its unity not only to the bonds of kinship but to the unity of the territory in which and on which they live. The size of the band is limited by the food resources of the territory, and the common enterprise of the hunt or the food quest imposes forms of co-operation and social discipline. These differences of environment and differences in the sources of food supply and the ways in which they are exploited involve a differentiation of culture. It does not need much scientific study to realize that mountaineers differ from plainsmen and that the way of life of men who hunt big game on the steppes will be very different from that of those who gather nuts and bananas in the tropical forest.

Nevertheless it was not until the anthropologists and ethnologists got to work that it was possible to understand how great were the achievements of the primitive cultures, and with what art and technical mastery man adapted his way of life to the requirements of a natural environment that often seemed hostile to human survival. In this respect no culture is more striking than that of the Eskimo peoples of the Arctic, which is remarkably ancient and stable, distinctive and highly specialized. It is a classical example of the way in which a people can learn to adapt itself to a harsh and unfavorable environment by creating a specialized way of life adapted to its peculiar circumstances.

Eskimo culture is a work of art—a primitive art of hunting and dog sledging, of blubber lamps and bone harpoons, of kayaks and igloos, but a work of art none the less, since it uses the poor material that nature provides with admirable skill and artifice in order to construct a social world which is the best of all possible worlds for the Eskimos—who call themselves *Innuit,* The Men.

This process of cultural creation was not simple or inevitable. It has a long history behind it, which anthropologists and archeologists are beginning to unveil. There are in fact a number of Eskimo cultures, and some of them have followed different paths, like that of the People of the Deer, who have based their way of life on the caribou rather than the seal, or that of the more advanced Point Barrow Eskimo in Alaska, who have learnt to hunt the whale. In the course of their history they must have had their inventors, their men of genius, their artists and poets, but their activities have been inevitably restricted to a narrow field by the rigid limits imposed by the difficulties of their physical environment, so that individual achievements sink into insignificance compared with the great communal achievement which has enabled them to survive.

Here we see the problem of culture defined in its simplest terms, as the adaptation of human society to its natural environment by a special way of life embodied in a series of related activities and techniques. And this adaptation of Eskimo culture to its physical environment is so close that at first sight the Eskimo seems to be as much a natural product of that environment as the other creatures of the Arctic. In fact, however, Eskimo culture is a work of art not of nature, and is comparable to the procedure by which a modern Polar expedition equips itself for its special task, with the difference that the Eskimos are not explorers but colonists who have created a series of techniques by which they are enabled to exist permanently beyond the frontiers of what we regard as the habitable world. A similar process of adaptation to an unfavorable environment is to be seen in most of the primitive cultures, which are generally marginal developments that have found a way to exist, like the Bushmen in the South African desert or like the Pygmies in the inner depths of the tropical forests.

Throughout the whole course of man's development we can discover no culture so primitive that it is entirely determined by the natural influences of environment and economic function, nor yet any that is so advanced that it is not conditioned by these influences. Even today in our cosmopolitan technological civilization, societies and cultures are still influenced by their natural environment and by their local economies as well as by their language and their form of social organization. We are inclined to lump all these differences together under the description of national character and national tradition. But nationality is simply a convenient label which simplifies the complexity of cultural realities to conform with the unitary pattern of the modern state, while at the same time it represents a reversion to primitive ideas in that it owes its appeal, like the old tribal units, to the myth of common blood and common ancestry. But the real unity of culture is not to be found in blood or soil or economic class and function. Each of these factors has its importance, but none of them suffice to explain the inner nature of a culture. In addition to all these elements of partial community, a culture is also and above all a moral order and involves a community of values and standards which provide its internal or moral principle of unity.

It is obvious that men cannot live together without observing rules, and there is no scientific basis for the traditional prejudice that regarded savagery or barbarism as synonymous with lawlessness. On the contrary it would seem that primitive societies exact a stricter standard of conformity from their members than civilized ones and that the life of the individual is regulated by an intricate system of prohibitions and rules of behavior. These rules are neither purely utilitarian nor exclusively moral in our sense of the words. The distinction between manners, morals, laws and rites which is clear to us does not exist in primitive society. All of them form part of one great whole which embraces every aspect of the life of the tribe and the individual. Nor is this order confined to man alone, it also extends to the life of nature and is related to the supernatural or divine forces that rule the universe.

It may be objected that this concept is too abstract and "metaphysical" for primitive man to grasp. But there is nothing abstract about the notion that there is a connection between the life of human society and the life of nature or in the belief that there are sacred and mysterious powers on which both nature and man are dependent. Such ideas are to be found in all primitive cultures, and everywhere the highest social importance is attached to the sacred rites and ceremonies by which the help of the higher powers can be obtained and the order of human life co-ordinated with the cycle of nature. The famous cave paintings of Cantabria and Dordogne are a visible proof of the existence of such rites in paleolithic times, and they suggest comparisons and resemblances with the religious practices of modern hunting peoples—for example, the cult of the animal guardian spirits among the American Indians.

The culture of the European paleolithic hunters is unique owing to the high quality of its artistic achievements. In comparison the culture of modern "primitives" like the Australians seems comparatively impoverished. But this Australian culture shows an equally rich development in another direction through its elaborate system of totemic ceremonies and rites which preserve the contact of the tribe with the sacred world of its divine ancestors on which the life of nature also depends. Thus primitive culture is a complicated interwoven structure of rites and sacred techniques, symbols and myths, beliefs and traditions, moral standards and norms of behavior which binds the people together as a moral unity.

Within their unity the individual lives his life. It gives him his status and his function, teaches him what he has to do and why he has to do it, and gives him the sense of partnership in a community which transcends his personal experience.

Indeed the famous passage that Burke wrote on social contract applies far better to the primitive cultures than it does to the eighteenth-century state—"It is not a partnership in things subservient only to the gross animal existence of a temporary and perishable nature. It is a partnership in all science, a partnership in all art; a partnership in every virtue and in all perfection. As the ends of such a partnership cannot be obtained in many generations, it becomes a partnership not only between those who are living but between those who are living, those who are dead and those who are to be born."[2]

Yet the universality and spiritual completeness of primitive culture have one drawback, and it is of a fundamental nature. A primitive culture is intelligible only to itself. To the world outside it has no meaning and no value. When the primitive is performing his great rites of world renewal which re-establish the life of the earth and protect it against famine and earthquake, the stranger sees nothing but a group of dirty savages prancing round with uncouth gestures and unintelligible sounds.

If the stranger is a man of understanding, he may eventually become aware of the meaning of these rites and learn to appreciate the spirit of the culture. But before this has happened, it is only too likely that the culture will have been destroyed and the tribe scattered by the forces of change. For a culture is a very fragile thing, and the delicate balance of its social structure is overthrown as soon as its spiritual limits are broken and its individual members lose their faith in the validity and efficiency of its moral order. The alien power may be a humane one: it may be careful to respect the lives and property of the natives. But in so far as it introduces its own law and destroys or disregards the traditional moral values of the

[2] *The Works of Edmund Burke*, Vol. III, *Reflections on the Revolution in France* (World Classics), p. 106.

people, it cuts the vital roots of their culture and saps their social vitality.

The world of primitive culture is a world of isolated units. Each culture is a closed world, which can survive only so long as it remains an intact whole. But if this is so, how did the higher civilization ever come to exist? We cannot ignore the existence of these civilizations, for they now fill the world, and the remnants of primitive culture only exist, as it were, on sufferance. Yet there was a time when these great cultural empires that we call civilizations did not exist and there was nothing in the world but a mass of primitive cultures, all small, all weak and all separated from one another by apparently insurmountable barriers of linguistic and cultural diversity. The fact that this change has actually taken place shows that there is a dynamic element in human culture which is capable of breaking down the barriers that divide men from one another and of creating increasingly wider areas of communication.

The civilizations, no less than the simpler cultural units, also involve a principle of moral order. We see this with exceptional clearness in the case of China—that is to say, Confucian China, which was preserved for more than two thousand years by what seemed to be a changeless norm based on the Confucian code of ethics and the Confucian standards of behavior. But the same thing is true of the other world cultures of India and Islam, of Tibetan Buddhism, of Judaism and finally of Christianity in the West.

For the world civilizations are the great beaten highways on which mankind has travelled through history, and in every case men believed that they were following a divinely appointed path. In the past they believed, and many of them believe today, that their civilization is not merely a form of social organization that has been developed through the centuries, but that it is dependent on a transcendent divine order which has been revealed in the inspired writings of the prophets and lawgivers who laid the foundations of their culture. All the great civilizations were originally, as the

Moslems say, People of the Book. They all possess a corpus of sacred scriptures, each has its own sacred language and its sacred order of teachers, who are trained in the study or interpretation of the sacred writings and rites, Confucian scholars in China, Brahmins in India, Ulema in Islam, Jewish rabbis and Christian priests.

Thus there has been a close relation between the world civilizations and the world religions which have endured for ages which we must study if we are to understand the spiritual ideals that have inspired these great cultural unities which far transcend the national and political unities, which we are apt to regard as the ultimate social realities.

Nor has the advent of a world technological civilization changed this. For it is a purely external order. It does not bring with it a new moral order. On the moral plane, therefore, influences of the old religious traditions still exist and mould man's ways of thought and behavior.

IV. THE GROWTH
AND DIFFUSION OF CULTURE

We have seen that what distinguishes human culture from the ways of life of animal societies is that it is not an instinctive way of behavior common to all the members of the species but something which can be learned and handed on from man to man, from group to group and from generation to generation. This unique human power of tradition or the transmission of culture is due to the faculty of language and to the processes of thought which are inseparable from it. Indeed language is itself a tradition, not an innate faculty, and it is by means of this linguistic tradition that the continuity of a culture is maintained and that the process of cultural change is made possible.

All the different elements of culture possess this traditional character. The economic life with its associated techniques is a tradition which is learned by the individual and transmitted by the society, so that the latter comes to possess an accumulated wealth of techniques which have originated at different periods and have been preserved by the tradition of the culture. In this way the most modern forms of culture are still dependent to a great extent on the technical achievements of the remote past. The domestication of cattle, the cultivation of grain, the plough and the wheel, are all integral elements of modern economy, and they have come down to us by a continuous tradition which had its origin in neolithic times.

So too with regard to the forms of social organization that determine the structure of society. Every social institution represents a stereotyped social tradition, and tribes and nations and states are the embodiments of continuous social traditions. Finally, every human religion from the lowest to the highest is a spiritual tradition, and it is through these spiritual traditions that man first attained the consciousness of culture. The rise of the higher cultures in the Near East, as also in Central America at a much later period, is closely related to the development of the institution of the temple and the temple priesthood—that is to say, a professional class of experts devoted to the maintenance of the sacred tradition of ritual order. The invention of writing, which has been of such inestimable importance for the transmission of culture, was the work of this class, and in this way the religious tradition became the source of historical tradition in the strict sense. Indeed there is no limit to the survival and influence of a cultural tradition when once it has attained literary expression, as we see in the cases of Chinese classical culture in the East and Greek and Latin classical cultures in the West.

These literary traditions imply an immense increase in the width and depth of social memory and cultural consciousness, but they are not indispensable. Every culture, even the lowest, has its tradition, and every tradition which depends on language rather than on direct imitation implies the existence of a social memory. Moreover, even in non-literate cultures this social memory may become so highly developed that it can make a society conscious of its past in a strictly historical sense, as in the case of the royal genealogies and the stories of migration and settlement characteristic of the Polynesians and of some African peoples like the Baganda and the Yoruba. It is therefore impossible to assume that historical consciousness and historical tradition are confined to the higher forms of culture.

On the other hand it is clear that cultural tradition transcends historical tradition. The higher cultures embody an accumulated wealth of tradition, much of which has been handed down from peoples whose very names are forgotten. We still know very little of the laws of cultural inheritance and of the processes by which a tradition is transmitted from one culture to another. Yet this is one of the most important of all factors in the maintenance and extension of culture. We are apt to regard "tradition" as a negative conservative, inhibiting force, but in reality it is the chief organ of change. Not that a tradition changes automatically by its own internal law of development, but because culture contact or the meeting of two different cultural traditions sets up a process of change which may go so far as to produce a new culture. Modern anthropology and archeology have tended steadily to increase the importance of the factor of external diffusion as against internal evolution in the development of culture; and the chief agent of diffusion is tradition. Indeed, when we speak of cultural diffusion, we mean the expansion or the communication of a tradition.

The importance of this traditional element in cultural change is often concealed by our terminology, which confines the word to the element in the culture process that resists change. But if we consider a typical case of culture change in historical times, such as the reorganization of the Russian States by Peter the Great or the modernization of Japan in the second half of the nineteenth century, we shall see that it is not just a case of the subversion of the traditional order by a revolutionary change, but rather of a conflict between two different traditions, one of them native and the other imported, so that the defeat of one tradition is the victory of another.

The importance of this kind of culture change is particularly obvious in modern times. During the last four centuries the civilization of the non-European world has been completely changed, not by internal evolution but by a movement of culture diffusion which had its origins in Western Europe. In some cases, as in America, this diffusion has taken the form of an actual transfer of population from Europe by colonization, accompanied by the wholesale transplantation of social institutions and economic techniques. In other cases, as in India and Indonesia, it was associated with European conquest and political control, while elsewhere, as in nineteenth-century Japan, there has been a voluntary acceptance of the European cultural tradition by Asiatic peoples in order to preserve their independence or to increase their power. Finally there are innumerable examples of the spread of European culture among the more backward peoples by European trade or missionary enterprise, on the one side, and by a spontaneous process of imitation or borrowing, on the other.

These simple forms of cultural diffusion by colonization, conquest and contact have always been of primary importance and can be traced back to prehistoric times. But they only represent one side of the process of culture change. They do not explain the process of internal change within the tradition itself, which is the source of the most fundamental changes in culture—the origin of agriculture, of the city, of writing, of Greek philosophy or modern science. This is the problem of cultural invention or discovery—the most mysterious and impressive factor in the culture process, and it is so often associated with the equally mysterious and impressive factor of individual genius that we cannot be surprised that man tended in the past to attribute it to some god or divinized hero who was regarded as the ultimate source of culture—like Athena, for example, the goddess of wisdom, who sprang fully armed from the brain of Zeus, or Prometheus the Fire-bringer, who stole the gift of fire from the jealous gods.

Even in modern times where the origins of a discovery can be traced in some detail, there has been a similar tendency to exalt the creative initiative of the individual genius and to make the history of science or exploration a pageant of great names. But while it is impossible to deny the reality of individual genius and the creative achievement of individuals, this is only one side of the story. A genius is also the member of a society, the bearer of a culture and a link in a tradition. Unless the conditions of his culture are favorable, the genius cannot do his work, and even if he did, his discovery would be sterile. For inventions are steps in a cumulative process. They do not appear out of the void, but originate as part of a social process of co-operation and competitive thought and discussion. And so behind the individual invention we have an inventive tradition and an inventive culture. Examples of these creative traditions are to be seen in the tradition of Greek thought and science from the sixth to the third centuries B.C., the European scientific tradition from the sixteenth century onwards, and the Western technological tradition since the eighteenth century. It is clear that similar creative traditions existed in the remote past, notably at the dawn of history in Mesopotamia, where so many of the elements of higher civilization appear to have originated simultaneously or in close association with one another about the beginning of the third millennium B.C.

The origin of these creative traditions is the greatest problem of human history, and the further back we go into prehistory the more mysterious does it become. Nevertheless in the case of the cultures for which we possess historical evidence, it is possible to point to certain general factors that seem to favor exceptional cultural originality. Cultural activity, for example, seems to be greater in regions of mixed race and social tradition where the opportunities for culture contact and cross fertilization are greatest; above all, in cases where two clearly marked and socially conscious culture traditions meet one another and become fused in a new cultural unity. Secondly, we have the case of the conquest of a relatively advanced and ancient culture by a "young" and vigorous people which adopts the conquered culture and acts as an agent for its diffusion. A striking example of this process is the adoption of Carolingian Latin and Slavonic Byzantine culture by the Viking settlers in North France and Western Russia in the eleventh century A.D., which was followed by the remarkable cultural expansion of the Normans in the West and the Kievan Ros in the East. Thirdly, there is the case of the non-military and non-colonial expansion of a higher culture by religious conversion and missionary activity, examples of which are the introduction of Latin Christian culture into Ireland and England in the fifth and seventh centuries, the introduction of Indian Buddhism into China and of Chinese Buddhism into Japan.

But however important such processes of culture contact may be, they are always secondary. They do not explain the genesis of the component factors, and we cannot exclude the possibility of a creative tradition arising on virgin soil without the external stimulus of culture contact or racial mixture. But it is difficult to find any example of this, since the only modern examples that we can study of "pure" cultures which owe nothing to culture contact tend, in the nature of the case, to be stationary and uncreative.

Every culture, in fact, has two different aspects. It can be seen as an organic growth, like a tree which is rooted in the earth and produces its leaves and fruit by the inner law of its own specific nature; or it can be seen as a continuous stream of tradition, like a river which is fed from a hundred springs and grows wider or deeper as it flows from the tributaries that it receives on its course. Thus when we study a culture sociologically as an organic whole we emphasize its vital unity and idiosyncrasy; and when we study it historically, as the development of a tradition, we stress its comprehensive and cumulative character—its capacity to borrow elements from other cultures, to accept and assimilate other cultural traditions.

Both these aspects are present to some degree in every culture. All cultures are in some degree closed systems or orders of life which resist change and eject what is alien to their traditions as barbarous or impious. Nevertheless even the most conservative culture has its history and its process of change, and none of them is entirely unaffected by the diffusion of culture unless it is completely isolated by geographical factors, as in the case of Tasmania before the nineteenth century. It is true that the borrowing of particular elements from an alien culture may not involve any lessening of cultural tension and conflict. The acquisition of the horse and the musket by the Indians of the Plains entirely transformed their culture, but at the same time it increased their resistance to European penetration. As a rule, however, the diffusion of material culture is accompanied by some diffusion of spiritual culture. The trader and the missionary follow in one another's traces, and the same process may have taken place in prehistoric times, when the diffusion of the megalithic religion or cult prepared the way for the development of trade and the diffusion of material culture along the Atlantic seaboard of Western Europe. In the past the anthropologists have concentrated their attentions on the simplest forms of culture, such as those of the Australian aborigines, the Melanesians and the Red Indians. Yet even so, they have found these cultures far more elaborate in structure and richer in tradition than the explorers and missionaries who first discovered them had ever guessed.

But the higher cultures with which the historian is concerned are immeasurably more complex, so that the academic historian has tended in the past to confine himself to the straightforward narration of events and to the criticism of the literary sources on which his narrative is based. But this was not always so. Herodotus was not only the "father of history" but also the father of ethnography and even of a kind of comparative study of cultures, while Thucydides and Polybius were not unaware of the sociological forces that determined the course of history. Nor is it so today, for in modern times history has steadily extended its range and depth, so that it is no longer satisfied to record events but devotes itself to the complete understanding of the past by the study of institutions and of the economic and religious development of society.

Thus history and anthropology alike culminate in the study and history of culture, and neither of them can dispense with the help of the other. In fact, the advance of scientific archeology is making the distinction between history and prehistory more and more artificial and we are coming to realize the essential unity and continuity of human culture.

This is to be seen with exceptional clarity in the case of ancient Egypt, which represents the most perfect example a culture which preserved its identity and individuality intact for thousands of years. Here we see the river of tradition flowing down like its mother the Nile from the darkness of prehistoric barbarism through the Old, the Middle and the New Kingdoms until at last it reaches the

Middle Sea and the Hellenistic world city of Alexandria. The study of this great tradition has become a special science which owes more to archeology than to literary evidence and is just as much concerned with predynastic prehistory as with the dynastic history of the second millennium B.C., and on the other hand it has thrown a flood of light on Hellenistic and Roman culture and on the religious movements of the "ancient" world (which from the Egyptian point of view was a very modern world indeed).

Throughout the entire course of its history and extending back into prehistoric times the factor which gave Egypt its internal unity and cohesion was its highly original and distinctive religious tradition, which dominated the whole social and political order of Egyptian life and without which Egyptian culture is inconceivable. As I have written elsewhere:

"It is indeed one of the most remarkable spectacles in history to see all the resources of a great culture and a powerful state organized, not for war and conquest, not for enrichment of a dominant class, but simply to provide the sepulchre and to endow the chantries and tomb-temples of the dead Kings. And yet it was this very concentration on death and the after-life that gave Egyptian civilization its amazing stability. The Sun and the Nile, Re and Osiris, the Pyramid and the Mummy; as long as these remained, it seemed that Egypt must stand fast, her life bound up in the unending round of prayer and ritual observance. All the great development of Egyptian art and learning grew in the service of this central religious idea, and when, in the age of final decadence, foreign powers took possession of the sacred kingdom, Libyans and Persians, Greeks and Romans all found it necessary to 'take the gifts of Horus' and to disguise their upstart imperialism under the forms of the ancient solar theocracy, in order that the machinery of Egyptian civilization should continue to function."[1]

When this religious tradition came to an end in the fourth century A.D. with the conversion of Egypt to Christianity, a cultural revolu-

[1] *Progress and Religion*, p. 116.

tion took place that was far more fundamental than any political catastrophe. The whole life of Egypt was changed. Nevertheless the result of this revolution was not what we might have expected. In spite of nearly a thousand years of Hellenistic domination, Egypt did not become merged in the ecumenical culture of Byzantine Christendom for which she seemed predestined by this lengthy period of Hellenistic influence. She was submerged and absorbed by the new world religion of Islam which had its origin in Arabia and spread with lightning speed over Western Asia and North Africa, from the Oxus and the Indus to the Atlantic and the Pyrennees, and thenceforward she has remained an integral part of this great "Afroasian" cultural unity.

This is a classical example of the kind of problem which requires a new science of culture history or culture change for its solution, since it transcends the scope alike of history, anthropology and comparative religion, as hitherto understood. Yet it is a genuine problem, which might be elucidated, if the scattered contributions of numerous independent specialisms could be co-ordinated and focused upon it.

And the same is true of the resultant world culture itself. There is no real history of Islam, nor can a knowledge of Islamic theology, however profound, fully explain Islamic culture. Nevertheless Islam is a reality which is a part of the contemporary world and extends in space from the Atlantic to the Pacific and from Central Asia to Central Africa. To the superficial observer it may seem a ramshackle collection of races and peoples—Arabs and Turks, Indians and Persians, Negroes and Berbers—with no material or social principle of unity. Yet, for all that, Islam is still very much alive, and the same power which broke the unity of the Byzantine Empire in the seventh century was still strong enough to break the unity of India only twenty years ago.

Here, then, we have the case of a new way of thought and life, arising 1,300 years ago in the heart of Arabia and perpetuating itself by an unbroken tradition which has spread East and West, absorbing the centers of the higher civilization in the Near East and penetrating deep into the African bush and the Malayan jungle. And wherever it has gone it has not only carried its law and its faith, but has also stamped its imprint deep on human character and personality, so that the Moslem Negro in the West Sudan is quite a different kind of man from his pagan neighbor—different not only in dress, speech and gesture, but also in his habits of thought and standards of value.

This expansion is undoubtedly one of the most remarkable examples of the diffusion of culture that is known to us, and it is one that took place within the historical world, so that we can trace its whole development from source to culmination. But while Islam is distinguished from the other world cultures by the rapidity with which it developed and was diffused, it is equally remarkable for its conservatism and its power of resisting change. Even today Moslem society is more impenetrable to alien ideas and more firmly anchored in its traditional way of life than any other culture.

In these respects Islam is untypical, since its extraordinary power of external diffusion has not been related to any process of internal development or growth. It attained its full stature at the beginning of its history and has preserved its original character like a stereotype that can be repeated again and again without change. As it was in the beginning, so it is today and so it must be as long as it exists.

This is due, above all, to its religious character. Islam is not, like Christendom, the secondary product of a world religion, it is the religion itself. For Islam is by definition nothing else but an act of surrender to the will of God as revealed by the Prophet. The community of Islam is the fellowship of believers and nothing else, and it is indissolubly linked with the unique experience of one man which has set its seal on the thought and life of hundreds of millions for more than a thousand years.

Thus the success of Islam was due to its simplicity. It created a faith and a community which transcended the complex divisions of Arab tribal society. This common faith inspired the community with a dynamic militant spirit which drove it to expand, and every new wave of expansion brought an influx of converts who, by their acceptance of Islam, became members of the new community. And since the community was all-inclusive—a state as well as a church—it was also the bearer of a common culture, which absorbed and transformed the cultures of the conquered peoples. To some extent this culture, in its earlier phases, was parasitic, since it was dependent on the unassimilated subject peoples not only for its economic resources but also for the skilled technicians and administrators who gave their services to the conquerors. Moreover, the institution of slavery has played a larger part in Islam than in any of the great cultures that were its contemporaries. In particular the institution of military slavery was peculiar to Islam and resulted in the formation of slave states like the Memluk sultanate of Egypt and the Turkish slave kingdom of Delhi which are perhaps the most remarkable examples in history of states that exist without any national basis or any roots in the soil. Nevertheless this parasitic element in Islam was not a symptom of decadence. The great age of Islamic culture, alike in the East and the West, was an age in which this element was prominent, and the non-Moslem element in society was largest. When the process of absorption was completed and the whole society became Moslem, Islamic culture became stationary and even to some extent retrograde and decadent, although it never lost its religious convictions and its power to resist the influence of alien cultures. We see this especially in Western Islam, where the brilliant cultural achievement of the Middle Ages, the age of Averroes and Ibn Khaldun, ended abruptly with the Christian reconquest of Spain and was followed by an age of stagnation and decay in which the cities of North Africa became the centers of predatory states which lived by piracy and the slave trade.

So too, in the nineteenth century, the one region where Islam continued to expand was in Negro Africa, where conditions still resembled those of primitive times and where the Moslem states of the Western Sudan and of East Africa could still carry on the Holy

War and incorporate new tribes and peoples into the domain of Islam. Nor was this a purely external movement of conquest and exploitation, it involved the development of a new form of Negro-Moslem culture, expressed by the creation of the Swahili language, which has become the living language of the greater part of East Africa.

Thus, in spite of its internal rigidity and conservatism, Islam is still a dynamic culture which has not lost its power of diffusion. Nevertheless it differs so widely from other cultures, and especially from the simple autochthonous type of culture such as we see in ancient Egypt, that it can hardly be compared with them. It is in fact a kind of *superculture* which incorporates a very large number of older cultural unities without altogether absorbing them. We shall see that this is not peculiar to Islam but is a situation present in the other world cultures, although none of them has dealt with it in the same way as Islam. But even though we accept this situation as normal, we must always remember the existence of these submerged cultures, for the failure to do this is responsible for the oversimplification that has been the bane of cultural studies and vitiated so many of the "philosophies of history" and the theories of the evolution of civilization in the past.

A subculture may possess a very rich intellectual and religious tradition. This was the case with many of the subject peoples of Islam—with the Parsis in Western India and above all with the Jews, who have attained the widest diffusion of all. In spite of all the efforts of the Jews to keep themselves apart from the Gentiles, and of the Gentiles to exclude the Jews from their social life, Jews have everywhere exerted a considerable cultural influence—alike in the Hellenistic and Roman worlds, in Islam and in Western Europe. And since they have often occupied key positions in the dominant cultures—as government officials, court physicians, bankers and merchants, scholars, and men of letters—their influence has been out of all proportion to their numbers.

It is difficult to exaggerate the importance of the part that such a subculture can play in the diffusion of culture, especially when, as in the case of the Jews, it is common to two world cultures and provides a bridge between East and West. It is true that the existence of a specifically Jewish culture has often been denied, and one of the leading authorities in the field of culture study, Professor A. L. Kroeber, has described Judaism not as a culture, but as "a social quasi-caste, based originally and primarily on religion."[2] Nevertheless the Jews are a true people with a distinctive way of life and an exceptionally strong social and religious tradition, and the mere fact that they have no geographical unity and even today little political autonomy is not sufficient to disqualify their cultural status.

A subculture of this kind is a genuine culture, and even though it exists in a submerged state and cannot achieve complete external expression, it may possess greater cultural activity than many normal cultures which are free to develop in their own territorial environment. In fact subcultures, cultures, and supercultures all play an indispensable part in the total process of the growth and diffusion of civilization. It is easy to imagine a world in which every culture has its own place in time and space and runs its course from birth to death according to Spenglerian pattern. But this is not the world we know; the historical world in which the river of tradition never ceases to flow and where cultural growth is inseparable from cultural contact and diffusion. Here the total culture process is an immense web of intercommunicating cultural patterns and traditions. A whole group of cultures may be brought together by the unifying influence of a superculture, so that they seem to lose their identity and even their existence. But some of their traditions are incorporated into that of the dominant culture and others live on under the surface in the life of the subculture.

When the Mongols destroyed the capital of the Moslem world in 1258, a representative of the Armenian subculture, Kiriakos of Kantzag, hailed its downfall in the same accents as those with which the Hebrew prophet had rejoiced over the fall of Nineveh nearly

[2] *Anthropology* (New York, Harcourt, 1948), p. 279.

two thousand years before. And the resemblance is not merely the result of a similarity of situation, it is due to the survival of a literary tradition and a spiritual attitude which had been handed on from one subculture to another, while successive world empires had risen and fallen. Thus the voice of a vanished culture will often make itself heard after it has been submerged and forgotten for ages.

It is, however, the cultures of the great world religions which have shaped the course of civilization, and these possess a kind of super-cultural position, though not usually to such a marked degree as Islam. Thus in the Far East we have the Confucian tradition of China which was intimately related to the state religion of the archaic Chinese Empire and continued to dominate not only Chinese culture but all the other cultures of the Far East down to the revolutionary changes of the present century.

Secondly, in India we have the no less ancient tradition of Brahmanism, the origins of which go back to the beginnings of Atyan culture in India and which has continued to mould the life of Indian society down to the present day. Closely related to this is the second Indian world religion of Buddhism, whose influence extends from Mongolia and Japan to Ceylon and Cambodia.

These are the three great religions of the East, and correspondingly we find three world religions in the West—Judaism, Christianity, and Islam—which are historically related to one another and share certain common features which distinguish them from the rest. Finally between East and West there formerly existed a seventh world religion—the Zoroastrian religion of Persia, which exerted a great influence on the culture of the Middle East in the past, but today has almost disappeared, being represented only by the small Parsi community in Western India.

These six or seven great religions have been the great unifying factors in the civilization of the world. They are, as it were, the spiritual highways which have led mankind through history from remote antiquity down to modern times. These ways are not equivalent or necessarily competitive. The three Western religions, all of which are monotheistic and dependent on the idea of a particular divine revelation, are no doubt competitive, and so in a sense are Buddhism and Brahmanism, which offer alternative solutions to a common series of problems. But on the whole it is true to say that in the case of India and China and Europe the factors of geographical and historical separation have been so great that their religions have developed, not as rival systems of thought and belief, but as the spiritual traditions of three different worlds which have been brought together only by the material and technological expansion of Western civilization in modern times. In the past all these world religions with the exception of Judaism have been what I have termed supercultures—common forms of faith and moral order which embraced and united large numbers of previously existing cultures with their own languages and histories.

The problem today is whether these great world cultures themselves are to become merged in one all-embracing world civilization, based on modern science and technology. But even though we may regard this as inevitable, we cannot say that any such world civilization at present exists. We have the material conditions for world unity, but there is as yet no common moral order without which a true culture cannot exist. The entire modern world wears the same clothes, drives the same cars, and watches the same films, but it does not possess common ethical values or a sense of spiritual community or common religious beliefs. We have a long way to go before such a universal spiritual community is conceivable, and meanwhile what we call modern civilization remains an area of conflict—a chaos of conflicting ideologies, institutions, and moral standards.

Part Two: Beginnings of Christian Culture

V. THE CHRISTIAN AND
JEWISH IDEA OF REVELATION

We have just seen how all the great civilizations of the world have been in the past associated or identified with a religious tradition, and that these traditions presuppose the existence of a divine revelation embodied in a canon of sacred scripture. These religious traditions were originally regarded as unique and exclusive. Each was the jealously guarded secret tradition of a holy class or caste, and in some cases, as in India, the most severe penalties were decreed against any outsider or member of a lower caste who attempted to become acquainted with the sacred mysteries. It was not until the coming of the World Empires that the idea arose that these sacred traditions were alternative ways of expressing the same truth—notably in the Mongol Empire, where the Great Khan explained this point of view to a Western missionary by comparing the five religions to the five fingers of his one hand. In this case the motive was probably not theological or metaphysical but political. The world empire must make the different religions co-operate within one all-embracing imperial system.

However that may be, there can be no doubt that the idea of revelation was developed independently within each of the great cultures, and that in many cases, notably in the case of Judaism and Christianity and Islam, it was anterior to them. There is in fact a remarkable analogy between the idea of human culture as developed by modern anthropologists and the idea of revelation as developed by the ancient theologians. Culture is the human way of life com-

municated by language, so that the word of man is both the creator
and the transmitter of culture. But in the case of religion, it is the
Word of God that is the dynamic principle. It is communicated to
man by the process of revelation, which is a creative act, since it is
the principle of a new spiritual society which transcends the temporal
order of culture and brings man into contact with a higher order of
reality.

Nowhere is this idea of divine revelation so strongly expressed or
so clearly identified with the tradition of culture as in the case of
Israel. For here the whole social form and historical destiny of the
people had been imposed on them by the Word of Yahveh, which
was not merely, as in other cases, a sacred tradition of learning, but
a way of life embodied in a moral law and a sacred history which
set it apart from all the other peoples of the ancient world.

From the beginning the Jewish tradition stood out in uncompromising hostility to the religious traditions of the more civilized
peoples that surrounded the Jews. While the rest of the ancient
world was being integrated into one great society by the influence
of Hellenistic culture and education and Roman government and
law, one little people obstinately refused to be assimilated. The
stronger the external pressure of the world society, the more intense
was the consciousness of the Jewish people of a unique destiny which
set them apart from the nations. For more than a thousand years
they had maintained their faith through the successive waves of
conquest that had overwhelmed the other peoples of the Near East.
The Assyrian and the Babylonian, the Persian and the Macedonian
had come and gone, but the hope of Israel still lived on, and through
the dark ages of conquest and oppression the remnant of the chosen
people still held fast to the sacred heritage of the divine law which
was the foundation of their national life.

This is an exceptional situation. The other world religions like
those of India and China were the religions of great cultures which
regarded themselves as world civilizations; they had no rivals in
their own worlds. But Israel was always conscious of its minority

status—as one people among many nations, and as smaller and weaker than the historic empires that surrounded it from the beginning—Egypt and Assyria, Babylon, Persia, Macedonia, and Rome. For the Jews themselves and the Christians afterwards this uniqueness was the result of a divine vocation and election. Israel was chosen from among the nations to be the witness to God and the bearer of divine revelation. This calling was placed far back in history in the middle of the Bronze Age—somewhere in the first half of the second millennium B.C. when Yahveh called Abraham—the father of all believers—to leave his home in Haran on the Euphrates and become the founder of a new people in a new land. And this is described not as part of a movement of tribal migration or conquest, but as the call of a particular individual who was set apart for a destiny which he was unable to comprehend, but which he accepted in the darkness of faith under the influence of the prophetic experience, which is described obscurely but impressively in the fifteenth chapter of Genesis.

Thus behind the national vocation of the Jewish people there stands this idea of a personal vocation based on a unique individual revelation. It is not even certain who the people were to whom Abraham belonged, for the "Hebrews" were probably the same as the *Habiru*, *Apiru*, who appear in the Syrian and Egyptian inscriptions and seem to have been a class rather than a race. The word *Apiru* appears to be a generic name for nomadic warriors who took service as mercenaries with the princes of Syria, like the "Apiru warriors" with whom King Idrimi of Alalakh took refuge in Northern Palestine during the seven years of his exile about 1420 B.C.

No doubt they must once have been a people—"The Sons of Eber" of whom we read in Genesis, who are reckoned by biblical tradition among the descendants of Shem—along with Elam and Asshur and Arpachshad—all of them peoples from the Northeast as compared with the descendants of Ham—Egyptians, Canaanites, Arabians and Babylonians. But when they first emerge into the light, or rather the twilight, of history in the middle of the second millennium B.C., they are already a broken people. They may have been driven from their original home by the great Southern movement of peoples which brought the Hurrian peoples down into Syria and Northern Mesopotamia and led to the establishment of the kingdom of Mitanni and finally to the Hyksos conquest of Egypt.

It was in the midst of this movement of peoples that the wanderings of Abraham from Haran in Northern Mesopotamia into Canaan took place. In Genesis xiv we see him as a Hebrew warrior raiding the victorious Elamite army after the battle of the nine kings. Nevertheless the part he played was not that of a conquerer. He was essentially an alien, a wanderer in strange lands, who "went out not knowing whither he went," following the divine command.

Thus the religious tradition preceded the national tradition of which it was the source. When the descendants of Abraham went down into Egypt, they were, according to tradition, but seventy souls in all, and in Egypt they were merged with the Syrian immigrants who were reduced to servitude by the Pharaohs of the nineteenth dynasty. The origins of Israel as a nation begin only with the Exodus and the Covenant at Mount Sinai which consecrated the whole people as Abraham had been consecrated by the first covenant. Here again it was a prophetic individual, Moses, who is shown as the saviour of his people from Egypt, as the channel of divine revelation and the giver of the divine law.

Consequently it is to Moses and to the Covenant of Mount Sinai that the whole of Jewish tradition looks back as the creators of the unique theocratic society and culture of Israel—the chosen people, the people of the Covenant and the people of the Law. Henceforward, according to that tradition, the history of Israel is the record of its faithfulness or failure in the fulfillment of this divine mission. Israel stood alone among the peoples of the ancient East as the one witness to the Law of the one God.

Every culture is a moral order, but the moral order of Israel was identical with the Law of Yahveh, as revealed to Moses and elaborated in the teachings of the priests and prophets. The gist of this teaching is, first, the Sacred History of Israel's call and deliverance; secondly, the Covenant of Yahveh with Israel as the constituent form of Israel's being; and, thirdly, the moral duties and obligations imposed on Israel by the Law which was the condition of the Covenant. "Yahveh thy God has chosen thee to be his peculiar people of all peoples that are upon the earth. Not because you surpass all nations in number has Yahveh joined himself to you and chosen you, for you are the fewest of any people. But because Yahveh has loved you and has kept the oath that he swore to your fathers and has brought you out with a strong hand and redeemed you from the house of bondage. . . . Keep therefore the precepts and ceremonies and judgments, which I command you this day to do." (Deut. vii. 6–8, 11)

This is the theme reiterated all through the Scriptures—not only in the Law but in the Prophets and in the Psalms, and repeated in summary form in the early apostolic preaching of St. Peter as described in the Acts of the Apostles. Nor has it lost its importance for modern Christians. For we still see in it not only "the mystery of Israel" itself, but the indispensable preparation for the Christian revelation and the life of the Church. This Jewish revelation is altogether different in kind from those revelations of esoteric wisdom of which we read in the Upanishads and the religious literature of the East. It was a creative revelation, a process of continuous training and education by which a half-savage tribe of wandering herdsmen were gradually remade into a unique instrument for the fulfillment of the divine purpose towards mankind. The Covenant or Berith of Yahveh with Israel was more than a contract, it was a living communion or, as the later prophets describe it, a sacred marriage. And this concept, which involves the introduction of a divine principle into history, not after the pagan fashion by the deification of the powers of nature but by the association of man with God in the fulfillment of a divine mission, is the key to the whole Judeo-Christian revelation.

The principle differed from the age-old tradition of the God of the City which had existed in Sumeria from the dawn of civilization. For Yahveh was not a member of a divine society or pantheon like the gods of Syria and Mesopotamia, nor was he a metaphysical principle like Brahman or Tao. He was a personality of whose presence Israel was always aware and whose will and power were continually manifested in all the judgments of its history.

This concept is already implicit in the Covenant at Mount Sinai and the whole story of the Exodus and the life of Moses, but it was difficult to maintain it after Israel had become settled in Palestine and was exposed to the influence of a new environment and to the religious and cultural traditions of the peoples of the land. Henceforward there was continual tension and conflict between the Mosaic tradition and the influence of Canaanite culture. Paradoxically, the higher material culture was bound up with a lower form of religion, and the religion of Yahveh and the Covenant was associated with the primitive culture of a warrior tribe and the tradition of the desert. This conflict became especially acute in the ninth century B.C., when King Ahab's Phoenician consort, Queen Jezebel, attempted to introduce the cult of the Tyrian Baal as part of the state religion of Israel. The story of the prophet Elijah and his opposition to the royal power and his conflict with the prophets of Baal gives a dramatic picture of the conflict between the two religions and the two spiritual ideals which contended for the soul of Israel; and his flight to the desert, to Mount Horeb, typifies the return to the Mosaic tradition which was characteristic of the prophetic reform.

Henceforward down to the fall of the Kingdom of Israel and Judah and thereafter, the Mosaic tradition was preserved and deepened by the witness of the prophets who contended for the "cause of Yahveh" against the sins and infidelities of Israel. Thus the entire corpus of the prophetic writings is a continuous dialogue between the spokesmen of Yahveh and his people which renews and reinforces the relation between Israel and Yahveh established at Sinai.

This partnership was not an easy one for Israel. "You only have I known of all the families of the earth: therefore will I visit on you all your iniquities" (Amos iii.2) "Do two walk together unless they are agreed?" "Does a lion roar in the forest when he has no prey?" (Amos iii.3-4) "The lion has roared, who will not fear? The Lord Yahveh has spoken, who can but prophesy?" (Amos iii.8)

Thus according to the teaching of the prophets from the eighth to the sixth centuries the destruction of the two kingdoms was the judgment of Yahveh on the failure of Israel and the House of David to keep the Covenant. Nevertheless the Covenant and the divine promises had become inseparably bound up not only with the national culture but also with the land of Palestine, the city of Jerusalem, and the royal line of King David. And this incorporation of the worship of Yahveh with a particular history rooted in place and time and embodied in institutions still retained its significance even for the prophets who were most conscious of Israel's universal mission. Yahveh is Lord and King not only of Israel, but, as the prophets declared, of the whole earth and all the nations. But he must have his own kingdom—one corner of the world in which his authority was recognized and his name sanctified. The rest of the earth was given up to worship of idols, but here, in the Kingdoms of Israel and Judah and in the holy city of Jerusalem, Yahveh was to reign alone without a rival. The destruction of Israel is not therefore final. In the end, the kingdom shall be restored, when the people cease to look to man or to "the arm of the flesh" for help, and put their trust in the power of Yahveh and his salvation.

This is the message of the great prophet Jeremiah at the end of the seventh century B.C., the man of sorrows who had the bitter mission of announcing and witnessing the doom of his people and the futility of resistance to the Babylonian armies. But to him it was also revealed that the old external observance of Yahveh's kingship and law was not enough. There must be a spiritual covenant "written on the heart" and in the conscience of every individual believer. (Jer. xxxi.31-33)

This hope in the spiritual rebirth and restoration of Israel had a transforming influence on the religion of Israel during the centuries that followed. Gradually the emphasis of Jewish religion was transferred from the past to the future and became centered in the future kingdom of God. The successive catastrophes and frustrations of Israel's history in the seventh and sixth centuries removed this hope from the political sphere and made it increasingly numinous or supernatural, altogether dependent on the will of Yahveh and his judgment of the nations.

In the same way the center of the Jewish community was no longer the nobles and rulers but became identified with an inner group of the devout who represent the chosen "remnant of Israel." And so during the exile and post-exilic period Israel became changed from a people into a Church—a religious society held together by its allegiance to Yahveh and its devotion to his Law. It was in these centuries that the universal character of the Kingdom of Yahveh became realized in all its implications, so that the hoped-for restoration of Israel was seen not merely as the return of the exiles or the re-establishment of the temple worship but as the cosmic triumph of Yahveh, the one true God, over the nations and their false gods. "It shall come to pass in the latter days that the mountain of the temple of Yahveh shall be established above the mountains and shall be raised higher than the hills. The peoples shall flow to it and many nations shall come in haste and say, 'Come, let us go up to the mountain of Yahveh, to the temple of the God of Jacob, so that he will teach us his ways and we will walk in his paths.' For the law shall go forth out of Sion and the word of Yahveh out of Jerusalem." (Micah iv.1-2; Isaiah ii.1-5)

All the glories of this future kingdom were concentrated in the person of the Messianic King, "He who is to come," who combines in his person the promised inheritance of the old Davidic royal line and the supernatural and universal qualities of the new divine kingdom. "There shall come forth a rod from the stock of Jesse and a flower shall rise up out of his root. And the spirit of Yahveh shall rest upon him, the spirit of wisdom and of understanding, the spirit of counsel and of fortitude, the spirit of knowledge and the fear of Yahveh. . . . He shall judge the poor with justice and give sentence with equity in favor of the meek of the earth. His word is the rod that will strike the violent, and with the breath of his lips he shall slay the wicked." (Isaiah xi.1–4)

In these prophecies of the Messianic Kingdom, especially in the wider development that they receive in the second part of the book of Isaiah, the hope of Israel finds its full and final expression. Nevertheless there remained an unresolved dualism between the spiritual universalism of this message and the national patriotism which was also an essential part of the Jewish tradition. For several centuries under the rule of Persia and Ptolemaic Egypt, Israel was left in peace to follow the law and the ritual order of the restored temple worship, but in the second century B.C. a new crisis arose, the attempt of a Seleucid king to assimilate the Jews to Hellenistic culture. Once more Israel took up the sword against the Gentiles, and under the leadership of the Maccabees they succeeded in securing political independence and creating a Jewish state. But though this was the work of the Hassidim, the strictly orthodox party, the result was not the glorious kingdom of prophecy. It was merely another kingdom among the kingdoms of this world—a weak and dependent kingdom which was forced to rely on "the arm of the flesh" and the help of a new Gentile world power—the Roman Empire. This was the worst frustration of all, since the Maccabean kingdom became the kingdom of the Herods, and the Roman Empire a more formidable enemy than any of the Gentile world empires of the past.

Thus the problem for the Jews was whether to look for the Messiah as a political deliverer, a new and greater Judas Maccabeus, or whether to abandon all political dreams and put their faith exclusively in the arm of the Lord and in the coming of a Messiah who will destroy the evil world empire by a miraculous act of power.

Messianic Expectations

This is the final step in the Jewish revelation, and it finds expression in the apocalyptic literature which was characteristic of the post-Maccabean period.

Thus at the coming of Christ in the first century A.D., there were three different schools of Jewish thought. First there were the Sadducees, the aristocratic ruling party who were ready to co-operate with the Romans and the Herodian dynasty. Secondly there were the Zealots, the party of active resistance who were determined to repeat the revolutionary violence of the Maccabean national insurrection. And thirdly there were the Pharisees, the successors of the Hassidim, and the ancestors of the Rabbis, who were the party of the strict observance, devoted heart and soul to the observance of the Law.

In addition to these Josephus mentions, after the Pharisees and the Sadducees, "a third sect," the Essenes, who formed a kind of monastic order and followed a strict ascetic rule of life. Though they are also mentioned by Pliny and Philo, their importance has been underestimated in the past; but today the discovery of the Desert Scrolls at Wadi Qumran, west of the Dead Sea, has thrown a flood of light upon the movement and has aroused intense interest and controversy. It is now evident that the sect is identical with the party of the New Covenant, or the Zadokites, whose existence was revealed half a century ago by the publication of two manuscripts discovered in Egypt and now stored in Cambridge, and that they were far nearer to the main tradition of Orthodox Judaism than was formerly supposed. They were, however, deeply influenced by apocalyptic and eschatological ideas, and in this respect as well as in their practice of baptism and of a common meal they showed some affinities to primitive Christianity.

Their messianic ideas, however, are peculiar in as much as they believed in the coming of *two Messiahs*—the Messiah of Israel, who would be the warrior leader in the war with the forces of evil which were identified with the Roman armies, and the Messiah of Aaron, who represented the priestly power and therefore had the pre-eminence.

But perhaps the most striking feature of the community of Kirbet Qumran is its military character, which is more akin to the spirit of the Zealots and the followers of Bar Cochbah than to the early Christians. This is seen most clearly in the remarkable document known as "The War between the Sons of Light and Sons of Darkness," which sketches a plan of campaign for the conduct of the Holy War against the Romans—heathen world power—who are referred to as "the Kittim." In spite of these differences, however, the documents of Wadi Qumran and the existence of this "community of the New Covenant" provide a new and most valuable source of evidence for the beliefs and practices of Judaism in the time of Christ and may force us to revise many of the theories that were current in the nineteenth century with regard to the non-Jewish influences on Christianity, especially perhaps in the case of the Fourth Gospel.

In any case this new evidence affords a further proof of that intimate connection between Christianity and Judaism—between the Old Israel and the New—which is the central theme of the Catholic liturgy, so that the Two Testaments or Covenants are shown as integral parts of one divine experience. It is not merely that Israel was for more than a thousand years the unique vehicle of divine revelation, it is also that in the tradition of Israel a unique relation was established between God and man and human society and history, a relation which was not broken by the defection of Israel but was carried on and extended in the Christian Church and its history.

Thus the Old and New Testaments or Covenants form a single integrated development which has no parallel among the religions of the world. The latter, as we have seen, especially the great historic world religions on which the civilizations of the ancient East and

India and China were founded, were essentially natural religions—
that is to say, they represented a human assent to the divine powers
that ruled the world, or co-operation with them. They sought to
maintain harmony between human life and the divine order of
nature which is manifested in the order of the seasons and the course
of the stars, and in so far as they went beyond this, as the religions
of India and China attempted to do, it was by the recognition of
the spiritual principle which lies behind this visible order and the
moral order which is at once transcendent and immanent, All and
more than All.

The Jewish revelation, on the other hand, shows a different
divinity and a different mode of divine action—a living personal
God who is essentially a creator—the creator of the world, of man
and of history. And his creative power is shown not only in what
he has done, but in what he is doing and is about to do; above all
in the creation of a new people who are destined to be the bearers
of the divine purpose in history through which God will change
human nature itself and renew the face of the world. And thus the
doctrine of the new creation, which holds such a central place in the
Pauline writings and indeed in the New Testament as a whole, is
deeply rooted in the Old Testament and the tradition of Israel.

The importance of the Old Testament for the understanding of
Christianity is twofold: on the one hand it is theological—the revelation of the Word of God as the ultimate reality, as Creator and
Judge: and on the other hand it is historical, since it shows how
the Word of God has been the creative force which has moulded
and transformed the life of the People of God and guided it through
the wilderness of history, preparing the way for the coming of the
Kingdom of God.

First of all, Yahveh enters into a particular relation with a particular chosen community which is given the Law of Yahveh, the Torah,
so that it becomes a holy people. Secondly, there is the Word of the
Prophets, by which the Covenant of Yahveh with Israel and his rule

over the Nations is reasserted in a new form. Through the voice of the prophets, Yahveh passes judgment on the failures of his people to keep the Covenant and displays the enemies of Israel and the successive world empires as Instruments of Divine Judgment in working out his purpose in history. This divine purpose is seen by the prophets as the coming of the Kingdom of God. The Kingdom is the goal of history, and all history is seen as a preparation for the coming of the Kingdom. But it is not in history, since the kingdoms of the nations, and even Israel itself in its obstinate refusal to hear the Word of God, were in a state of open rebellion against God's Kingdom. Hence the prophets announced the coming of the Kingdom as a revolutionary event—a judgment on man and the kingdom of man which was a work of destruction as well as salvation. Thus the literary tradition of the Old Testament finds its conclusion in a new expression of the prophetic spirit—the apocalypse or revelation of the last things—in which the coming of the Kingdom is associated with the end of the world or the end of the present world order. More and more the hopes of Israel became centered on the personal coming of one who was destined to found this Kingdom and to introduce a new dispensation.

It is a unique record and in a sense the source of three great world religions. It also shows, more clearly than anything else, the sociological function of religion and the way in which the religious law and ritual order become identified with the moral order and finally with the social, so that it was the Law that made the people and the polity, not the latter the Law.

The New Testament shows us how deeply Christianity was rooted in the Old Testament and in the Jewish tradition, though this is, of course, not fully admitted by the Jews themselves.[1] In this respect we must remember that Judaism as well as Christianity underwent great changes in the early centuries of our era. Judaism was rebuilt

---

[1] This attitude is explained in an interesting essay by Arthur Cohen in the volume of essays edited by Philip Scharper called *American Catholics*.

after the two great wars with Rome, and it is the Talmud and the age of the Talmud that has formed the mind of later Judaism. In the same way Christianity during the same centuries was deeply influenced by Hellenism; and the primitive Judeo-Christian tradition gradually faded out after the first century.[2]

The Church inherited the old Greek version of the Old Testament—the Septuagint, which was originally the common heritage of Christian and Jew, but which was abandoned by the latter after the fall of Jerusalem, when the break between Jews and Christians became total. The West has followed the Jewish tradition of Scriptures, i.e., the Massoretic text—first with St. Jerome and the Vulgate which became the official Bible of the Catholic Church, and then with the new translations of Scripture made from the Hebrew after the Reformation. The Eastern Church however, as was natural, adhered to the tradition of the Septuagint.

The influence of the Old Testament on the Church was extraordinarily strong, as one can see from the liturgy, especially the All Night vigil of Easter. After the Reformation, it declined, owing to the emphasis put on it by the Reformers, so that Bible reading became a mark of Protestantism, at least in the case of the Old Testament. But in the nineteenth century the situation changed again owing to the development of biblical criticism in the Protestant world, especially in Germany, which led to the discrediting of the historical value of the biblical tradition. This again has changed in the present century owing to the neo-orthodox reaction among Protestants and the development of biblical studies among Catholics.

The extreme Liberal Protestant tradition tended to reduce the importance of the Jewish tradition in Christianity not only by its criticism of the historicity of the sources, but even more by its one-sided emphasis on the ethical content of Christian teaching. It is now, however, generally recognized by Protestant as well as Catholic theologians that an interpretation of Christianity which confines itself to the moral teachings of the gospel deprives Christianity of

[2] See Gregory Dix, *Jew and Greek* (1953).

its historical and theological roots. Christianity without the Old Testament ceases to be Christianity and becomes quite a different religion, as the Fathers saw when they condemned the Gnostics, Marcion and the Manichees. The continuity of Christianity with the tradition of the Old Testament and the conception of the Church as the new Israel is a fundamental part of the Christian faith.

To the Old Testament we owe a whole series of religious traditions which are characteristic of Christianity and have no place in the purely ethical interpretation of Christianity of Renan, Strauss and the other nineteenth-century Liberals. Not the least important is the Christian interpretation of history, which was in fact the creation of the Hebrew prophets and was handed on without essential change to St. Paul, St. John and St. Augustine.

In the Old Testament, especially in the Prophets, we find first the guiding idea of divine providence and divine intervention in history —the conception that the great events of history are all integrated in a divine plan leading to a divine judgment.

There is also a historical dualism—there are two principles at work in history. True history—sacred history—is not the same as apparent history or secular history. The spiritual meaning and value of history are hidden under the veil of outward political and economic change.

There is the vital role of individuals who are called by God, often against their will or without their knowledge, to carry out a particular mission. This is seen in the calling of Abraham and Moses and in the prophetic vocation of Elias and the great writing prophets: especially in the case of Jeremiah, which shows us most vividly the psychological aspect of the process—how the prophetic individual is forced to accept a vocation which sets him in opposition to all the dominant forces of his contemporary world. And on the other hand, we see the vocation of a historic figure like Cyrus who is in tune with the dominant forces of his age but nevertheless becomes the unconscious or semiconscious instrument of divine purpose.

Finally there is the theme of divine judgment—the end of history. Each of the great empires and civilizations is judged by God and by history. They successively fail and are rejected, but God's purposes for man, Israel and the Church are realized in the midst of historic catastrophe and temporal failure.

All these themes are repeated and reinterpreted by Christian teachers throughout the ages, by St. Paul and St. John, by St. Augustine and by the leaders of the ecclesiastical reform in the eleventh century, by the Franciscans, by the Protestant Reformers and finally by modern Catholic writers like Joseph de Maistre and Newman, whose early preaching, especially in his Anglican Sermons, is largely devoted to the development of the second and third themes just described. First the dualism between external and internal history, between the concurrent and conflicting processes of the world and the Church, and secondly, the decisive function of individuals—of the few who are called to bear witness against their age and then to change the current of history. I do not know any writer whose mind was more deeply permeated by the imagery and ideas of the Old Testament than John Henry Newman, especially in the decisive period of his career.[3]

---

[3] This Jewish-Christian theory of history has also had an immense influence on the modern secular philosophy of history. In fact the book which initiated the German school of the philosophy of history—Lessing's *Education of Humanity*—was merely a generalized and rationalized version of the traditional doctrine.

It has also had a considerable influence on social action, but not always for the good. It inspired the Jews to make their two desperate and disastrous revolts against Rome and also many millenniarist and utopian movements in Christian history. It has been especially important in America, owing to the intense Biblicism of the seventeenth-century Puritans (see their writings generally and also Professor Perry Miller's books), and consequently had a considerable effect on later American history.

VI. THE COMING OF THE KINGDOM

In the history of Israel a unique religious tradition was born into the world of history. In contrast to all other religions, this tradition was not the expression of a world civilization: on the contrary, the culture—the unique theocratic culture of Israel—was the expression and embodiment of the religion, and apart from religion the culture of Israel was almost nonexistent. Thus the Old Testament, which is the record of the tradition of Israel, is also the record of divine revelation in the Covenant of Sinai, the Law of God and the Word of the Prophets; and the latter culminated in the announcement of the coming of the Kingdom of God which would be realized by the advent of a Messiah—at once a king and saviour—and by the judgment of the Nations.

In the first century of the Christian era this Messianic expectation reached its climax: on the one hand, in the coming of Christianity, and on the other, in a tremendous catastrophe, the revolt of the Jewish people against the Gentile world power, which led to the destruction of Jerusalem and the reconstruction of Judaism on a new foundation.

At first sight it seems incredible that the Jews, who were one of the smallest peoples of the ancient world, should have dared to challenge the world power of Rome, whose armies had subdued the whole world from the Western Ocean to the Euphrates and the Red Sea. Yet three times in the course of seventy years they rose in a series of desperate revolts—in the time of Nero and Vespasian, from 66 to 73; under Trajan, during the Parthian War in 115–117, and finally under Hadrian, from 132 to 135. These

were overcome only after years of bitter warfare which did not
end until the whole country was almost reduced to a desert and
the Jewish people were almost exterminated. The Tract on the
War between the Forces of Darkness and the Forces of Light,
which is one of the most interesting of the recently discovered
documents from Wadi Qumran, illustrates the mentality of the
men who fought these wars and shows how their resistance was
intensified by their very literal belief in a sudden supernatural intervention which would give them total victory at the end, after
successive defeats.

The coming of Jesus and the emergence of Christianity were
almost contemporary with the later stages of the Qumran community, during the final period of truce when the Jewish people
was nerving itself for the great struggle with Rome. Like the
men of Qumran, the disciples of Jesus lived in expectation of the
imminent advent of the Kingdom, which would mark the end of
the age and the beginning of a new world order.

Nevertheless, the kingdom which Jesus preached was not the
kingdom that the Jews were expecting, nor did the course of his
mission as Messianic Saviour and Son of Man correspond with the
picture which the Jewish people had cherished of a triumphant
warrior king who would destroy the power of the Gentiles and
restore the kingdom to Israel. It is true that the kingdom in Hebrew, Malkut Shamaiim, is not precisely what we mean by the
term—it is "kingship" or "kingly authority" (perhaps the Latin
imperium is closer to the meaning than *regnum*); but even so, it
does carry political connotations which are absent in the gospel.
The "kingdom" of the gospels is much closer to that of the apocalyptic writers, since it involves the idea of a new world, a new
dispensation, or a new world order. But even here there are vital
differences, since the kingdom of the gospel is already here, "The
kingdom of God is among you." "The kingdom of God has come
upon you." Here the kingdom is seen above all as divine power
manifested in the supernatural works of Jesus. Elsewhere and more

commonly, the kingdom is shown as a new state to which men are called, or a new discovery—it is compared to a wedding feast, a seed, a harvest, a hidden treasure, a pearl of great price.

Throughout the preaching of the kingdom, the mission of Jesus, the Son of Man, as central figure in the new dispensation is taken for granted rather than asserted. And when at last Peter does confess Jesus to be "the Messiah," "the Son of the Living God," this is immediately followed not by any declaration of future triumph, but by Jesus' announcement of his passion and death. The revelation of the mystery of the kingdom is at the same time the revelation of the mystery of the cross.

This is the supreme novelty of the gospel of Jesus: the coming of the kingdom, and the new spiritual covenant which the Prophets had foretold is realized only by the passion of the Messiah. "This is the Blood of the Covenant that is shed for many." "This cup is the New Covenant in my Blood." From this point onwards everything is changed. The enactment of the New Covenant at the Last Supper is immediately followed by the rejection of Jesus as Messiah by the Jews, and his condemnation and death at the hands of the Gentiles at the instigation of the Jews, and finally by the Resurrection.

These events, in the Christian view, are the final manifestation of the divine mission of Jesus, they are the historical fulfilment of prophecy and the gateway to a new age. With them the Messianic Kingdom has already come, since Jesus is now sitting at the right hand of the Father with supreme authority over both the earthly and heavenly powers. And already it is to this Messianic authority that he alludes in his charge to the apostles after he had risen. "All power is given to me in heaven and on earth; go, therefore, and make disciples of all nations, baptizing them in the name of the Father, the Son and the Holy Ghost."

And as the old Covenant of Sinai had created the old Israel, so the new Covenant in the blood of Christ created a new people, a second spiritual Israel which would receive the promise and enter into the new kingdom. This kingdom was a universal one extending to all things in heaven and on earth, as St. Paul says: "that in the name of Jesus every knee should bow, of those that are in heaven, on earth, and under the earth; and that every tongue should confess that Jesus Christ is in the glory of God the Father" (Phil. ii.10–11). But the Church which was constituted by the outpouring of the Holy Spirit at Pentecost, as had been promised by the risen Christ, was the organ of the kingdom in a special sense, since it was the body of Christ and it was in and through the Church that Jesus established his kingdom on earth.

It was by the Spirit, which was the Spirit of Christ, proceeding from the Father, that the Church was created and was guided throughout the New Testament. This is emphasized as the distinguishing mark of the new society, which was not conceived as a human society but rather as a new creation, reborn in Christ and destined to extend beyond the boundaries of Israel to the Gentiles and the whole human race. This last truth, however, was only gradually realized. To an outsider who visited the primitive Church at Jerusalem, it must have seemed just another of the Jewish sects which were so characteristic of this period, as we see from the recent discoveries at the Dead Sea.

In reality, however, the Messianic crisis of the Way of the Cross was the turning point in the history of Israel and of the world. The Jewish people as a whole were carried onwards irresistibly into the vortex of war and destruction which destroyed the bridges between the Jewish and Gentile worlds and forced them to fall back on the Study of the Law as the ultimate citadel of Jewish national being, while the Christians took the opposite path and began, tentatively at first, to draw nearer to the Gentile world that surrounded them.

We must remember, however, that even before the Christian apostolate to the Gentiles there was already a marked difference between Palestinian Judaism and the Judaism of the Hellenistic cities. The Judaism of Palestine had been formed in response to the challenge presented by the Seleucid Empire during the Maccabean period, whose aim was to make Jerusalem into a Hellenistic city and replace the worship of Yahveh with that of Zeus. The success of the Maccabean revolt against the Seleucids gave the Jews of Palestine confidence that God was on their side in terms of military insurrection against the Gentile world powers. Moreover, the coming of the Roman Empire and the complete subjection of the Holy Land to hated foreign rule increased the feeling of opposition to paganism and the resistance to intercourse with Hellenism.

The Jews of the Hellenistic cities, on the other hand, while keeping their basic religious tradition, and indeed trying to propagate it among the Gentiles in the cities where their communities were located, were much more open to the influence of Hellenic culture—as indeed their translation of the Bible into the Greek of the Septuagint showed.

On the one hand, we have a reaction to Hellenism which involved greater emphasis on the purity of the Jewish tradition and as sharp a separation as possible from non-Jews; on the other hand, in the diaspora communities, we have an acceptance of Hellenic language and culture in so far as these did not conflict with monotheism and an attempt to make the Gentiles aware of *their* obligation also to worship the one true God, the God of Israel. And since the Jews of the diaspora numbered over seventy-five per cent of the total Jewish population in the Roman Empire (the latter variously estimated at from five to eight million), their importance as a bridge between Judaism and Hellenism can readily be understood.

However, as H. Daniel-Rops remarks: "This extension of Judaism had its difficulties and encountered some resistance. Rigorist Jews distrusted the converts. Moreover, the rite of circumcision was obligatory upon any male who wished to become a true child of Yahweh and a full member of the Jewish community, and a large number of would-be proselytes drew back when faced with this. So, torn between an exclusivism which was to become increasingly violent right up to the time of the catastrophe known as 'the Jewish War,' and a universalism which, though admirable, dared not go to its logical conclusion and declare that there were no longer 'circumcised nor uncircumcised,' the Jewish conscience seemed poised in a state of unbalance."[1]

Thus it was Christianity rather than Judaism which reaped the harvest of these early missionary efforts that had been made by the Jewish communities of the Hellenistic cities. Moreover, after the revolt of A.D. 66 to 70 which resulted in the destruction of Jerusalem, and the two subsequent revolts in 115-117 and 132-135, the Jewish community in Palestine gradually set the model for Jewish communities in the diaspora as well. And this model was not one of missionary apostolate but of the careful development of the Law and elaboration of commentary upon its precepts, a development which increasingly isolated the Jews from contact with the Gentile world, however much it may have contributed to strengthen the bonds of the Jewish communities against disintegration or dissolution.

The extension of the Apostolic preaching to the Gentiles and the creation of an Hellenistic Church was the work of St. Paul, who took the revolutionary step of insisting on the right of the Gentile Christians to membership of the *ecclesia* without the need for circumcision or the observance of the Mosaic Law. He taught that as the Old Law was abrogated by the blood of Christ and was replaced by the New Law, which is the Law of Liberty, there is no longer room for any distinction between Jews and Gentiles. "For you are all the children of God, by faith in Christ Jesus. For as many of you as have been baptized in Christ have put on Christ. There is neither Jew nor Greek: there is neither bond nor free: there is neither male nor female. For you are all one in Christ

[1] *The Age of the Apostles and Martyrs* (New York, Doubleday Image ed., 1962), Vol. I, pp. 43-44.

Jesus. And if you be Christ's, then are you the seed of Abraham, heirs according to the promise." (Gal. iii.26–29)

It was this new preaching that created the great network of Greek-speaking Churches strung out along the shores of the Mediterranean from Antioch through Asia Minor and Macedonia and Greece to Rome itself. This is the theme of the Acts of the Apostles, which is authentic history but which is at the same time a kind of Christian epic. It is the spiritual Aeneid of the Church from Jerusalem to Rome with St. Paul as the heroic figure who carries out the divine mission by superhuman labors and sufferings. Unfortunately we have no comparable record of how the Church spread eastward and how the Syriac-speaking Christianity of Mesopotamia came into existence (for the traditions about the foundation of the Church of Edessa are legendary). But it is probable that Syriac Christianity was derived from the Gentile Church, possibly from Antioch, and not from the Jewish Church at Jerusalem. The latter maintained its own tradition all through the cataclysm of the First Jewish War and the destruction of Jerusalem, and even through the no less serious crisis of the Third Jewish War, in spite of much persecution from their own countrymen. But it gradually lost touch with the Church of the Gentiles so that by the third century we find it sinking into the position of a heterodox sect—isolated alike from the Gentile Church and the Jewish Synagogue and divided against itself by the schism of the Ebionites, and by the strange sect of the Elkesaites which arose about 101.

But meanwhile the Church of the Gentiles had become the Christian Church, the Catholic Church. In the first generation it was, of course, not purely Gentile, but rather the Church of the Dispersion, and its leaders, like St. Paul himself, were Judeo-Christians. Above all, St. Peter, the chief of the Apostles, who had been the center of the Jerusalem Church in its early days, was most active among the Churches of the Dispersion, first at Antioch and finally at Rome, where, according to an ancient and well-attested tradition, both he and St. Paul were put to death in the days of Nero.

The part of St. Peter is of outstanding importance in this development, because it was his authority and influence that preserved unity between the revolutionary propaganda of St. Paul to the Gentiles and the old Judeo-Christian tradition. Moreover, there is good reason to believe that it was under Petrine influence and as representing the Petrine tradition that the earliest Gospel, that of St. Mark, was written at Rome during the sixties, and this provided the stable historical framework which was accepted by both Judeo-Christians and Gentiles as the foundation of their faith. And later when St. Luke repeated this same gospel narrative in an enlarged form, he combined it in a single consecutive narrative with his history of the foundation of the Church at Jerusalem and its expansion by the apostolic preaching, and above all by the mission of St. Paul to the Gentiles.

Thus there was created an authoritative classical scripture into which all the elements of the Christian tradition—the sayings of Jesus, the foundation of the Churches, the Pauline epistles and the other apostolic traditions could be incorporated.

By this time, in the later part of the first century, the Judaizing problem was no longer so acute. To converts from a purely Gentile environment, Christianity no longer appeared to be a kind of Judaism. It was to all intents and purposes a new religion—the Gospel of the Salvation of Mankind in Christ, the Son of God. But the more they were detached from the Jewish community, the more they were exposed to the hostility of the pagan world, since they no longer had the status of a recognized national community to protect them.

Thus the early Christians seemed to be living in a social vacuum, suspended between the Jewish and the Gentile worlds, and this cultural isolation was but the social expression of the deeper spiritual issue of which they were so highly conscious. They felt themselves to be living in two worlds and two world-ages. The coming of Christ had wound up the old order; the old world was dead, the old Israel had lost its mandate, a new world order had been born, of which the Christians themselves were the first fruits. They already possessed the Kingdom in faith and hope; they had only to wait for its final manifestation and triumph. Consequently the external conditions of their present life did not matter. They were merely travelling through the debris of a wrecked world towards a certain goal. The Church was the society of the world to come, and they possessed in it already "the pledge of the Spirit" and the foretaste of the life of the new world.

The author of the Epistle to the Hebrews expressed this sense of tension and expectation in a wonderful passage in which he explains the continuity and the contrast of the Jewish and Christian dispensations. He sees the whole history of the Chosen People as a pilgrimage of faith from the time when Abraham left his country in obedience to the divine call not knowing where he was going, living in tents in a strange land and looking forward all the time to the real city whose founder and builder was God. In the same way his spiritual descendants, "the heirs of the same promise," travelled all through history, overcoming every obstacle and hardship by the power of faith. "All these died in faith, not having received the promises, but they saw them and hailed them from afar, confessing that they were pilgrims and strangers on the earth." Christians are the heirs of this great tradition, but now the pilgrimage has reached its end and the promise is being fulfilled—not in the cloud and darkness and fire of Mount Sinai where men could not bear to hear the awful voice of God. "You have come to Mount Sion and to the city of the living God, the heavenly Jerusalem, to an innumerable host of angels and to the Church of the firstborn whose names are written in heaven and to God the Judge of all, and to the spirits of the just made perfect. And to Jesus the Mediator of the new covenant, and to the sprinkling of his blood which speaks better than the blood of Abel."

All things are being changed. Heaven and earth will be shaken. Only the Kingdom will stand fast. (Heb. xi, xii, passim)

In the face of these tremendous world-transforming events all differences of class, race and culture among the early Gentile Christians vanished. They applied to themselves the parable of Jesus in which he spoke of the marriage feast of the King's son to which the invited guests refused to come so that their places were filled by the sweepings of the streets—the poor and the maimed and the blind and the lame. (Luke xiv.16–24) The unity of the new community was essentially a supernatural unity, depending not on external circumstances but on the spiritual union of the faithful with one another in Christ. This union was realized above all in the sacraments which were the channels for the transmission of the life of the Spirit and the means by which the faithful were incorporated into the divine organism or mystical body of which Christ is the head. "On him all the body depends; it is organized and unified by each contact with the source which supplies it; and thus, each limb receiving the active power it needs, it achieves its natural growth, building itself up through charity" (Ephes. iv.16, tr. Knox).

This supernatural organic unity is not limited to the internal spiritual life of the Christian—the life of faith and charity—it is also a principle of external organization and hierarchical authority. The different offices or ministries in the Church represent the organic functions of the one Body, and as the physical organs have their separate functions and their mutual interdependence and coordination, so it is with the organized communal and hierarchical life of the Church. From the first the Christian communities were not regarded as independent autonomous bodies. Though they were scattered through the Roman world among many cities and peoples, they were one as Christ was one. As Christ had been sent into the world by the Father, so the apostles had been sent by Christ, and the ministers of the local Churches—presbyters, episcopi, deacons—derived their office and authority from the apostles.

This insistence on apostolic unity in tradition, in doctrine, and in authority runs through all the teaching of early Christianity, alike in the New Testament and in the writings of the post-apostolic period.

In the beginning the question of organization was relatively unimportant. Everything depended on the authority of the central group of apostles who were the founders and supervisors of the new community and, secondarily, on the other representatives of the higher ministry—prophets, teachers and missionaries—whose activities were not confined to any particular place. The local ministry was indeed of secondary importance, as we see from St. Paul's list of the different ministries or "charismata" in the Church—"first apostles, secondly prophets, thirdly doctors, after that miracles, then the graces of healings, helps, governments, interpretations of tongues" (I Cor. xii.28). The importance of the apostles, the founding fathers of the local churches, was overwhelming both as the source and rule of the faith and as the source and center of authority, and even the churches that were not directly founded by them looked to them for guidance and accepted their supervisory authority no less than the rest.

But when the apostles had passed away, the problem of ecclesiastical organization became of urgent importance for the Church. The insistence on the unity of the Church and the maintenance of the apostolic tradition remained as strong as ever, but to be effective it had to be reinforced by the strengthening of the local ministry and of the bond of hierarchical subordination. We possess a valuable piece of evidence for this transitional period in the letter written by St. Clement on behalf of the Roman Church to the Church of Corinth which had deposed its leading presbyters from their offices. The whole of his epistle is devoted to a defense of the principle of hierarchical order and authority as derived from the tradition of the apostles. "The Apostles received the gospel for us from the Lord Jesus Christ and Jesus the Christ was sent from God . . . They preached from country to country and from city to city and they appointed their converts, testing them in the Spirit to be bishops and deacons of the future believers." "Moreover the Apostles knew through our Lord Jesus Christ that there would be contention for the title of bishop. And so they appointed those already mentioned and added the provision that if they fell asleep other approved men should succeed to their ministry, men who were appointed by them, or afterwards by other leading men with the consent of the whole Church."[2]

Now St. Clement's insistence on the principle of authority and apostolic succession in the Church is the necessary consequence of his belief that the Christians are a separate people—"the people of God" in the literal sense. Although the breach with Judaism had been completed for more than a generation, the thought and language of St. Clement is still rooted as strongly as that of the author of the Epistle to the Hebrews in the ancient Hebrew tradition. He speaks not as a Gentile but as a spiritual son of Israel. As in the First Epistle of St. Peter the unique vocation of the Christians is identified with that of the chosen people, and the words of Scripture on the unique prerogative of Israel are applied to the Church: "For there it is written 'When the Most High divided the nations, when He scattered the children of Adam, He determined the bounds of the nations according to the number of the angels of God. [But] His people Jacob became the portion of the Lord, Israel was the lot of His inheritance.' And in another place He says, 'Behold the Lord takes to Himself a nation from the midst of the nations, as a man takes the first fruits from the threshing floor, and the Holy of Holies shall come forth from that nation.' "[3]

And as Israel had been separated from the nations by the elaborate obligations and restrictions of the Law, so now the Church was a separate people with its own law and way of life which separated it from Jews and Gentiles alike.

[2] *Clement* xlii-xliv.
[3] *Clement* xxxix.

At first sight it seems difficult to see how this separation could be maintained, since Christians were no longer divided from their neighbors either by nationality or cultural differences. But from the beginning the pressure of external hostility and persecution was so great that it provided a natural barrier that separated the Christians from the rest of the Roman world. For two and a half centuries a long war was waged between the Church and the Empire which began in the age of Nero and never entirely ceased, in spite of occasional periods of truce and relaxation, until the conversion of the Emperor Constantine.

The causes of the persecution are not immediately obvious, since the Roman Empire was not usually intolerant in religious matters and the Christians were not merely politically inoffensive, but inculcated obedience to the Roman government as a religious duty.

We must, however, remember that the second half of the first century and the first half of the second century was the period that witnessed the life-and-death struggle of the Jewish people against Rome, and the distinction between Jews and Christians was not so apparent to the Roman authorities at this period as it becomes later. Suetonius mentions the prosecution, in the reign of Domitian, of those "who concealed their origin and did not pay the tribute levied upon their people."[4]

The reaction of this persecution on the Christians themselves was inevitably serious. It was in the first century, probably in the reign of Domitian, that the Christians' experience of persecution and their consequent hostility to the Roman Empire found its most passionate expression in the pages of the Apocalypse. Rome is Babylon, the great mother of harlots, drunken with the blood of the Saints and the blood of the martyrs of Jesus, the Empire the kingdom of the Beast which seeks to destroy the Church but which is itself destined to destruction by the triumphant return of Jesus and the establishment of the Kingdom of the Saints.

This remarkable work which is so entirely different from the

[4] *Lives of the Caesars*, Domitian xii.

other New Testament writings and from the *First Epistle of Clement*, which is almost contemporary with it, shows how intense the hostility between the Church and the Empire had become, in spite of the fact that the Christians had never become involved in the successive Jewish revolts against Rome. Nevertheless it is not surprising that their attitude of passive hostility, their refusal to take any part in the public ceremonies and their deliberate separation from the civic life of the Roman-Hellenistic world, should have provoked the suspicion and hostility of the authorities.

The Empire felt itself in the presence of a vast underground movement which it did not understand, but which it feared and suspected. And when, as in the third century, the Empire became involved in a series of social crises, Christianity was singled out as the most obvious representative of the subversive forces which threatened the Roman way of life.

By the Christians, on the other hand, persecution and martyrdom were taken for granted as normal conditions of the Church's life. They had been foretold in the gospels and had found their supreme archetype in the example of Christ himself. The martyr was following in his master's steps, and his death expressed that identity between the Head and the Members which was the key principle of the Pauline theory of the Church. Consequently it is not surprising that the idea of martyrdom is the dominant motif of early Christian literature and thought throughout the whole of this period from the New Testament to Eusebius. In the first age of the Church the ideal of sanctity was embodied in the figure of the martyr—the man who "bears witness" with his blood to the Christian faith. The ideal and even the name itself goes back to the very beginning of Christianity—to St. Stephen, to Antipas, "my faithful witness who was slain among you at Pergamum" (Apoc. ii.13), and St. John's reference (I John v.8) to the Three Witnesses —the Spirit, the water (of baptism) and the blood (of martyrdom); and throughout the age of persecution the martyrs play an increasingly important part in the life of the Christian community.

The literature dealing with the subject—the *Epistles* of St. Ignatius, the *Martyrdom of Polycarp*, the *Epistle to Diognetus*, the *Letter to the Churches of Lyons and Vienne*, the *Acts* of Perpetua and her companions, and the *Letters* and *Acts* of St. Cyprian—give us a more intimate knowledge of the early Christian mind than any other documents. They show how the expectation of martyrdom was one of the permanent factors of Christian life and how the martyrs' triumph was shared by all the faithful as their common possession and their common glory. Writing in a time of relative peace, Origen looks back to the previous persecution as a golden age of the Church: "The days of real faith were the days when there were many martyrs, the days when we used to take the martyrs' bodies to the cemetery and come straight back and hold our assembly. They were the days when the whole Church was in mourning and the instructions the catechumens received were meant to prepare them to acknowledge their faith right up to the moment of their death, without wavering or faltering in their belief in the living God. Christians saw amazing signs and wonders then, we know. There were few believers then, but they were real ones; they followed the narrow road that leads on to life."[5]

Thus in early Christian culture the figure of the martyr took the place of that of the hero in pagan culture, and the lives and legends of the martyrs replaced the heroic myths and legends which were one of the most popular and persistent elements in the old culture.

It is difficult to exaggerate the importance of the ideal and cult of the martyrs for Christian culture. Every important church had its own martyrs who were regarded as its special intercessors and whose cult strengthened the solidarity of the spiritual community. And there were also more famous figures whose story was familiar to the whole Christian world—"megalomartyres," as they were

[5] *De principiis* 3, 3, 2. Quoted in Jean Daniélou, *Origen*, trans. by Walter Mitchell (New York, Sheed and Ward, 1955), p. 41.

called by the Byzantines—like St. George and St. Sergius and SS. Cosmas and Damian, whose cult was equally widely diffused in the East and West, from Persia to Gaul.

The cult of the martyrs also found very early expression in art and architecture, as in the art of the catacombs and in the influence of the "martyrion," or tomb chamber, on the development of the circular type of church plan. At Rome, above all, the life of the Church centered in these great suburban cemeteries which grew up on private estates outside the walls of the city. Here were the tombs of the martyrs where their feasts or anniversaries were celebrated, so that the Church worshipped in the presence of the martyrs. Moreover, these underground cemeteries by their permanence provided an opportunity for the development of Christian art. Deriving its technique and motifs from the contemporary popular art of the Hellenistic tradition, it transformed them to its own purpose by a system of symbolism, in which a naturalistic representation of forms like the vine, the fish, the dove, the anchor, the crown, etc., acquired an esoteric significance which was clear enough to the faithful but meaningless to the uninitiated. In other cases a mythological motif like that of Orpheus or Hermes Kriophoros is translated into Christian terms as a figure of Christ, the Good Shepherd. Most frequent of all is the figure of the Orante— the female figure with outstretched hands, which is a symbol at once of the Church in prayer and of the Christian soul. Finally there are paintings that clearly illustrate scenes from the Old Testament or from the liturgy. There is one scene in the catacomb at Naples of three maidens building a tower which is undoubtedly an illustration of the vision of Hermas, the second-century Roman prophet—a unique example of the co-operation of early Christian art and literature to create a new kind of poetic imagery, which foreshadowed the art of the coming ages of Christian culture. No less important than the ideal of martyrdom was that of virginity, which also goes back to the first age of the Church. Indeed the two ideals were associated—first by the cult of virgin martyrs, like St. Agnes, which was so popular, and secondly by the idea that virginity was a kind of living martyrdom, a witness to the power of the faith to transcend human weakness. Thus the ideal of asceticism as an heroic struggle to overcome the world and the flesh goes back to the beginnings and is associated by the early Christian writers both with the idea of martyrdom and with that of virginity. In the words of St. Cyprian, "*Habet et pax coronas suas*"—"Peace also proffers her victors their garlands."

And as both the confessors and the virgins had a recognized status—an *ordo*—in the early Church, so was it with the ascetics. The "Sons of the Covenant"—Benai Queyama—to whom St. Aphraates, the earliest Syriac teacher, writes, were not monks, but they came very near to the monastic life, since they were Christians living an ascetic and celibate life which distinguished them from the rest of the faithful. They were, so to speak, pre-monks, and it is easy to understand how such an institution would inevitably develop into the full monastic life under favorable circumstances.

It was a very modest beginning, and in the second century it is hardly possible to speak of the existence of a Christian culture, but the foundations had been laid of a new way of life which was neither Greek nor Jew, but which united the two traditions under the inspiration of a new spirit.

This is brought out very strongly in the *Epistle to Diognetus*, which is one of the most striking of the post-apostolic writings. The author describes how the Christians are scattered everywhere in both Greek and barbarian cities, living externally like other men but entirely different in their inner life. They are, he says, "a third race," neither Jews nor Greeks, but something new. In fact, he concludes, "Christians are in the world what the Soul is in the body. . . . The Soul is spread throughout all the members of the body and the Christians throughout the cities of the world. The body may rebel against the Soul, and the world may perse-

cute the Christians, but although the world hates them, they are
the principle of life on which the world depends. For God has
called them to this great office and they cannot shirk this responsibility."

VII. CHRISTIANITY AND
THE GREEK WORLD

By the middle of the second century the great conflict between the Jewish people and Rome had been brought to a conclusion, and the ancient world had entered on an age of peace and prosperity under the Antonine emperors. The hope of a great catastrophe or world revolution which had hitherto sustained both Jews and Christians in different ways in their resistance to persecution had now become more remote, and they began to adapt themselves to the new situation. But they did this in different ways. The Jews tended to withdraw from contact with Greek civilization and to reorganize their national life round the new but intensely conservative cultural centers which grew up in Mesopotamia at Sura and Pumbeditha.

It is not possible for me to discuss, as I should like to do, this development of Babylonian Judaism in the third century. Unfortunately it tends to be overlooked in most of the histories of early Christianity and of the Roman Empire. It was, however, of very great importance. For it involved the progressive detachment of the Jews from Hellenistic and Western culture and their closer relations with the Aramaic- or Syriac-speaking world of Babylonia, which was at this time under the rule first of the Parthian empire and then of the new Sassanian monarchy, which was the most formidable enemy of the Roman and Byzantine empires.

Here at Sura and Nehardea and afterwards at Pumbeditha, there arose the great Jewish schools under a succession of famous teachers, from "Rab" or Rabbi Arika (c. 220–247) to Rabashi, head of the School of Surea from 372 to 427. It was here that the great Babylonian Talmud was created which was the foundation of medieval and modern Judaism. Its importance cannot be exaggerated. Unfortunately, of all the religious classics, it is the most difficult for the ordinary reader to assimilate. He is confronted not only by its length, which in the modern English translation extends to thirty-six large volumes, but still more by its style and its lack of unity. As I. Abrahams writes, "It is not a book, it is a literature. It contains a legal code, a body of ritual customs, poems, prayers, histories, facts of science and medicine and fancies of folk lore." Thus it has formed a barrier rather than a bridge between Jewish and Gentile culture, and explains to a certain degree the cultural isolation of the Jews in later times.

The Christians, on the other hand, entered into closer relations with the Hellenistic world and inaugurated that long dialogue with Greek thought which was carried on first by the Apologists, then by the Christian School of Alexandria, and finally by the Greek Fathers of the fourth and fifth century, like St. Basil, the two Gregorys, and Theodoret of Cyrrhus.

But by the second century A.D., Hellenism was a very different thing from the Hellenism of classical Greece, it was a real world culture which embraced the whole civilized world, which extended from Rome to Antioch and Alexandria and reached far to the East into the heart of Asia. From the first it had been a cultural rather than a national phenomenon. A man became a Hellene not by birth but by education, and anyone who had undergone the training of the Greek School and the Greek gymnasium was as much a Hellene as the man who had been born in Attica. But in addition to this kernel of genuine cultural Hellenism, the Hellenistic world included the vast multitude of those who had come under the rule of the Greek cities and kingdoms and who spoke Greek, though they still retained their contact with older, non-Hellenic cultures. Throughout the Roman period, this secondary form of Hellenistic culture was expanding, especially in Asia Minor, and the old vernacular languages were being replaced by Greek, just as Gallic and Iberian languages were being replaced by Latin in Gaul and Spain.

The religious attitude and needs of these two forms of Hellenistic society were very different. The unassimilated or imperfectly assimilated subject peoples remained faithful to the pre-Hellenic religions and cults, and it was through them that the Hellenistic world was exposed to an invasion by the oriental cults and ideas which threatened its spiritual independence.

The Hellenic culture itself had almost from the beginning possessed its own tradition of spiritual wisdom which found classical expression in the Platonic dialogues. Later in the Hellenistic period, this tradition was adapted to the needs of a cosmopolitan society until it became a rational world religion common to the whole Hellenistic world. It was a species of spiritualist pantheism, based on the universal spiritual principle or Logos which was at once the immanent cause of order and harmony in the cosmos and the principle of moral order in human life. In its later development, especially with Epictetus at the beginning of the second century, and with the Emperor Marcus Aurelius, the religious element in this philosophy becomes more and more pronounced, so that it is transformed, in spite of its original pantheism, into a monotheistic religion inspired by a high ideal of moral perfection.

But this, after all, is only one side of the Hellenic tradition, though it is the most authentically Hellenic one. There were also the traditions of the Hellenistic world which are derived from the East and not from Hellas—from the countless peoples who had undergone a superficial process of Hellenization and who at least had learned to talk Greek, but had remained at bottom faithful to the religions and beliefs of the old oriental world. It was through this imperfectly Hellenized element that the Hellenistic world was exposed increasingly in the second and third centuries A.D. to the rising tide of oriental influences. The Jewish Christians themselves represented one element in this movement, but in so far as they were non-Hellenic, they represented the distinct religious and national tradition of the Jewish people. But in addition to these there was the anonymous, faceless multitude of peoples who had lost their distinct national traditions and had become absorbed into the cosmopolitan society of the Hellenistic monarchies, and above all by the world empire of Rome.

These people remained spiritually alien to the dominant Western civilization. They did not share the typical Hellenic attitude of religious reverence towards the natural world as a visible manifestation of intelligence and order. On the contrary, they were profoundly pessimistic in their attitude to life and the whole cosmic order, which they regarded as under the domination of demonic powers; and they looked for some way of salvation which would deliver them not only from the body but from the world and from the evils of birth and procreation.

This attitude finds expression in that whole series of religious and theosophical movements which are usually grouped together under the common name of Gnosticism. But they also include the new world religion of Manicheanism which was to endure for at least a thousand years, as well as heresies like Marcionism, and sects like Mandaeism, which has survived almost to the present day. In their essential nature all these religious systems belong to a totally different world from that of Western Hellenism or even from the Judeo-Christian tradition: on the other hand, they often show a remarkable resemblance to the religions and philosophies of ancient India. They are all, like Buddhism and Jainism, essentially ways of "deliverance"—*Moksha*—which teach man how he may extricate himself from the world and from bodily existence.

They agree with the Indian philosophies in their profound pessimism, which views the soul as an exile that has been cast into the world of darkness—"You see, O child, through how many bodies, how many ranks of demons, how many concatenations and revolutions of the stars, we have to work our way in order to hasten to the one and only God." "Having once strayed into the labyrinth of evils, the wretched soul finds no way out. She seeks to escape from the bitter chaos and knows not how she will get through."

"Grief and woe I suffer in the body—garment into which they transported and cast me. How often must I put it off, how often put it on, must ever and again settle my strife (i.e. die), and not behold the Life in its Sh'kima."

One may compare with these passages the passage I have quoted from the *Maitrayana Upanishad*, in the ninth chapter of *Religion and Culture*,[1] which describes the same sense of dereliction and thirst for enlightenment and deliverance.

In the same way the Gnostic doctrine of the Saviour—"the one true Messenger altering his forms with his names carries through the Aeon until he shall have reached his time, and anointed by God's mercy for his labor, attained to eternal rest"—resembles the Indian doctrine of the successive Buddhas or *Jivas* who bring the message of deliverance to successive ages. And this resemblance was appealed to by Mani, in his history of revelation: "From aeon to aeon the apostles of God did not cease to bring here the Wisdom and the Works. Thus in one age their coming was in the countries of India through the apostle that was the Buddha; in another age into Persia through Zoroaster; in another into the land of the West through Jesus. After that in this last age, their revelation came down and this prophet-hood arrived through myself, Mani, the apostle of the true God, into the land of Babel."[2]

But the most remarkable parallel between Gnostic and Indian thought is the belief that finds its clearest expression in the Jain religion—that the world is full of souls which exist not only in men but in animals and vegetables and in every particle of matter, and that the man of enlightenment must abstain scrupulously from any act which could destroy or injure these lives. Now a

[1] Op. cit., p. 180. *Sacred Books of the East*, XIV, 287–290.
[2] Quoted by Al-Biruni in his *Chronology* from the *Shahpurakan* of Mani.

similar idea is found in the Manichean scriptures, which relate
how the higher spiritual nature of Jesus, the Saviour and Messenger of Life, has become dispersed and bound in all the material
creation.

This, in Manichean language, is "the passible Jesus" who hangs
on every tree, is served up bound in every dish, and who every day
is born, suffers and dies."[3] Thus the Manichean "Elect," like the
Jain ascetic, is bound by the strictest rules of abstinence and non-
violence. "It behoves man," it is written in the *Kephaleia*, "that
he look down at the ground when walking on his way, lest he
tread under foot the Cross of Light and destroy the plants." Accordingly the later medieval Manicheans, like the Jains, saw the
highest act of virtue in a total abstinence from all food, even
though this involved a voluntary death.

All these resemblances do not, of course, prove a direct influence
of Indian thought on the West or the Middle East, but they do
suggest that the world of oriental peoples that had been submerged
by the victorious advance of Hellenistic culture and Roman imperialism was reasserting its spiritual independence. This development would, no doubt, have taken place, if Christianity had never
existed, and but for Christianity it might well have conquered and
absorbed Hellenistic religion and philosophy, and created a new
syncretistic world religion, comparable to the Mahayana form of
Buddhism which was spreading from Northern India to Central
Asia and China during the same period.

Different as these various creeds are from one another, they all
possess common features which distinguish them from Christianity. They are all dualist and anti-material, teaching that the material creation is evil and that God is not the creator of the world:
they all agreed in regarding the Saviour not as true man but as
an angelic or celestial power which manifested itself in the appearance of humanity, and they all taught that salvation was to
be found not in faith in an historical revelation, but by initiation

[3] Hans Jonas, *The Gnostic Religion* (Boston, Beacon, 1958), p. 229.

into a secret knowledge—a *gnosis* or theosophy which contained the ultimate secrets of cosmology and metaphysics.

When this flood of strange doctrines invaded the ancient world and attempted to transform Christianity into their own image, the Church was faced with a new problem. She was a living organic society conscious of possessing a sacred tradition, a divine gospel and a new way of life. But hitherto she had no ideology or *gnosis* in the Hellenistic sense. Now she had to construct a reasoned defense of Christianity as a consistent body of doctrine capable of providing an answer to all the abstruse questions the new movements raised. This development of a scientific theology was not completed until the age of the great councils. But it was in this age—at the end of the second century and during the first half of the third—that the foundations were laid by St. Irenaeus and Tertullian in the West and by Clement of Alexandria and Origen in the East.

It is the earliest of these—St. Irenaeus—who is the most representative figure, since he belongs both to the West and the East and in a special sense is the Father and Doctor of the Universal Church. He was the disciple of St. Polycarp at Smyrna who had himself been the disciple of the apostles, and he spent his life as a missionary in the far West when he succeeded the martyr St. Pothinus as the bishop of Lyons at the time of the persecution in the days of Marcus Aurelius.

His great work against the Gnostics is far more than a controversial refutation of heretical errors. It is a profound and original statement of the whole Christian plan of salvation—a Christian philosophy of history, a theology of creation and Incarnation and a definition of the mission of the Church as the guardian of the apostolic tradition and the organ of the life of the Spirit. Against the Gnostic cosmological and theosophical speculations, he insists on the necessary limitations of human knowledge and even of the Christian revelation. For the latter was never intended to be an initiation into cosmic mysteries and divine theogonies. It is simply the story of God's dealings with the human race, his progressive education of humanity through the earlier dispensations recorded in Scripture and his final summing up or recapitulation of the process in the Incarnation of the Word by which humanity at last reaches its predestined divine goal. Thus all the mysteries of the faith are relative to the conditions of human nature and human knowledge. They are all concerned with the one single theme—doctrine regarding the education and regeneration of the human race which is the reason of creation and the purpose of history. And since man is a material creature, this purpose embraces the body as well as the soul. Man is not saved *from* the body, as the Gnostics taught, but *in* the body. The gift of the Spirit was fulfilled in the body, as the work of the Incarnation was contained and completed in the Church. The divine plan is worked out through the successive ages of the existing physical universe in the concrete realities of human nature and human history. This spirit of historical realism is expressed by St. Irenaeus in his doctrine of the Church. Christianity, he argues, is not like Gnosticism, an ideology or an hypothesis; it is the historic tradition of the historic Church which can be traced by direct succession to its apostolic founders.

In comparison with the other Greek Fathers St. Irenaeus owes little or nothing to philosophy. His thought is wholly Christian and biblical both in source and content, although he was a man of considerable literary culture and a powerful and original thinker. But, partly no doubt owing to his isolated position in the Celtic and Latin West, he founded no school and left no literary tradition. The mainstream of Greek theological development followed a different course which was determined by the leaders of the catechetical school of Alexandria, Clement and Origen.

This approach had already been initiated by the Greek apologists, especially Justin Martyr and Athanagoras. For they recognized the existence of a basic knowledge of truth which was common to both Christians and philosophers, and Justin explains this as due to the Indwelling Logos (λόγος σπερματικός) which led the wisest of the Greeks to anticipate to some degree the truths now manifest in the Incarnate Logos.

This conception of Greek philosophy as a preparation for Christianity was developed much further by Clement of Alexandria and the Alexandrian Catechetical School. Clement goes beyond Justin not only in claiming philosophy as a sort of "third dispensation" leading the Greeks to a knowledge of God, but as necessary for Christians also, if they were to understand all that their faith involved, so as to advance from faith to knowledge, *gnosis* (for Clement is not afraid to use this word, in spite of its heretical associations). Thus the School of Alexandria was no longer satisfied with the strictly traditional theology of St. Irenaeus. They boldly accepted the challenge of Hellenistic thought and proceeded to show how the Christian revelation was the true answer to the intellectual no less than the moral quest of Hellenic philosophy.

By far the greatest representative of this tendency was Origen, who was the most learned, not only of the school of Alexandria, but of all the theologians and scholars of the ancient Church. Thus it is inevitable that he should have exerted a profound influence on Christian theology and culture. But this influence was not unchallenged, and eventually Greek orthodoxy was to reject his theology and condemn his works. This was the penalty of his success, for his synthesis with the Hellenistic thought of his age (which was the age of the founders of Neo-Platonism, like Plotinus) was too complete to be acceptable to the orthodox.

This was above all the case with the bold speculations of his fundamental treatise—*De Principiis*—which today only survives in Rufinus' somewhat Bowdlerized Latin translation. As with his predecessors, like Justin, and his successors, the Greek theologians of the fourth century, it is the creative function of the Logos which is the center of his thought. His world, like that of the Neo-Platonists with whom he has so much in common, is a hierarchical universe in which the Logos is the intermediate link between the Father who is αὐτοθεός—God in his own right—and the λογικοί, the created spiritual beings, whether angels or men, who receive from the Logos all the spiritual knowledge they possess, since they see in him the image or reflection of the supreme divinity. The visible world in turn owes its beauty and order to the spiritual creation by which it is ruled. Yet at the same time Origen was keenly aware of the forces of evil—the spiritual, even angelic, powers which exert such a profound influence on this visible material world. It was to free mankind and the whole material creation from these evil powers that the Logos became man and suffered death upon the Cross. And the Christians are carrying on the same work of salvation when they in turn defeat the powers of evil by bearing witness by their blood to the triumph of the Logos over death. Ultimately, Origen believed, this work of cosmic redemption would be a total one and the whole creation, including even the powers of evil themselves, would be brought back to God and restored to its original integrity.

This idea of universal salvation—this *apocatastasis*—as Origen calls it, was one of the points in his theology which was singled out for special condemnation by the theologians of a later age, as were also his views of the pre-existence of all human souls. But it was in reality his cosmological and hierarchical doctrine of the Trinity which constituted a much greater danger to Catholic orthodoxy, since it had such a deep and sometimes unconscious influence on the whole tradition of Greek theological speculation. For there is no doubt that although Origen regarded the Logos as the Eternal Image of the Invisible God, his doctrine is frankly subordinationist and he views the Logos as inferior in the scale of being to the Father in the same way as the rest of the spiritual creation is inferior to the Logos. This is so much in accordance with the tradition of Greek philosophy from Philo to the Neo-Platonists that it was readily acceptable by educated Greek Christians and largely contributed to the success of Arianism and semi-Arianism in the following century. Yet Origen must also be regarded as the source of the main tradition of higher Christian studies, both biblical and theological, in the Orthodox Church. The school at Caesarea in Palestine which he founded after he had been forced to leave Alexandria in 232 became the great center of study for Christians in Palestine and Asia Minor and at a later period produced one of the greatest of Christian scholars—Eusebius the historian. Moreover, in the fourth century the great Cappadocian Fathers, St. Basil and the two Gregorys, who have always been regarded as the glory of orthodox theology, undoubtedly owed their inspiration to Origen's thought, as we see in the anthology from his writings compiled by St. Basil and St. Gregory Nazianzen, entitled *Philocalia*.

This Hellenization of Christian culture, to which the influence of Origen and the School of Alexandria bear witness, was a very far-reaching movement which came to include almost the whole Mediterranean world. The Church of Rome itself remained Greek-speaking far into the third century, and the early Western theologians like Irenaeus in Gaul and Hippolytus all wrote in Greek. It seems paradoxical that Latin Christian literature and the whole theological tradition of the Western Church should have originated not in Europe at all, but in Africa, in the countries that are now known as Tunis and Algeria.

But this does not mean that the new Latin literature was a pale reflection of the dominant culture of the Hellenistic East. Far from it—it was profoundly and disconcertingly original, owing, no doubt, to the fact that the first Latin Christian writer was a man of genius and had a greater natural talent for writing than any of his Greek contemporaries. At this time classical Roman literature had practically come to an end.

A strange silence had fallen on the Latin pagan world. And in this silence a new voice of passionate intensity and conviction suddenly made itself heard. It was the voice of Tertullian, the founder of Latin Christian literature and one of the most powerful formative influences in Western Christian culture. Tertullian, the son of a Roman officer at Carthage, was a born writer and a born fighter with a passion for theological controversy and a gift for creating telling phrases which pierce the armor of indifference and prejudice and strike the heart of the matter. Nothing could be more unlike the style and thought and temperament of his great contemporaries at Alexandria—Clement and Origen. They wrote as Greek intellectuals for a cosmopolitan, Hellenistic audience. He wrote as a Roman to Romans, as a citizen to citizens, as a lawyer to lawyers. Although his strange, difficult, baroque style has always been a scandal to the purists and has caused him to be treated as a kind of outlaw by the conventional literary historians, his Latin was a living tongue and he did more than any other writer to create the language of the Church.

Moreover he was no less a Roman in his thought and his ideals. He is the last representative of the great Roman moralists, like Lucretius and Juvenal and Tacitus, and the moral indignation which made Lucretius an atheist and Juvenal a pessimist makes Tertullian the champion of the Christian faith against the corruption of the pagan world. No doubt it also made him a puritan and eventually a heretic, but even in these respects also he is only too representative of the later developments. But unlike other heretics he retained his theological and literary influence on the Church from St. Cyprian to St. Jerome, and he has always been recognized as the first of the Latin Fathers.[4]

The second Latin Father, St. Cyprian, also shares the same preoccupation with moral issues and a similar sense of social and juridical values. But though Cyprian was intellectually the disciple of Tertullian, no two men could be more unlike in character. The one a born writer, a fiery, erratic individualist, the other a born ruler, a man of order and moderation, who governed the Church of Africa with the authority and prudence of a great Roman magistrate. Nothing in literature is more purely Roman than the laconic

---

[4] His sect, the Tertullianists, was reconciled with the Church by St. Augustine himself, and their basilica was a well-known place of worship in Carthage.

heroism of St. Cyprian's trial and martyrdom, as recorded in the *Acta Proconsularia Cypriani*,[5] and it is his episcopate and his death that explain the immense prestige of his memory in both East and West, even more than his theology and his writing.

St. Cyprian's letters and his treatise on the Unity of the Catholic Church are among the most important documents that we possess for the history of the Church of the third century. They show us the high degree of constitutional organization and canonical authority that the Church had come to possess. The Roman world could no longer dismiss Christianity as just another of the oriental sects and mystery religions which swarmed in the religious underworld of the Mediterranean. It was an organized social power with its own autonomous system of government and jurisdiction. In provinces like Africa or Asia or Pontus, every city had its church, every church had its bishop, and bishops and churches were united by ecclesiastical councils within the province and by a regular system of correspondence and communication. It is true that these wider relations were still liable to interruption, as we see from the conflict between St. Cyprian and Rome on canonical issues. Nevertheless the ecumenical character of the organization was so strong that the Church was already potentially coextensive with the Empire.

Indeed in the East it had already begun to transcend the imperial frontiers in the debatable lands between the Roman and Persian empires, above all in Northern Mesopotamia. Here the conversion of King Abgar IX of Edessa, who reigned c. 176–214, brought about the Christianization of the little kingdom or client state of Osrhoene, so that Christianity gradually became the national religion of the Syriac-speaking population of Mesopotamia and the door was opened for the further spread of Christianity into the heart of Asia.

Thus by the end of this period—in the early fourth century—

---

[5] Cf. P. Monceaux, *Histoire littéraire de l'Afrique chrétienne*, Vol. II, pp. 179–190.

the Church had become an international and interracial society which extended from the Atlantic to the Persian Gulf or beyond. It was one in faith, in order, and in worship, but it had already permeated three different cultural and linguistic worlds. From the cultural point of view there was not one Christendom but three— Greek, Latin and Syriac—and each of these already possessed its own version of the Scriptures, its own form of the liturgy and its own literary tradition. The Latin tradition was still far less rich than the Greek, and the Syriac was poorer than either. This is not surprising, since the Syrians were always a subject people— first of the Greeks and the Parthians, then of the Romans and the Persians, and finally of the Byzantines and of the Arabs, so that they were never in a position to develop an independent national culture. The Greeks, in spite of their cosmopolitan spirit, had always ignored the languages and cultures of the "barbarian" peoples, and this attitude was maintained by their Byzantine descendants or heirs. In this situation the coming of Christianity brought new hope to these peoples who had been subject for so many centuries to the heavy yoke of alien conquerors. The Church became a national home for them, and they found in it a spiritual citizenship and a new culture which were denied to them elsewhere. The Greeks and the Latins always remained conscious of a double tradition—that of the Church and that of the classical past—and their rejection of paganism did not involve a complete break with the philosophy and literature of the past. But the Syrians had no such problem to face. The educated classes had adopted Greek as their literary language and there was no longer a living tradition of Aramaic literature. The renaissance of Syriac culture coincided with their conversion, and their new literature was completely Christian and predominantly didactic and liturgical. But though they remained dependent on the Greeks for their theology and philosophy and history, they had an important influence on Christian culture as a whole. They formed a bridge between East and West by which Christianity passed from the

Greek-speaking world of the Eastern Mediterranean to the peoples of alien speech and culture beyond the frontiers of the Empire—Armenians and Georgians, Persians and Arabs, and ultimately as far as Central Asia and Southern India.

VIII. THE CHRISTIAN EMPIRE

The infant Church was born at a time when the greatest state the world has ever seen was attaining its full development. The whole civilized world west of the Euphrates was united under a single head. The age of civil war, of social unrest, of the exploitation of the conquered peoples was at last over. Everywhere new cities were springing up, trade was flourishing and population increasing. It was "the hour of the prince of this world," the apotheosis of triumphant material power and wealth.

Yet the whole splendid building rested on non-moral foundations—often on mere violence and cruelty. The divine Caesar might be a Caligula or a Nero, wealth was an excuse for debauchery, and the prosperity of the wealthy classes was based on the institution of slavery—not the household slavery of primitive civilization, but an organized plantation slavery which left no room for any human relation between slave and master.

The early Church could not but be conscious that she was separated by an infinite gulf from this great material order, and that she could have no part in its prosperity or in its injustice. She was in this world as the seed of a new order, utterly subversive of all that had made the ancient world what it was. Yet, though she inherited the spirit of the Jewish protest against the Gentile world power, she did not look for any temporal change, much less did she attempt herself to bring about any social reform. The Christian accepted the Roman state as a God-given order appropriate to the condition of a world in slavery to spiritual darkness, and concentrated all his hopes on the return of Christ and the final victory of the supernatural order. Meanwhile, he lived as a stranger in the midst of an alien world.

Thus the Christians stood apart alike from the Gentile and from the Jew, living a hidden life which had only an external and accidental connection with the life of the heathen world around them.

This withdrawal from social life, this passive acceptance of external things as matters of no consequence, seems at first sight to prove that Christianity had no direct influence on social and economic conditions. In fact, this attitude produced the most revolutionary consequences. Ancient society and the civic religion with which it was bound up centered in a privileged citizen class, and under Roman rule citizenship was directly based on economic status: that is to say, a man's position in his own city and in the Empire at large was determined by his property assessment under the census. There was a constant process of competition under the early Empire, by which freedmen and tradesmen became landowners, landowners raised themselves to the curia of their city, and rich provincial decurions became Roman knights and even senators.

Christianity substituted membership of the Church for membership of the city as a man's fundamental and most important relationship to his fellows. In the new religious society, rich and poor, bond and free, Roman citizen and foreigner all met on an absolutely equal footing. Not only were these earthly distinctions overlooked, they were almost inverted, and it was the poor who were privileged and the rich who were humbled. This world was for the rich, but the new world—the only world that mattered—was above all the inheritance of the poor. "Hath not God chosen the poor in this world, rich in faith and heirs of the kingdom which God hath promised to them that love him?" says St. James. "But you have dishonored the poor man" (if you have respect to persons). "Do not the rich oppress you by might, and do not they draw you before the judgment seats? Do not they blaspheme the good name that is invoked upon you?"

No external change was made in status and possession, apart from that involved in charity. Indeed, the poor are expressly counselled not to seek riches, not to take part in that social competition for individual advancement which was going on all around them. But the personal factor is utterly altered. To Cato[1] the slave is a chattel, to be sold when he becomes old or sickly, he is purely an economic instrument, to whom even the practices of religion are forbidden— all that must be left to the master. St. Paul sends the runaway slave Onesimus back to his master to be "received not now as a slave, but instead of a slave, a most dear brother, especially to me. But how much more to thee, both in the flesh and in the Lord?"

This contrast is not economic. The old legal rights are the same in either case, but an inner revolution has been effected which must necessarily produce in time a corresponding change in all external social and economic relationships.

Consequently, the conversion of the Roman Empire to Christianity, when it came, marked a revolution not only in the history of Christian culture but in the history of the world. From being the religion of a persecuted minority, Christianity now became the established religion of the greatest power that existed—an empire which was regarded by the peoples of the Mediterranean as embracing the whole of the civilized world—the *oecumene* and the *orbis terrarum*.

It is true that this was a gradual process extending from the edict of toleration published at Sardica (Sofia) in 311 to the definitive establishment of Christianity as the only licit religion of the Empire by Theodosius and Gratian in 380. But the revolutionary character of the change was already apparent when Constantine founded the new Christian capital of the Christian Empire. Church and Empire entered into a partnership which was to endure for more than a thousand years, and to have a profound influence on both partners. It was during the first two and a half centuries—from Constantine to Justinian—that the new forms of Christian culture arose which were to continue in the East as long as the Byzantine culture existed,

[1] Cato, *De Re Rustica* ii. 142, etc.

while in the West they became the foundation of a new development.

This alliance of the world Empire and the Catholic Church, important as it was, was nevertheless only the outward form of a deeper change. For the Empire was the political organ of a civilization much more ancient and wider than the power of Rome. This was Hellenism—one of the greatest and most original cultures that the world has ever known: a culture more universal than any of the great civilizations of the oriental world, since it was practically the creator of the younger culture of the Latin West and, on the other hand, had penetrated eastward into Asia as far as the Indus and the Oxus, influencing and transforming the older cultures of Western Asia. Its importance was not due to its political power but to its educational character—it was essentially paideia—a training of the mind and the character, and wherever it penetrated, it carried with it its tradition of literature and learning, its philosophy and science, its art and physical culture.

Moreover, though it was never a political unity, it also possessed a strong and original political tradition. It was the culture of the city, and it carried with it its civic institutions, its ideal of citizenship and its ideas of democracy, liberty and law.

The only civilization that is comparable to it is that of China, which also represented an educational tradition and ideal. But the Chinese culture was limited by its identification with the ideographic Chinese script and was bound up with the unchanging traditional pattern of Chinese patriarchal authority, whereas the Hellenistic tradition was communicable through different idioms and its political forms were essentially multiple. The thousand cities and the successive monarchies of the Hellenistic world were all potentially different in constitution. Yet all alike were capable of sharing in the common life of the Hellenistic world and contributing to its culture.

But in spite of its rich intellectual development, this great civilization was inferior to the original cultures in that it possessed no common religion which could provide an internal principle of spiritual unity. There was a separation between the traditional polytheistic cults of the Greek city and the esoteric theology of the philosophers which sometimes expressed itself in open conflict, as in Heraclitus' denunciation of the mystery mongers and in Plato's attack on current poetic mythology.

Hellenism, that is to say, was a world civilization in search of a world religion; and this quest reached its culmination in the first centuries of the Christian era, especially in the third and fourth centuries. On the one hand, the Neo-Platonists attempted to reconcile the higher philosophy and the lower religion by providing a philosophic or mystical interpretation of pagan mythology, and on the other, the Christian apologists presented the doctrine of the Incarnate Word as the true answer to the quest of the philosophic Logos. In the third century, both these movements found their highest expression in the two leading thinkers of Alexandria, which was then the metropolis of the Hellenistic world—in Plotinus, the greatest of the Neo-Platonists, and in Origen, the Christian theologian.

Christianity, as we know, was victorious, and from the fourth century onwards, the whole of the Greek-speaking world, with the exception of a highbrow minority of scholars at Athens and Alexandria, accepted the new religion as the common faith of the civilized world.

It had not been an easy victory. There was much in the Christian, and still more in the Jewish, tradition that was antipathetic to the Hellenic spirit, as is evident from the writings of Marcus Aurelius, Lucian and Celsus in the second century. It required a long and patient effort on the part of the Fathers of the Church to make Christianity comprehensible to Hellenism and Hellenism acceptable to Christianity.

An acceptable synthesis between Christianity and the Hellenic philosophic tradition was not fully worked out until the third quarter of the fourth century, when we find it in the writings of St.

Basil, and in those of his brother, St. Gregory of Nyssa, and of his friend, St. Gregory Nazianzen.[2] All three were bishops from Cappadocia in the Middle of Asia Minor who had acquired their intellectual formation at the University of Athens and their spiritual training in the oriental monastic tradition. But by this time the Empire was already Christian and the foundations had been laid of that union between the Roman world empire, the Hellenic world culture, and the Catholic world religion which was the basis of the Byzantine culture for a thousand years.

It is the political aspect of this process that has been the most exhaustively studied ever since Gibbon wrote his *Decline and Fall of the Roman Empire* nearly two centuries ago, and a whole series of different theories have been put forward by historians on the nature of the Byzantine state. The view that is generally accepted by historians today is that the conversion of Constantine and the foundation of the new capital at Constantinople did not mean the creation of a new state. The Empire continued to be Roman, though it no longer had its center at Rome. It was only after the conquest of Egypt and Syria by the Moslems and the reconstruction of the Empire by the Isaurian emperors in the eighth century that it became Byzantine in the strict sense of the word. The new Byzantine Empire continued to exist until the Latin conquest of Constantinople in 1204 and in a diminished and mutilated form until the Turkish conquest in 1453.

But though this view has the great weight of modern scholarship in its favor, it fails to take sufficient account of the tremendous political and social changes that passed over the ancient world in the third and fourth centuries A.D. From the standpoint of Gibbon, which was Western, Latin and classical, this period was the Decline and Fall of the Roman Empire, and the new order and the new empire that emerged from the ruin no longer represented the domination of the Mediterranean world by Rome but rather the

[2] For a discussion of the elements involved in this meeting between Christian theology and Hellenic humanism, see the following chapter.

resurgence of the Oriental and Hellenistic elements which had been temporarily submerged. In this new order, Eastern and Western influences were united to a degree that has never been reached before or since. The position of the new capital at the point where Europe and Asia meet is a symbol of the way in which the Christian Empire drew together the divergent traditions of Western and Oriental culture and forced them for a time to follow the same path.

In this synthesis, it was the Oriental element that was predominant. The genuinely Roman imperialism, that of a constitutional monarchy based on a privileged citizen class and a society of self-governing cities, had broken down in the revolutionary crises of the third century. In its place, there had arisen a new state which resembled the sacred monarchies of the ancient East more than the Augustan principate. It also has considerable resemblance to the Russian Czardom in its great days, i.e., from Peter the Great to Nicholas I (1689-1855). It was a state in which every class, profession and individual had a fixed place under the all-seeing eye of the emperor and his omnipresent bureaucracy. The peasant was bound to his holding, the citizen to his curia, the soldier to his legion and the workman to his guild. No man was free to change his profession or his place of residence or the price he asked for his work or his merchandise.

It is a system that is not unfamiliar to us in Europe today after our recent experience of war economy and universal national service. But in the later Empire, the state of emergency was permanent and the regime of universal state service and control endured for centuries.

This system had been created under the pressure of necessity by the grim Illyrian soldier-emperors who struggled for decades against barbarian invasions, civil war, famine and bankruptcy and who finally re-established the broken unity of the Empire by hard fighting and ruthless authoritarianism.

I do not think it is ever sufficiently realized that the Roman Empire in its later development from the middle of the third century to the age of Justinian was ruled neither by Westerners nor by Easterners, but by men from the Balkans—Illyrians, Dalmatians, Pannonians, and Thracians—the only important exception being Theodosius the Great, who was a Spaniard. The greatest of these emperors and the one who really restored the stability of the Roman Empire was Diocletian (284–305), the founder of the Tetrarchy. This meant the division of the Empire into an eastern and western half, ruled by the two Augusti, Diocletian and Maximian, each of whom was assisted by a subordinate Caesar, Galerius in the East, Constantius Chlorus in the West.

This system involved an enormous increase of both the army and the civil service, which in turn involved an increase in taxation, so that eventually, as Lactantius writes, the numbers of officials became greater than the number of taxpayers. But Diocletian succeeded in maintaining this elaborate and expensive system intact from the time that he divided his authority with Maximian in 286 throughout the period of the first Tetrarchy down to his abdication together with that of Maximian in 305. This was no small achievement, for Diocletian was not a great military leader. Nevertheless, he imposed his will on his two ambitious and power-hungry colleagues, Maximian and Galerius. And it was not until the breakdown of his health in 303 and the beginning of the great persecution of the Christians, which was the work of Galerius, that his system failed. Nevertheless, the religious question remained of vital importance.

But this precarious equilibrium could not be maintained by purely military means. The new empire required new moral and spiritual foundations. At first, attempts were made to find such a basis either by a conservative reaction in favor of the Roman state religion, under Decius and Valerian, or by the new movement towards solar monotheism and emperor worship which was initiated by Aurelian, perhaps influenced by the prestige of the new Sassanian monarchy in Persia. Diocletian and his colleagues were not affected by these oriental religious developments. They were essentially conservative, and Diocletian put the new constitution under the protection of the old Roman Gods by taking Jupiter, the Father and Ruler, as his patron and assigning to his colleague Hercules, the divine patron of active heroism and labor.

But no artificial stimulus could revive the declining energies of Graeco-Roman religion, while the power of Christianity was continually growing, and was never stronger than when the new Empire launched the last full-scale offensive against the Church in the first years of the fourth century.

The failure of the policy of persecution left the Empire more spiritually divided than ever. Constantine's genius led him to the only possible solution: acceptance of the new religion by the Empire and the co-operation of the two hitherto hostile societies in the creation of a new order. This solution gave the Empire what it most needed—a new moral basis which was common to the whole Mediterranean world and was not identified with the declining fortunes of the old ruling class and the old civic culture. On the other side, it gave the Church the toleration it had always desired. It also gave power, wealth and prestige, but these were perilous gifts, since they brought with them dangers to spiritual freedom undreamt of in the days of persecution. It also meant that the new spiritual society had become yoked with a moribund or stationary social order which allowed little scope for free social activity. For freedom was totally lacking in the social life of the new state, and the conversion of the Empire to Christianity did nothing to check the progressive decline of civic institutions and the rights of the old citizen class.

Consequently, we cannot look to the Christian Empire for any thorough working out of Christian social principles. The social revolution had already occurred, and Christianity was called in at a later stage, not to reverse it, but to make it spiritually tolerable. For though the revolution was totalitarian, it differed from modern totalitarianisms in accepting its limitations and recognizing the existence of a reality which transcended the world of the bureaucrat, the tax-gatherer and the recruiting sergeant.

Thus the Church provided a spiritual substitute for the lost freedom of the city. In this new spiritual community, the ordinary man found a citizenship which was at once wider and deeper than that of the old city-state. In the first place, it was not confined to a privileged class but was open to all men—to the poor even more than the rich. And, in the second place, it was not based on the shifting foundations of political circumstances but on eternal spiritual verities. In an age when death was the only thing that was certain, the hope of immortality meant a great deal more than any political franchise, and the fellowship of the great community which offered a man help in temporal suffering and the hope of eternal glory was infinitely more valuable than the secular citizenship which subjected the citizen to burdens of public service and the crushing weight of corporate fiscal responsibility.

Christianity during the first two centuries of the Roman Empire had spread chiefly among the classes that had least economic influence—independent craftsmen, shopkeepers, freedmen, household slaves and so forth. It affected neither the ruling classes nor the lowest grades of slave labor, which were found not so much in the great cities of the Levant, the cradle of Christianity, as in the mines and on the great agrarian estates of the Western provinces. When Christianity finally established a position for itself among the educated and the wealthy, the great economic transformation of the ancient world had already begun, and civilization was henceforward engaged in a continual and desperate battle with barbaric invaders from without and economic decline from within. The one great problem now was how to save as much as possible of the inheritance of the past, and there was no room for any economic development other than that which was imposed by the hard law of necessity. Even so, however, the social changes in the Christian Empire were by no means all for the worse. In place of a society of capitalists and financiers, where wealth was ultimately derived from usury and from the exploitation of slave labor, there grew up a hierarchic society of officials and nobles, in which each class and occupation became a fixed caste, each with its own privileges and its own obligations. Instead of the slaves of the ergastula and the chain-gang, the land was cultivated by servile or semi-servile peasants, who had acquired the right to a family life, and even to a certain amount of economic independence.

The greater part of these changes was undoubtedly due to economic and political causes—to the inherent tendency of the imperial organization, to the Orientalization of Graeco-Roman civilization, and above all to the decline of the lesser cities and the return to agricultural self-sufficiency on the rural estates. Nevertheless, the influence of the Church imprinted a distinctively Christian character on the whole process. Her ideals were opposed to all the main features of the earlier imperial society—to the luxury of the rich, the idleness and dissipation of the poor and the oppression of the slaves. In place of the classical contempt for manual labor and "vile mechanic arts," which was the inheritance of Hellenistic culture, she did all in her power to substitute the duty and the honor of work. "Blush for sin alone," says St. John Chrysostom, "but glory in labor and handicraft. We are the disciples of One who was brought up in the house of a carpenter, of Peter the fisherman and Paul the tentmaker. By work, we drive away from our hearts evil thoughts, we are able to come to the aid of the poor, we cease to knock importunately at the doors of others, and we accomplish that word of the Lord: 'It is better to give than to receive.'"

At the same time, the Church held trade in little honor, and condemned unhesitatingly the usury which was the foundation of so much of the prosperity of the upper classes of Roman society. The nobles whom she honored were not the great financiers and independent aristocrats of the old type, but the conscientious bureaucrats and soldiers who served the new ideal of divine authority, vested in an hereditary imperial house, men like Lausus, the Chamberlain, Pammachus, the Consul, and the Count Marcellinus.

But above all, the influence of Christianity was shown in the protection of the weak in a time of universal suffering and want.

From the earliest times, the Church had exercised charity upon the most lavish scale, and when at last she had the power to influence the rich, the extent of Christian almsgiving became so great as to cause a real economic change in the distribution of property. The great Fathers—St. Basil, St. Ambrose, St. Jerome, St. Augustine, above all St. John Chrysostom—insist on the duty of almsgiving in language which is as disconcerting to modern ears as it no doubt was to the rich men who first heard it. "What you give to the poor man," says St. Ambrose, "is not yours, but his. For what was given for the common use, you alone usurp. The earth is all men's and not the property of the rich. . . . Therefore you are paying a debt, and not bestowing a gift."[3] And St. Basil even more forcibly declares: "He who strips a man of his garments will be called a thief. Is not he who fails to clothe the naked when he could do so worthy of the same title? It is the bread of the hungry that you hold, the clothing of the naked that you lock up in your cupboard."[4]

And as a practical commentary on these exhortations representatives of the great senatorial families such as Pinianus and Melania sell their vast estates and distribute all to the poor. The enfranchisement of slaves was an essential part of this work of charity. At first, the economic position of Christians rendered it almost impossible, although even poverty could not prevent the heroic charity which St. Clement describes in the *First Epistle to the Corinthians* (lv): "Many among ourselves have given themselves to slavery and provided food for others with the price they received for themselves."

But under the Christian Empire, enfranchisement on a large scale became common. Melania is said to have freed eight thousand slaves in the year 406 alone, and it was usual to give not only freedom, but also the land or money with which they might earn their living.

In addition to this, the Church was everywhere the protector of the poor, the orphan and the criminal. The bishop was not only the administrator of the charity of the faithful, he also acquired a recog-

---

[3] St. Ambrose, *On Naboth* xii.
[4] St. Basil, *Hom. in Lucam.*

nized position as the representative of all the oppressed classes, as their defender not only against the rich, but against the government and the tax-collector. How widely these activities extended may be seen, for example, in the correspondence of St. Basil and in the record of his work for the people of Cappadocia during the famine of 367–368. The Church was gradually becoming an economic as well as a moral power, and as the economic condition of the Roman world declined, her relative wealth and importance increased until she became, above all in the Western provinces of the Empire, the only social force which retained life and vigor.

Thus, while the Church could not cure the social evils that had become endemic in the Roman Empire and the Mediterranean world, it did bring into that world a new hope and a way of life which were to be the source of a new Christian culture. We call this culture Byzantine because it had its center in the new Christian capital which Constantine had founded and because it was in the Eastern Empire that it found its classical development. Nevertheless, it was originally common to the whole Empire, and in spite of a gradual divergence between the Greek-speaking East and the Latin West, the great Christian Fathers of the fourth and fifth centuries still belonged to the same world and shared the same cultural background. From the fifth century onwards, the Western provinces were brought into increasingly close contact with the Germanic barbarians, but in spite of the social changes this produced, they remained faithful to the intellectual and religious tradition of the earlier period. Consequently the rise of the new Christian culture in the fourth century is an event of incalculable importance since it was the foundation on which the two twin cultures of Eastern and Western Christendom are based.

It is true that the barrier of language between the Greek-speaking world and the Latin West was always serious, so that the writings of the Greek Fathers were little read in the West, and those of the Latin Fathers were even more neglected in the East. But the separation was less marked in the fourth and fifth centuries than at any other period. The common culture of the Roman Empire was a synthesis of two elements, never completely fused. Greeks and Romans retained their own cultural traditions, so that in spite of the Hellenization of the West and the Romanization of the East, the Greek and the Latin cities continued to be distinct social organisms with their own social and political institutions. But this was not so in the case of the new Christian culture. The Church from the beginning was Catholic and ecumenical, and Christian communities everywhere possessed the same institutions and the same form of organization. It is true that the Church had adapted itself to the pattern of political order, so that the frontiers of the ecclesiastical provinces corresponded with those of the provinces of the new Empire. The Catholic Church was a society of city-churches, as the Roman Empire was a society of city-states, and the terms commonly used to describe the two elements that made up the Church—the clergy and the laity—were the same as those used for the magistrates and the people in the city—*ordo* and *plebs*.

But the parallelism does not extend beyond this relatively superficial level. Each city was in theory an autonomous community with its own exclusive franchise. But all the churches were one Church and all their members, members of one another. The whole Christian world from Western Europe to Persia was united by a common spiritual citizenship and shared the same rites of initiation and communion by which they were made not only members of a universal society, but partakers of a new life.

The Byzantines were so conscious of this all-embracing unity that they tended to regard the Empire as the embodiment of this universal spiritual society and thus to overlook or minimize the essential duality of Church and State. Even as early as the time of Constantine, his biographer and admirer, Eusebius of Caesarea, developed the parallelism between the divine order of the universe and the political order of the new Christian Empire. He sees a providential harmony between the spiritual unity of the cosmos in the Divine Word, which frees mankind from the spiritual tyranny of false gods, and the political unity of the Roman Empire which has freed the civilized world from the perils of civil war within and from barbarian invasions from without, so that "the whole world is like one well-ordered and united family. For our Emperor, invested as he is with a semblance of heavenly sovereignty, directs his gaze above and frames his earthly government according to the pattern of that divine original, finding strength in its conformity to the monarchy of God."[5]

This identification of the political order with the divine order and of the universal Empire with the universal Church is characteristic of Byzantine culture and gave the emperor a sacred and theocratic character which was to prove a danger to the unity of the Church. It was not that the emperors were opposed in principle to the freedom of the Church; on the contrary, as the Emperor Justinian explains in his carefully worded statement which forms the preface to his *Sixth Novellum* (535), it was the function of the emperor to maintain harmony between the two powers and a due observance of the dogmas and canons of the Orthodox Church. But this concern of the emperors with the cause of religious unity led them to interfere in every theological controversy by imposing an official solution which they then proceeded to enforce by bureaucratic action.

The history of the Byzantine Empire from Constantine I (324) to Constantine IV (668–685), for three and a half centuries, is the story of conflicts that arose from these imposed solutions—first the semi-Arian formulas of Constantine II in the fourth century, which were upheld by Valens, then the Henoticon of Zeno in 482 which gave rise to the Acacian schism, next the Condemnation of the Three Chapters by Justinian in 543 and finally the Ecthesis of Heraclius in 638 which caused the Monothelite Schism. All these conflicts defeated their object since they tended to identify heresy with disloyalty and to convert every theological dispute into a cause

[5] Eusebius, *Oration in Praise of Constantine* (English translation, 1845), p. 301.

of national or local resistance. For the Churches of the East and West looked for spiritual guidance not to the Byzantine Emperor and the Patriarch of Constantinople, but to the authority of the more ancient apostolic sees—to Rome in the West, to Alexandria in Egypt, to Antioch in Syria, while the Christians of the Persian Empire looked to the Church of St. Thomas at Edessa and the School of the Persians at Nisibis. Each of these centers had its own theological tradition and tended to take its own line in theological controversies, but they also represented independent cultural or national traditions, so that, for example, the loyalty of the Egyptians to the theology of St. Cyril was inseparable from their national patriotism, and their resistance to the theological decisions of the Byzantine government in the fifth century acquired the character of a national resistance movement.

The position of Rome was somewhat different, since the Papacy was not identified with any particular school of theology, but claimed to be the moderator of the universal Church. Thus its interests were the same as that of the Emperors since both were concerned with the preservation of Catholic unity. But the Papacy could not accept the claims of the Empire to be the final court of appeal and arbitrator in religious disputes, and it constantly opposed attempts of the Emperors to impose a theological decision in the interests of the political unity of the universal Empire, since its own decisions were dictated by the primary importance of the unity of the Church and the unity of the faith.

Thus from the beginning there was a latent opposition between the Roman Papacy and the Byzantine *Caesaropapism,* the open expression of which was delayed for many centuries by the political loyalty of Rome to the Byzantine Empire and the loyalty of the Empire to the Orthodox faith. Nevertheless, throughout this period the West was becoming increasingly detached from the Empire in spite of Justinian's temporary success in restoring Byzantine control in Italy and North Africa, and in the following age the Roman tradition of independent apostolic authority and ecclesiastical freedom became the basis of the new religious development which shaped the new Catholic culture of Western Europe.

But while there were strong social and political forces making for the division of the East and the West, there were also very strong religious forces making for their unity. The great religious innovation which was developed in this age—the monastic life—was neither Greek nor Latin in origin. It first developed in the Egyptian desert as a protest against any compromise between the Christian ideal of perfection and the worldliness of life in the cities.

Yet in the course of a century it was fully adopted by the Church alike in the East and the West, as the accepted norm of the Christian life. Although it was rapidly assimilated and adapted to different environments, it remained extraordinarily faithful to its original ideals; the lives and sayings of the monks of Egypt—the Desert Fathers—were translated into every language, and seekers after perfection used to visit Egypt to learn from the examples of the monks. Cassian, Palladius, Jerome and Paula, and Rufinus all visited Egypt for lengthy periods at the end of the fourth century and have left full and fascinating accounts of what they saw and heard.

Thus monasticism was one of the most important religious creations of the patristic age and one that was purely Oriental in origin— for the early monks were Coptic-speakers, like St. Anthony and St. Pachomius. It is a remarkable paradox that such a movement originating as a protest against culture and an escape from culture should become one of the characteristic institutions of Byzantine culture and later of Western Catholicism.

From the beginning, however, we can discern several distinct tendencies in the monastic movement, and in the course of the following centuries these tendencies continued to develop. The original Egyptian monasticism of St. Antony and the early hermits was essentially a flight (*anachoresis*) from the world and secular culture, and it is remarkable that this word was already being used in Egypt during the third and fourth centuries as a technical term for the act by which the peasants and curiales attempted to escape from the crushing burdens of taxation and compulsory services. But already, as early as the time of St. Pachomius, from 323 to 346, a different type of monasticism was being established at Tabbenisi and Akhmin in Upper Egypt which resembled what we know as monasticism today—that is to say, a religious community living in obedience under a common rule and a common superior, and devoting their time not only to solitary prayers and meditation but to organized common work and common worship.

This was the type of monasticism which was to spread all over the Christian world from the Atlantic to Persia, and it was St. Pachomius and his Rule (which was originally written in Coptic) that were the starting point of the whole movement. The original Antonian or eremetical type, it is true, also had a very wide diffusion, especially in Syria and Mesopotamia.

But it was in Asia Minor soon after the middle of the fourth century that the cenobite, or congregational, form of monasticism attained a more complete development owing to the teachings of the great St. Basil, who at this time presided over a monastic community on the River Iris in Cappadocia. He was opposed alike to the undisciplined individualism of the solitary hermits and the excessively rigid mass discipline of the great Pachomian monasteries which left little room for personal contact between the abbot and the individual monk. He believed that community life is superior to the life of the solitary on account of man's essentially social nature, and he taught that the higher a man went in spiritual life, the more necessary it was for him to use his spiritual gifts for the good of others. The monastery was essentially a spiritual community, the members of which shared not only their material possessions but also their spiritual goods. The law of charity was the supreme principle, and it was extended even to the outside world by the foundation of monastic orphanages and schools. Thus it is not too much to say that St. Basil humanized and socialized the monastic life, which in its primitive Egyptian form tended towards an ideal of superhuman asceticism and austerity.

This more temperate monastic ideal not only influenced the Church in the Byzantine world but was diffused in the West through the translation or condensed version which Rufinus made into Latin and which became well known to St. Benedict and the other founders of monasticism in Western Europe.

Monasticism spread to Italy and Gaul in the fourth century, and to Britain and Spain in the fifth. It was above all the French Riviera which became the great center of early monasticism in the West with the island monastery of Lérins near Cannes, founded by St. Honoratus, and Cassian's monastic foundations at Marseilles where he composed his famous and most influential works on Egyptian monasticism. But even before this, in the fourth century, St. Martin, the Pannonian ex-soldier, had founded an important center of monasticism at Tours Ligugé, while in Italy St. Eusebius of Vercelli had adapted the monastic ideal for his clergy—an adaptation which was carried by St. Augustine to Africa and which was to become a characteristic feature of the Western Church.

However, it was not until the sixth century—the age of St. Benedict and Cassiodorus in Italy, of SS. Columba and Columban in Ireland, of St. Isidore in Spain and of St. Caesarius of Arles in France—that Western monasticism achieved its full development.

But already in the East we can distinguish the different causes which led to this development. In the first place, monasticism arose as a protest against the secularization of the Church that followed the conversion of the Eastern Empire. The life of the monk in the fourth century, like that of the martyr and confessor in the third, was regarded as a visible proof of the miraculous power of Christianity to overcome the powers of the world. His heroic feats of asceticism were, like the suffering of the martyrs, signs of the completeness of his victory.

On the other hand, the communal organization of the later monasticism, introduced by St. Pachomius and improved by St. Basil, shows how the total break with secular culture which marked the original monasticism might become the principle of a new social development, based on Christian principles, so that monasteries would be, as it were, the cells of a new culture. This was the development which would prove of such immense significance for the history of Western Europe in the following centuries.

IX. THE INFLUENCE OF LITURGY
AND THEOLOGY ON THE DEVELOPMENT
OF BYZANTINE CULTURE

The spiritual unity of Christian culture finds its fullest embodiment in the early liturgies, which are not only the most intimate expression of the faith and life of the ancient Church, but also the first creative achievement of the new Christian culture. Nowhere is the spirit of the ancient Church more fully manifested than in the rite of baptism and the associated rites and ceremonies which have left such a deep mark on the Roman liturgy of Lent, Easter and Pentecost. We have also the evidence of the art of the catacombs and the ancient Christian baptisteries, especially that of St. John Lateran with the inscription of Pope Xystus III (432–440).

These final rites were preceded by the long period of instruction of the catechumenate, of which there are examples in the discourses of St. Cyril of Jerusalem and the homilies of St. Augustine. This was the first Christian education by which the new Christians were initiated into the sacred tradition of the Scriptures. And this was not only the source of Christian theology, it was also one of the primary elements in the formation of a Christian culture. For behind the change of culture, there is the spiritual change, "the re-creation of a new people," the theme that runs through all those liturgical rites and which finds poetical expression in the above-mentioned inscription of Pope Xystus:

Gens sacranda polis hic semine nascitur almo
quam fecundatis Spiritus edit aquis
Virgineo fetu genitrix Ecclesia natos
quos spirante Deo concipit amne parit

. . . . . .

Fons hic est vitae qui totum diluit orbem
sumens de Christi vulnere principium

. . . . . .

Nulla renascentum est distantia quos facit unum
unus fons, unus spiritus, una fides.[1]

The first external result of the Peace of the Church was the
erection of the Constantinian basilicas in which all the artistic inheritance of the Roman-Hellenistic culture served the liturgy of
the Church. And the liturgy was itself a work of art—perhaps the
greatest and the most elaborate ever created by man. Everything
that the Christian world possessed of doctrine and poetry, music
and art was poured into the liturgy, moulded into an organic
whole which centered upon the Divine Mysteries.

The liturgy, it is true, was not the creation of any individual: it
is the anonymous work of centuries of growth, so that it may be
compared to the growth of a natural organism rather than a work
of art in the ordinary sense of the word. As a modern Austrian
writer—Sigismund von Radecki—has well said, "It is not art, but
rather the archetype towards which art strives to ascend."[2]

It is difficult for us today to realize the immense importance of
the liturgy in the life of the Christian community in the first centuries after the Peace of the Church. It was their literature, their

[1] "Here of fertile seed is born a people consecrated to heaven whom the spirit
brings forth from the pregnant waters. Here in virgin birth mother Church by
the baptismal stream bears the children conceived by the breath of God. . . .

"Here is the fountain of life, sprung from Christ's wound to cleanse the world
entire. . . . No separation is there among the regenerate made one by one fountain, one spirit, one faith."

[2] *Wort und Wunder* (1942), p. 51.

poetry, drama and art, but above all it was a common social act which occupied the central place in their lives. It even came to dominate secular activities, as we see in Constantine Porphyrogenitus' account of the public ceremonies of the Byzantine court in the tenth century. For in the Byzantine Empire, Church ceremonies and state ceremonies were very closely related, since the latter, as Constantine says, were intended to "reflect in their rhythm and order the harmony and movement of the divine order of the universe." It is this liturgical character of Byzantine culture which differentiates it most sharply from that of the modern world. To us the social aspects of secular and sacred activities are essentially disparate and unconnected; to them there was one sacred order running through everything, and it was only natural that the Church and the Empire should resemble one another in their external behavior.

In the West this unity did not exist, owing first to the more gradual conversion of the Western provinces to Christianity and the strength of the pagan opposition within the Empire, and secondly to the cultural opposition between the barbarian State and the Latin Church. Nevertheless the cumulative influence of the liturgy on Western culture was no less strong. Indeed in some respects it was even stronger, because Western culture was in a more fluid state and the influence of classical literature and art was too weak to compete with that of the liturgy. In the newly converted countries like Anglo-Saxon England the only centers of higher culture were the monasteries, and the culture of the monasteries was entirely religious and liturgical.

Moreover, since the laity in the new kingdoms of the West were entirely illiterate, the liturgy was practically the only channel for the diffusion of Christian culture, and the whole life of the people revolved round the Church, followed its annual cycle of feasts and fasts.

Thus the liturgy was the focus which integrated other manifestations of Christian culture. Christian art and architecture, music and poetry, all grew up in the service of the liturgy and were moulded by its influence. The Church took the existing forms of late Roman culture and used them for liturgical purposes, and by doing so transformed them into something new, as we can see in the evolution of the basilica from its Roman-Hellenistic to its Christian-Byzantine form.

But this was only one side of the Christian cultural inheritance. If the body of the new culture was Hellenistic or Roman, its spirit was Semitic, since it was derived from the sacred tradition of Israel. There is a direct link between the liturgy of the Church and that of the Synagogue. The entire liturgy, even today, is permeated by the language and imagery of the Bible, and this was one of the main factors which separated the new Christian culture from that of the Roman-Hellenistic world and gave it a new history and a new world of sacred archetypes and symbolic imagery which took the place of the old mythology which had formed the background of classical literature.

Not the least important aspect of this process was the birth of a new Christian liturgical poetry. For a new poetry is the expression of a new soul. It involves new psychological attitudes and new emotional reactions to life. From its earliest beginnings the Christian Church possessed the inheritance of the Jewish poetry of the Psalms, which had already been employed for liturgical purposes by the Synagogue. This was a new poetry indeed. It expressed what had never been expressed in classical poetry and it expressed it in a new language and a new rhythm. Nevertheless it became immediately popular with the Gentile converts as well as with the Jewish Christians. It expressed spiritual things with a much greater intensity and with more intense personal feeling than classical poetry had ever attained, even in a narrower range and on a lower level. It was a poetry which could be applied by the individual Christian to express his own thoughts and feelings, yet it was at the same time the voice of the Church and the voice of Christ, as St. Augustine writes in a wonderful passage: "Who is this one man who calls from the ends of the earth? Only that heritage of which it was said to the Son, 'Desire of me and I will give the heathen for thine inheritance and the uttermost parts of the earth for thy possession.' This is Christ's inheritance, this is Christ's possession, this Body of Christ, this one Church of Christ, this unity that we are, calling from the ends of the earth. He moves us Himself through all nations, in the whole world, in great glory but in great temptation. He is in heaviness and He calls to God from the ends of the earth, but He is not forsaken. . . . It is His voice we hear in all the Psalms, 'whether in praise or lamentation, rejoicing in hope, or groaning in present sorrow' —'*vel psallentem vel gementem, vel laetantem in spe, vel suspirantem in re.*'"

This tradition of Hebrew psalmody was continued in the early Church—first in the four evangelical canticles of St. Luke's Gospel, and then in the "psalms and hymns and spiritual songs" of which St. Paul speaks. The first thing the Church did was to sing, and it continued to sing, until out of that song a new Christian poetry was developed in Greek, Latin and Syriac.

The original home of this new Christian poetry was in Syria and Mesopotamia, and it was there that it developed earliest and most luxuriantly. Syriac Christian literature is pre-eminently a poetic literature, for the Syrians used poetry not only for liturgical purposes but also as a medium for theological teaching. The originator of the new poetry was Bardesanes, the second-century Gnostic, but it was brought into the service of the Church in the fourth century by St. Ephrem, who was at once the greatest doctor and the most famous poet of the Syrian Church. His biographer has described how the love of the people of Edessa for folk songs and dances led him to compose hymns and spiritual instructions divided into strophes and refrains. "He divided the virgins into choirs to sing alternately and taught them different musical tunes. They met on Sundays, on the great feasts and at the commemoration of the martyrs while he, as a father, stood in the midst accompanying them on the harp."

Thus there developed not only the antiphonal chant but also the poetic dialogue between two persons or groups in dramatic form with a short introduction. Finally we have the long metrical homilies and instructions which St. Ephrem composed in defense of the faith against the heretics.

It seems probable that this Syriac poetry was not only the earliest in date, but also had a direct influence on the rise of the new Christian poetry in the Greek and Latin world. There is an extraordinary resemblance which can hardly be fortuitous between these Syriac metrical homilies and the rhythm composed by St. Augustine against the Donatists—*psalmus abecedarius contra partem Donati*—which is also based on number and accent instead of quantity with a recurrent refrain as in Syriac poetry.

This, however, is an altogether exceptional work. The true origins of Christian poetry in the West are to be found in the Latin tradition. There we see most clearly how the tradition of Hebrew psalmody met the tradition of classical Latin poetry and how their meeting produced the Latin hymn which was a living literary form for a thousand years and which, apart from its liturgical importance, has had a deep and wide influence on Western religious poetry.

We are exceptionally well informed about the genesis of this literature, owing to the fact that St. Augustine was a witness of the circumstances under which the new liturgical poetry was popularized at Milan by St. Ambrose; and he also provides evidence for the genuineness of several of the existing Ambrosian hymns. It was peculiarly fortunate that the rise of Latin hymnology should have been dominated by St. Ambrose. For the standard of Latin liturgical poetry was therefore set by a man who even more than St. Augustine or St. Jerome united in himself the Latin genius and the Christian spirit. As Archbishop Trench wrote more than a century ago, "Only after a while does one learn to feel the grandeur of this unadorned metre, and the profound, though it may have been more instinctive than conscious, wisdom of the poet in choosing it; or to appreciate that noble confidence in the surpassing interest of his theme, which has rendered him indifferent to any but its simplest setting forth. It is as though, building an altar to the living God, he would observe the Levitical precept, and rear it of unhewn stones, upon which no tool has been lifted. The great objects of faith in their simplest expression are felt by him so sufficient to stir all the deepest affections of the heart, that any attempt to dress them up, to array them in moving language, were merely superfluous. The passion is there, but it is latent and represt, a fire burning inwardly, the glow of an austere enthusiasm, which reveals itself in deed, but not to every careless beholder. Nor do we presently fail to observe how truly these poems belonged to their time and to the circumstances under which they were produced—how suitably the faith which was in actual conflict with, and was just triumphing over, the powers of this world, found its utterance in hymns such as these, wherein is no softness, perhaps little tenderness; but a rock-like firmness, the old Roman stoicism transmuted and glorified into that nobler Christian courage, which encountered and at length overcame the world."[3]

The Ambrosian use of the iambic dimeter was not the only early form of Christian Latin poetry. On the other hand, we have the more elaborate and literary Christian poetry of Prudentius, who may have been a greater poet than St. Ambrose, but who was so conscious of his classical learning and tradition that he fails to give full expression, as Ambrose had done in his simpler style, to the new spirit represented by the poetry of the psalter and the liturgy. And on the other hand we have the great rhythmical prose poem of Nicetas of Remesiana—the *Te Deum*—which is much closer to the tradition of Hebrew psalmody but which stands practically alone and founded no tradition. It was the Ambrosian type of

[3] R. C. Trench, *Sacred Latin Poetry*, pp. 81–82.

hymn which became the archetype of Western hymnology, and its influence has survived all the changes in fashion and metrical form and has continued to bear fruit down to modern times, as in the hymns of J. B. de Santeuil in the seventeenth century and of Charles Coffin in the eighteenth.

By far the greatest monument of Christian culture is the theological work of the Fathers of the fourth and fifth centuries, which has remained the common patrimony of the universal Church and the foundation on which all later theologies have been built.

The Age of the Fathers is roughly co-terminous with the later centuries of the Roman Empire and the early Byzantine period, from the time of Marcus Aurelius to the Mohammedan conquest of the Eastern provinces, so that their writings record the whole process of the conversion of the ancient world to Christianity and the development of Christian doctrine through the conflict with paganism and heresy down to its final definition by the great Ecumenical Councils.

Here again, the tradition of Christian culture is threefold— Greek, Latin and Syrian, but in this case there can be no question which was the predominant element.

As in the classical world Greek had been the language of philosophy, so in the Christian world it was the language of theology. In the earlier period, in the apostolic and post-apostolic age, Greek had been the common language of the Church throughout the Empire—at Rome no less than at Antioch and Alexandria; and it remained the theological and liturgical language of the West down to the time of Hippolytus of Porto in the third century, of the East as late as the age of Severus of Antioch and the author who used the name of Dionysius the Areopagite in the sixth century. Above all in the first century and a quarter of the Christian Empire, from the Council of Nicea in 325 to that of Chalcedon in 451, the Greek or Byzantine world was the scene of a consecutive series of theological debates, through which the orthodox faith received its final theological formulation. It was under these conditions that the Greek patristic literature was composed. It was essentially a literature of controversy, most of it written under the stress of some particular theological conflict, and it was composed by men who had the Greek passion for philosophical discussion and who brought to the study of the faith the whole armament of logic and dialectic which they had learned in the schools of Athens and Alexandria. This makes it a difficult literature for the modern reader who does not possess this dialectical equipment. Indeed it was one of the main causes which led modern Liberal Protestantism, above all the Ritschlians, to reject the whole tradition of patristic theology as an alien importation and a Hellenistic deformation of evangelical Christianity. Even in the age of the Fathers themselves we find a certain resistance to Greek theology, particularly among the Syrians, who were temperamentally opposed to the rationalism of Greek thought. St. Ephrem, above all, devotes much of his poetry to an attack on the spirit of dialectical argument and disputation which the Greeks had brought into theology. They were the Disputers, "the children of strife," who destroy the Faith by seeking to explain it. "Blessed is the man who has not tasted the gall of the wisdom of the Greeks or let slip the simplicity of the Apostles." For true wisdom is to be found not in speculation but in contemplation and in "tuning the harp of the soul to the order of the mysteries."

This is the way of the mystic, but it is not the way of the theologian. It was only by a sustained effort of theological discussion and definition that Christianity was able to overcome the intellectual resistance of Hellenism and make the faith comprehensible and acceptable to the higher culture of the ancient world. Thus the assimilation of Greek thought by the work of the great theologians of the fourth century is comparable to the assimilation of Aristotelian logic and metaphysics by medieval Scholastic philosophy, and the resistance of St. Ephrem foreshadows the attitude of St. Bernard towards Abelard and of the traditional Augustinianism towards thirteenth-century Aristotelianism. At the same time we must remember that the polemic of St. Ephrem was directed not against theology as such but against the theological rationalism of the Arians; and the Greek Fathers themselves were at one with him in their condemnation of the excesses of unbridled theological speculation. Where they differed was in their recognition of the validity of a philosophical treatment of religious questions and of the need for a synthesis of the Christian tradition with the Hellenistic culture.

The key to this approach is to be found in the doctrine of the Logos, which from the time of the early Christian apologists down to the end of the patristic period forms the bridge between Christian faith and Greek philosophy. It was the central conviction of the Greek mind from the time of Pythagoras and Heraclitus that the visible world is an intelligible order or harmony and that the creative principle behind the universe is Reason—*Nous* or Logos. This view was accepted by the Christian apologists who indentified the Greek cosmological principle with the creative Word of the true God who has become manifest in Jesus Christ. As Tertullian, following the earlier apologists like Justin and Tatian, writes, "It is abundantly plain that some philosophers also regard the Logos, that is the Word and Reason, as the Creator of the universe. For Zeno lays it down that he is the creator having made all things according to a determinate plan—Cleanthes ascribes all this to Spirit which he maintains pervades the universe. And we, in like manner, hold that the Word and reason and power, by which we have said God made all, has spirit as his proper and essential substance, as the soul is in the speaker, and thought in the planner and power in the maker. And we have learnt that he was brought forth from God, and by being brought forth was begotten, and therefore is named Son of God and God from unity of substance."

But it is with Origen, the last of the great apologists and the first of the great theologians, that the philosophic and cosmological implications of the Logos doctrine were most fully developed in relation to Hellenistic thought. As we have already seen, he stood in close relation to contemporary Neo-Platonism, and his system developed under the same philosophical influences. His conception of the universe, like theirs, is that of a hierarchy of spiritual natures and states which descends from God to the world of sense and the frontiers of nothingness. This intelligible world is created in the image of the Logos, the supreme archetype, who is himself the image of the Father or the mirror through which his light illuminates the whole spiritual creation. By the contemplation of the Father, the Logos creates the world, and by the contemplation of the Logos the creation returns to the Father. Only in the Logos is the divine pattern preserved pure and intact. Everywhere else there is a falling away, a descent from unity to multiplicity, from Being to Not-Being, from good to evil. And this fall is the cause of the diversity and inequality of created natures. For all spiritual natures were created free and equal, and their present state of degradation and inequality is the result of their own guilt, which they have incurred in their previous states of existence.

Despite Latin ecclesiastical condemnations Origen's philosophical theology, with its cosmological treatment of the Logos doctrine, its ideal of spiritual hierarchy and its affinities with Neo-Platonism and Hellenic culture, continued to exert an enormous influence on the thought of Eastern Christendom throughout the patristic period.

It finds complete expression in the apologetic writings of Eusebius, the most learned Christian scholar of the age. In his *Theophany* especially, in spite of its verbose and rhetorical style, the aesthetic idealism of Greek thought found its complete expression and fulfilment in terms of Christian theology. Moreover, the case of Eusebius is especially significant, because it shows the organic connection between this Christian Hellenic cosmology and the political ideal of the Christian Byzantine Empire. For as we have already noted, Eusebius sees a providential harmony between the unity of the cosmos in the Divine Word, which frees mankind from the spiritual tyranny of false gods, and the social unification of the world by the Roman Empire, which has freed the civilized world from internal war and from the attacks of the barbarians from without, and in the Emperor a semblance of heavenly sovereignty.

Thus the Age of the Fathers, when Christianity was becoming the dominant religion of the Empire, saw Christian culture accord a much larger place to the traditions of Hellenic and Latin culture than it had done in the post-apostolic age. From the time of Clement of Alexandria and Tertullian to that of St. Jerome, St. Augustine and Theodoret, the Fathers were men steeped in the literary and philosophic culture of the classical world, and they had to adapt the sacred literature of the Church to the needs of a public which accepted the standards and values of classical culture. Thus the educated Christian belonged to two worlds, had inherited the cultural traditions of both. The task of explaining the language and thought of the Bible to men who thought in different terms and regarded anything that did not conform to Hellenistic standards as barbarous, was one of immense difficulty. There is in fact a dualism in early Christian and patristic culture, which means between two different worlds of thought: a dualism exemplified by the Latin of Jerome's letters and that of his translation of the Bible, or again between the old classical poetry of Juvencus and the new liturgical poetry of the author of the *Te Deum*.

Nevertheless the main intellectual effort of the patristic age was devoted to the development of the biblical tradition and its adaptation to the understanding and needs of Gentile culture. As Cuthbert Butler wrote: "There is a sense in which nearly the whole of the writings of the early Christian Fathers may be truly said to be the expositions of Holy Scripture," and in the later periods the Fathers who were most Greek in culture, like Origen and St.

John Chrysostom and Theodoret, were also the ones who did most for the study and exposition of the Bible.

The essential achievement of the patristic age was the synthesis of Eastern religion and Western culture, or, to be more precise, the uniting of the spiritual traditions of Israel and of the Christian Church with the intellectual and artistic traditions of Hellenism and the political and social traditions of Rome. This synthesis has remained the foundation of Western culture and has never been destroyed, in spite of the tendency of the Reformation to re-Hebraize Christianity and that of the Renaissance to re-Hellenize culture.

And this synthesis has been no less important for Christianity itself. No form of Christianity since the days of Marcion has attempted to disavow its basis in the Old Testament, and Catholic Christianity has always been fully conscious of its debt to Hellenic thought, primarily for its contribution to the theology of the Fathers and the definitions of the Ecumenical Councils, but also in a secondary degree for the development of its philosophy and the formulation of its jurisprudence. Nor do the Oriental forms of Christianity reject this Hellenic element. Syrian literature derives from the same tradition as that of the West. There has been no attempt to produce an exclusively Oriental version of the Christian faith.

The original decision concerning the harmony between Christianity and Hellenism was made by the Apostolic Church when it turned from the Jews to the Gentiles, from the closed world of the Synagogue and the Law to the cosmopolitan society of the Roman-Hellenistic world. In spite of his apparent anti-intellectualism, St. Paul was by no means unconscious of the value of humane letters in the work of evangelization. In fact he was himself the first Christian humanist, and his speech to the Athenians, with its appeal to the Hellenistic doctrines of the unity of the human race, of divine providence and of the natural affinity between the human and divine natures, is the basic document of Christian humanism. All this is much more than a method of apologetic devised for a Hellenistic audience. It is an expression of St. Paul's sense of a certain affinity between Christianity and Hellenism, owing to which the Hellenistic cities of the Eastern Roman Empire provided the necessary milieu for the propagation of the new faith.

What was the nature of this affinity? On the one hand Hellenism provided a humane ethos and a philosophy of human nature which were not to be found in other cultures, while on the other hand Christianity is distinguished from other religions by its doctrine of the Incarnate Word, through whom the divine and human natures have been substantially united in the historic person of Jesus Christ, the mediator between God and Man.

It is clear that this essential Christian doctrine gives a new value to human nature, human history and human life which is not to be found in the other great Oriental religions. The more the latter insist on the transcendence and absoluteness of the Divine Nature, the more they widen the gulf between God and Man, so that they tend either to deny the reality of the material world or to regard it as essentially evil, so that the body is a jail in which the human soul has been imprisoned. These ideas were so powerful in the ancient world that they have often threatened to invade Christianity, and it was only by using the methods of Hellenic culture and with the help of Christian humanists like St. Irenaeus and St. Gregory of Nyssa that the Church was able to vindicate the Christian doctrine of man.

To St. Gregory there is a profound analogy between man's natural function as a rational being—the ruler of the world and the link between the intelligible and sensible orders—and the divine mission of the Incarnate Word which unites humanity with the divine nature and restores the broken unity of the whole creation. The natural order corresponds with the supernatural, and both form part of the same divine, all-embracing plan of creation and restoration. The Incarnation restores human nature to its original integrity, and with it the whole material creation, which is raised through man to a higher plane and integrated with the intelligible or spiritual order.

These doctrines are no doubt fundamentally Pauline, but with St. Gregory of Nyssa they are explicitly related to the tradition of Greek thought and to the Hellenic ideal of humanity. Moreover, St. Gregory of Nyssa with his brother St. Basil and their friend St. Gregory Nazianzen were also humanists in the more technical sense—great students and lovers of humane letters who had a decisive influence on the development of the culture of Orthodox Christendom. Today there is a tendency to view Eastern Christianity through Russian eyes and to stress those elements in the Byzantine tradition which are most remote from the humanist tradition—as expressed, for example, by Avakkum, Khomiakoff and Dostoevsky. But these represent the spirit of Russia rather than the Byzantine tradition. The founders of the Byzantine culture were the great Cappadocian Fathers, and behind all the later developments of Eastern Orthodoxy, which found so many different expressions in different ages and peoples, there lies this Christian Hellenism of the fourth century which was also a Christian humanism.

It is true that there is another element in Orthodox Christianity which is neither Western nor humanist—I mean the tradition of the monks of the desert. But whereas the Byzantine culture was able to incorporate and Hellenize this tradition, thanks largely to St. Basil himself, the purely Oriental element in monasticism, as represented by such leaders of Egyptian monasticism as Bgoul and Schenouti, became unorthodox as well as non-humanist and was one of the driving forces behind the religious revolt which separated Egypt and Syria from the Orthodox Church.

It is therefore no accident that this great Orientalist reaction against Hellenic culture should have found its theological justification in a doctrine which denied the full humanity of Christ.

Nor did the Oriental reaction stop at this point. For Monophysitism is only the first step in a far-reaching movement which carried the East away from Christianity and found its final expression in the uncompromising unitarian absolutism of Islam which rejects the whole idea of Incarnation and restores an impassable gulf between God and Man.

And thus while it is easy enough to conceive of an Oriental Christianity which has no affinity with any form of humanist and Hellenic culture, we must admit that it is very difficult in practice for such a Christianity to hold its own against the various forms of unorthodox or non-Christian spirituality—Manichean, Moslem or Monophysite—which make such a profound appeal to the Oriental mind.

It is true that Western Christianity also has witnessed attempts to eliminate the Hellenistic-Patristic tradition from Christianity. These have occurred among the more extreme forms of Protestant sectarianism, which appeal to the Bible alone or to some form of direct prophetic inspiration—for example, some of the Puritan sects in seventeenth-century England and in nineteenth-century America. These movements tend to such an extreme reaction against secular culture that they become movements of social revolution—like the Munster, and the Diggers under the English Commonwealth.

The only true Oriental Christianity is that of the Syriac Churches, which became separated from Byzantine Orthodoxy in the fifth century. Nevertheless, in spite of their primitive and ultra-conservative tradition, they represent a similar synthesis of Christian and Hellenic traditions to that of the rest of Christendom. They also look back to the literature of the patristic period as the source of their religious culture. And it was through them that Greek philosophy and science, above all the works of Aristotle, were transmitted to the medieval Moslem world.

It is only their sacred poetry, derived from the ancient Syriac tradition of St. Ephrem, that is entirely their own and owes nothing to Western or Hellenic influence. Here, as we have seen, it is they who influenced the West, not vice versa.

This community of inheritance from the patristic age unites the Churches of the East and the West in spite of their dogmatic and ecclesiastical differences.

Alike in theology and liturgy, in the cult of the saints and the monastic institution, they share the same traditions which go back to the formative age of the Fathers, and especially to the fourth century.

Hence this period is of crucial importance for the study of Christian culture in East and West, first, as the age of religious unity which we must study in order to find the religious elements which transcend differences of culture, but secondly, as the point of divergence where we can see the effect of cultural differences in producing religious schism.

From the sociological point of view this period is of unique importance as affording almost the only example of the process by which one of the higher civilizations is transformed from within and achieves a completely different form. The parallel process of change which affected Chinese culture in the Buddhist period is less significant because the change was less profound and less permanent, and it is also less easy to study because of the absence or inaccessibility of historical material.

In conclusion, to sum up the debt which Europe owes to the Byzantine culture is not easy. The influences were so manifold and passed through so many channels. There was the influence of Byzantine Ravenna upon the West in the fifth and sixth centuries, the contact through Venice and Amalfi and Southern Italy in the early Middle Ages, the influence through the Latin conquerors of Constantinople in the thirteenth century and the last contribution by the Greek refugees at the time of the Turkish conquest of the Aegean. And on the other hand, there is the direct influence of Constantinople on Eastern Europe through the culture of the Balkans, the conversion of the Slavs and the wholesale importation of Byzantine art and culture into Christian Russia, so that the whole culture of Eastern Europe still rests on Byzantine foundations. But beyond all this there is the incalculable importance of the existence of a great Christian civilization behind the medieval world of Western Europe. It was the Byzantine culture that created the view of life that we call medieval, and whatever in the West was not purely barbaric, participated in the spiritual and intellectual atmosphere that came from the Christian East. Only when the East had ceased to be Christian, and a Mohammedan sultan ruled at Adrianople and Byzantium, did the civilization of Western Europe finally form for itself a new way of life and a new conception of the universe.

X. THE CHURCH AND THE
CONVERSION OF THE BARBARIANS

I.

In spite of the great achievements of the patristic period in religion and life, in theology, liturgy and art, which were embodied in the great age of Byzantine culture, the period ended catastrophically and tragically. As medieval culture ended in the Protestant Reformation and the separation of Northern Europe from Catholic unity, so the Patristic-Byzantine age ended in the loss of the Christian East. The great schisms of the fifth century after the Councils of Ephesus and Chalcedon led to the formation of new national churches—Nestorian in Persia and Monophysite in Egypt, Syria and Armenia.

The attempts of the Byzantine Empire to maintain religious unity took the form either of compromises which produced a new series of heresies and schisms like that of the Monothelites, or of a policy of repression which increased the disaffection of the Eastern peoples and provinces towards the Empire. Finally the whole fabric of the Orthodox Byzantine Empire in the Eastern Provinces collapsed under the sudden unexpected onslaught of the Arabs from the desert, who were welded together and launched on a career of world conquest by the new religion of Mohammed (634–644). Under his inspiration the Arab armies swept across the world from Central Asia to Spain (632–732).

This was a world revolution which changed the whole history

of West Asia and North Africa, and it was undoubtedly made possible by the religious disaffection of the Eastern and Southern provinces of the Byzantine Empire. Thus the vast opportunity that was opened in the patristic age for the conversion of the oriental world to Christianity was thrown away in a series of disastrous and unnecessary disputes, and lost forever.

For when Islam had taken form and set its roots in the soil of Asia and Africa, it remained for a thousand years and more a fixed barrier against the spread of the Church in the East and in Africa. More than that, it was destined to destroy the Christianity of the homelands of the Byzantine and Greek culture in Asia Minor and to make the Christian capital itself the center of a Mohammedan empire.

Thus the coming of Islam seems to be nothing less than a divine judgment on the Byzantine world for its failure to fulfil its mission. And the cause of that failure was the same as that for which St. Ephrem, the greatest of the Syrian Fathers, reproached the Greeks in the fourth century—the unbridled lust for theological controversy which made the most sacred dogmas of the faith slogans of party warfare, sacrificed charity and unity to party spirit.

Islam in the East

In the West the patristic age also ended tragically. Here, however, the disaster was political and social, and from the religious point of view the conquest of the Western provinces by the Northern barbarians did not put an end to the expansion of the Catholic Church. The collapse of the Empire took place earlier than in the East by two centuries at least, and this meant that it took place when Latin patristic culture was at the height of its activity in the age of St. Augustine, instead of being in a state of decline as was the Byzantine patristic culture in the seventh century.

Barbarian in the West

In any case the decline and fall of the Roman Empire was a long-drawn-out process, and though the forces of order rallied again and again, the relief was only temporary, and after a few years the defeated barbarians renewed their attacks and another frontier was lost, another province devastated. All this went on for more than five hundred years, so that the Church was thoroughly acclimatized to the atmosphere of catastrophe. At the beginning of the fifth century the great Maginot Line of the Roman defenses in Western Europe, from Scotland to Rumania, was finally broken, and the Roman Empire in the West gradually gave place to a series of barbarian kingdoms—Goths, Vandals, Franks, Anglo-Saxons and Lombards. In the East the Empire had hardly had time to rally from these disasters before a fresh series of catastrophes began, so that finally all the richest provinces of the East—Syria, Mesopotamia, Palestine and Egypt—were lost to the Arabs and the new religious empire of Islam, while the Balkans were overrun by the Slavs.

Thus the united Christian world of Constantine and Theodosius became separated into three parts:

1. In Asia Minor and the Aegean the Christian Empire and the Byzantine culture survived and kept the old traditions alive.

2. In Syria, Egypt and Africa the Christians survived as a subject class, cut off from their co-religionists in the West and deprived of the opportunity to develop their own culture, at least externally.

3. Finally, in the West, where the material setback to culture was more serious than in either of the other parts of the Christian world, the spiritual opportunities for building a new Christian culture were also greater than elsewhere. Though the Empire had fallen, the Church survived and was free to undertake the task of spreading the Christian faith among the barbarians. In Northwestern Europe, unlike the Near East, there were no long-standing traditions of ancient civilizations, no rival religions. For the new peoples of the North, in spite of their strength and vitality, were barbarians in the strict sense of the word. That is to say, they had no written literature, and only a rudimentary form of political organization, so that the Church came to them not only as the teacher of a new faith but also as the bearer of a higher culture.

II. Decline of the West

Even in the fourth century the situation in the West was already more unstable than that of the East. The Western Empire was more exposed to barbarian inroads, owing to the length of the frontier and the warlike character of the barbarians who lived on the other side of the Rhine and the Danube. And in addition to this external danger, there was the internal instability due to the indiscipline of the Western legions and their tendency to set up their commanders as rival emperors, especially in Britain, which produced a succession of pretenders to the crown, from Carausius in the time of Maximian to Maximus in the reign of Gratian and Constantine III in the time of Honorius, as well as Magnentius in Gaul in the time of Constans and Constantine.

The Roman armies themselves were recruited largely from barbarian sources, and by the fourth century the highest positions in the Empire were open to them—were occupied by Stilicho, Ricimer and Odovocar in the West, Gainas the Goth and Aspar the Alan in the East. Thus, during the fourth century, the population of the Western provinces already contained a considerable German and barbarian element, particularly in the army, which was largely commanded by barbarian officers, but also in the countryside, where barbarians had been introduced as peasant serfs or free settlers in very large numbers. The older Roman civilian population was steadily decreasing, owing to the decline of the cities, itself a result of the decline of trade and the increasing burden of taxation. Western society based itself more and more on a natural economy in which every large rural estate tended to form a self-sufficient economic unit. Hence, when the general breakdown of the imperial administration occurred after the death of Theodosius the Great—because of the weakness of the two boy emperors and the renewed wave of invasions which flooded the Western provinces with barbarian armies and led for the first time to the foundation of independent German kingdoms on Roman soil—the result was not a catastrophic end to civilization but merely a general deterioration of conditions which had already existed for a considerable time.

The Roman provincials settled down as well as they could under their new barbarian masters, and the ruling class, the great land-owners, continued to lead much the same life on their estates as before, as in the case of the family and friends of Sidonius Appolinaris, whose extensive correspondence throws such invaluable light on the society of Southern Gaul in the second half of the fifth century.

One might certainly have supposed that the effect of this conquest on Christian culture would have been disastrous, since Western society was still largely pagan and the main factor making for Christianity had been the support of the imperial government, which was now lost, while the German invaders were either Arians like the Goths, the Burgundians and the Vandals, or still pagans, like the Angles and Saxons in Britain and the Franks in Belgium and Northeast France.

Yet history seems to show that it was the barbarian invasions which led educated opinion to rally to Christianity, so that they mark the end of the old conservative aristocratic tradition of paganism represented by Symmachus and Rutilius Namatianus.

It is difficult to say why this should have been so. It is possible that many good Romans shared the opinions of Prudentius, the Spanish Christian poet, who believed that there was a providential connection between the Roman ideal of world unity and the higher spiritual unity of the Christian Church. Certainly the old Roman ruling class, who no longer had a political career in the service of the Empire, found a new vocation of spiritual leadership as bishops of the Catholic Church. This had already happened under the Empire, as in the case of St. Ambrose, who was already high in the civil service when the people of Milan practically forced him to become their bishop; while after the fall of the Empire, the majority of the leading bishops, above all in Gaul

—men such as St. Paulinus of Nola, St. Avitus, St. Sidonius Appolinaris and St. Caesarius of Arles—were men of this class and were now able to stand between the oppressed provincials and their barbarian rulers as representatives of a higher spiritual authority.

The fact that the episcopate was drawn from the upper classes of the old Roman society was important, not only because it gave them the social prestige necessary to impress the barbarian rulers, as well as a well-established tradition of public service, but also because it enabled them to carry on the traditions of higher culture and classical learning on which the continuity of Western culture depended. A man like Sidonius Appolinaris spans the gulf between two different cultures and worlds; as a young man, he had risen to high office at Rome and had married the daughter of one of the late shadow-emperors, Avitus. Later, after he had withdrawn to his estates in Aquitaine, he was elected bishop of Auvergne in 471 and led his people in their courageous resistance against the Gothic conquerors. After the conquest, he was a prisoner of the Gothic king Euric, who was an Arian, but he succeeded in gaining his favor by writing a panegyric in his honor, and he was finally allowed to return to his diocese, where he spent his last years as the protector of his Roman and Catholic flock.

Sidonius is exceptional in his awareness of the cultural issue and of the importance of preserving the higher standards of Latin literary culture. But there was no lack of bishops drawn from the old Gallo-Roman aristocracy who played a leading part in the new semi-barbarian culture that was emerging, like St. Remigius of Rheims, who baptized King Clovis, St. Lupus of Troyes, St. Germanus of Auxerre, who undertook an historic mission to Britain, and St. Avitus of Vienne, who exercised a considerable influence on the Burgundian kings.

In the course of time, however, the gradual unification of the population reduced the gap between the old aristocracy and the new class of barbarian nobles, so that the former tended to become barbarized, at the same time as the latter became Catholic.

We see the result of this process in the pages of Gregory of Tours'
History of the Franks. Gregory himself was a typical example of
the old aristocratic class, who numbered many bishops and saints
on both sides of his family, and himself became one of the leading
bishops of the Gallican Church. But he no longer had any preten-
sions to classical culture, and his history shows that the episcopate
of his time included many unworthy bishops who followed the
example of the lawless Frankish nobles among whom they lived.

*Church forged Xtiandom from
diverse elements.*

III.

For five hundred years and more the Church pursued the double
task of making the pagans Christian and making the barbarians
civilized, and these two tasks were one, since as we know even
today, religion and education—Church and school—are two sides
of one reality which is both spiritual and social.

Thus the unity of medieval Europe was not a secular or political unity. It was conceived as the unity of the Christian people or
Christendom, a unity constructed by the Church out of the most
diverse materials—the relics of Imperial Rome, the native traditions of new peoples from beyond the old Roman frontiers, Latin
literature and scholastic tradition, the sacred learning of the age
of the Fathers, and the Christian liturgy, art and music which had
their sources in the Christian East.

It is therefore not altogether an exaggeration to regard medieval
culture as Christian culture *par excellence,* since it is the only
great culture that we know which was created by Christian forces
and directed towards Christian ends, so that it is difficult to study
any aspect of medieval life unless we understand something of the
Catholic Church and the Christian way of life. This, of course,
does not mean that medieval culture was an ideal culture, as the
romantics of the last century tended to suppose. Barbarism, as well
as Christianity, was an essential ingredient. It was the culture of

Christian barbarians—of barbarians who were becoming Christians and of Christians who were themselves in part barbarians.

One has only to consider the conditions of a missionary Church to see how this was so. A barbarian warrior chieftain is converted to Christianity. He accepts the faith, sincerely, according to his lights. He abandons the traditions of his forefathers and the old sacred customs. He accepts a new god, builds new temples and endows the Church with wealth and lands. But when he has done all that, he feels that he has done all and more than can be expected of him; he expects to be treated by God and the Church as a privileged person, and he does not realize that his nature is still deeply rooted in the pagan past. Something similar occurred in the case of the conquered peoples who remained Christian. They had suffered the shock of barbarian conquest. They had lost their security and their rights as citizens. They had kept the Faith often at the cost of great sacrifices. And so they, too, felt that they were privileged people from the religious point of view, and that having kept the Faith, they had done enough.

The Christian Culture process, therefore, had to begin from a low level with poor materials, and when the first great step had been accomplished by the conversion of the pagans it was only the beginning of a much longer and more arduous struggle to overcome the inherent barbarism of the Christianized barbarians. We have only to compare Gregory of Tours' *History of the Franks* with Bede's *Ecclesiastical History of the English People* to see that the second stage of Christian acculturation was more difficult and more thankless than the first.

Above all, in our study of medieval culture we must remember that war was not so much the endemic malady of European society as the condition of its existence and the principle of its organization. In the East, the Church had to acclimatize itself to despotic government, to the absence of political freedom and personal liberty. But in the West, the Church was forced to exist in a world of perpetual war and violence—not only the organized war of states and kingdoms, but private wars and family feuds from which it was hard for any man to hold aloof without breaking the sacred bonds of kinship and loyalty. This theme runs through all medieval literature from the earliest heroic poems of the Celtic and Germanic peoples through the Icelandic Sagas, and from the French *Chansons de Geste* down to the vernacular ballads and folk songs at the close of the Middle Ages.

This factor in Western culture is shown in relation to the conversion of Iceland by the greatest of all the Northern Sagas—the *Njul Saga.*[1] It is, of course, not a contemporary record like Bede's history, but a work of creative imagination by one of the greatest medieval writers.

In such a world, the Church had to undertake the task of introducing the law of the Gospel and the ethics of the Sermon on the Mount among peoples who regarded homicide as the most honorable occupation and vengeance as synonymous with justice. It is not surprising that some found the task appallingly difficult and that medieval culture was in a state of continual tension between the opposing ideals of the Christian and the warrior.

[1] An excellent English translation is available in the Penguin series.

Part Three: Formation of Medieval Christendom: Its Rise and Decline

XI. THE FOUNDATION OF EUROPE:
THE MONKS OF THE WEST

The great social institution by which the Church carried out the work of Christian acculturation and which dominated the whole development of early medieval culture was the *monastic community*. This institution, as we have seen, already existed all over the Roman world in the last centuries of the Empire, and it continued to spread with extraordinary rapidity in the following period, even beyond the old imperial frontiers.

In Gaul, it steadily increased during the sixth and seventh centuries. In the fifth century it was mainly concentrated in the South, at Lérins and Marseilles and Arles, where it was associated with the last great school of theological writing in the West—the school of Lérins—represented by St. Honoratus, St. Vincent, St. Faustus and St. Caesarius. Several of these became bishops, notably the Briton, Faustus, who was Abbot of Lérins, Bishop of Riez and the most prolific theological writer of the West. But in addition to these monastic centers of higher culture, there was the even more widespread movement of ascetic and evangelical monasticism, which had its origin with the great St. Martin of Tours and gradually spread through central and northern France from the Loire to the Jura. This type of monasticism recruited its members from every class from the highest to the lowest, and its value as a means of spreading the faith among the pagan and barbarian peoples of Gaul was recognized by the great bishops. Thus, the biographer of St. Germanus of Auxerre describes how he founded a monastery outside

the city in order "to provide two roads to Christ so that the surrounding population might be brought to the Catholic faith by
contact with the monastic community as well as by the ministrations
of the Church."[1] We find the same thing at Rheims under St.
Remigius, who founded the neighboring monastery of St. Thierry,
and at Troyes, under St. Lupus.

This monastic apostolate was especially suited to the conditions of
the new barbarian society, because it provided little oases of Christianity amid the destruction and anarchy of the barbarian invasions.
Thus we have a very valuable record of the work of St. Severinus,
a monk from Pannonia, who established himself on the middle
Danube, west of Vienna, and devoted his life to protecting and
rescuing the remnants of the Christian population left at the mercy
of the barbarians in the Danube towns after the abandonment of
the Roman military frontier.[2]

Similarly in Britain, after the collapse of Roman government, the
monasteries became the rallying point of British Christianity in
Wales and Cornwall, where they created a new type of Celtic
ecclesiastical organization based on the monastic rather than the
episcopal system. The first apostle of the monastic movement in
Britain is said to have been St. Ninian, a disciple of St. Martin at
Tours, who founded his monastery of Candida Casa at Whithorne
in Galloway in 397. In the following century, St. Germanus, who
did so much to help the Christians in Britain, is said to have been
the teacher of St. Illtyd, the founder of the important monastic
movement in South Wales, which in the next generation numbered
St. David, St. Cadoc, and St. Gildas among its leaders. But the
greatest British contribution to the spread of Christianity was St.
Patrick, a Roman Briton of middle-class origin without classical
education, the son of a deacon who was also a decurion (that is to
say, a member of a Roman town council or *curia*), who had a farm
in an unidentified place called Bannaventa Taberniae (which may

---

[1] Constantius, *Life of St. Germanus*, ch. vi.
[2] Eugippianus, *Life of St. Severinus*.

have been near Daventry, or more probably in the Southwest near the Bristol Channel).

When he was still a boy of sixteen, early in the fifth century, Patrick was captured in an Irish raid and taken to Ireland as a slave. During his captivity, he underwent a religious conversion and spent his days and nights in prayer, while he was engaged in herding swine in the forests and mountains of Ulster. After six years, he escaped and returned to his family, but he had a vision in which he received a letter containing "the voice of the Irish," and while he was reading it, he seemed to "hear the voices of those who were near the wood of Foclut, which is by the Western Sea, and they cried out, 'We entreat thee, holy youth, that thou come and henceforth walk among us.' " It was not for many years after this that he was able to undertake the conversion of Ireland. From 418 to 432 he was in Gaul, a monk in the monastery over which St. Germanus presided at Auxerre.[3] His *Confession*, which was written towards the end of his life, is singularly lacking in information about the details of his later career. He speaks in general terms of "the success of his preaching, of the many thousands he converted of the sons of the Scots and the daughters of the chieftains" who became monks and virgins of Christ, of the persecutions he endured and his continual travels "amid many perils to remote places where there was no one beyond and where no one else had ever penetrated to baptize or ordain clergy or to confirm the people."

Nevertheless, his *Confession* is a priceless document—the only authentic voice that has come down to us from the great mass of the Christian Roman population who were involved in the revolution which followed the breakdown of Roman government in the Western provinces. For in spite of St. Patrick's lack of classical culture, of which he is only too aware, he felt himself to be a true

---

[3] The Bollandist Père Grosjean has proved this, largely from place names preserved in later lives of St. Patrick. In his opinion it was Germanus who unsuccessfully attempted to prevent Patrick's consecration as a missionary bishop by revealing the secret sin confided to him by Patrick. *Analecta Bollandiana*, Vol. LXXV, Fasc. i-ii. Notes d'Hagiographie celtique, 27.

Roman and showed a certain pride in his free citizenship, as we see in his other genuine work—the *Epistle to Coroticus*—in which he contrasts the barbarism of the Strathclyde ruler, ally of the pagan Scots and apostate Picts who slays and enslaves free-born Christians, with his true fellow citizens, the Roman and Gallic Christians, who sent holy men to the Franks and other barbarians to ransom Christian captives at great cost.

St. Patrick's work did not bear its full fruit until the following century, when the age of the great expansion of Irish monasticism took place, probably under the influence of the slightly earlier Welsh monasticism of men like St. Illtyd, St. Cadoc, St. Samson and St. Gildas. But by the middle of the sixth century there was a sudden and widespread expansion of monasticism in Ireland that rivalled the first great expansion of Egyptian monasticism, which in many ways it resembled, two centries before. With St. Columba of Iona, this monastic movement spread to Scotland and thence to England, and with St. Columban to the continent of Europe—first to Burgundy and ultimately to Bobbio in Northern Italy.

The effect of this Irish monastic movement on the fortunes of the Church in Northern Europe was very great. In Scotland and England, with the disciples of St. Columba at Iona and eventually at Lindisfarne, it began a new missionary movement, which was adapted to the conditions of barbarian tribal society, since it had never known anything else. In Ireland, there was no civilization in the Roman sense—that is to say, cities and city life were nonexistent and the word *civitas* as used by Irish writers normally means a monastery. In Northeastern Gaul, the decline of Latin culture was already far advanced when Columban founded his great monastery at Luxeuil in the Ardennes, and the influence of the earlier monastic movement of Southern Gaul—Lérins and Arles—was losing its impetus. Thus, the coming of the Irish, whether as monks or missionaries, revived the declining fortunes of Christian culture in Gaul and gave birth to a long series of monastic foundations in East Gaul and the neighboring territories as far as Northwest Italy, which in turn were the starting points of a new development.

But in Italy the situation was very different. There the Ostro-Gothic kingdom founded by the great Theodoric at the end of the fifth century was the protector of Roman civilization, though not of Catholicism. The ministers of Theodoric, like Boethius himself, were Romans of high culture, and though Boethius was executed on a false charge of conspiring against the Gothic king, even his misfortunes were fruitful, since they led him to compose the *Consolation of Philosophy*, which became one of the great legacies of later Roman civilization to medieval culture. In the same way, Cassiodorus, on retiring from public service, devoted himself in his monastic retreat at Vivarium in Calabria to the service of higher Christian culture, by collecting and transcribing manuscripts and compiling the encyclopaedic *Institutions* which was one of the main links between the dying classical culture and the new Christian culture of Western monasticism. It is significant of this process that the library which Cassiodorus had collected ultimately seems to have passed to St. Columban's Italian foundation of Bobbio.

But the greatest contribution that Italy made to the monastic institutions was the work of St. Benedict, who lived in the first half of the sixth century and founded the famous abbey of Monte Cassino about the year 525. It was here that he wrote his famous Rule which was eventually to become the standard and pattern of the monastic life throughout Western Christendom.[4] St. Benedict's Rule is characterized by three qualities—its moderation, its completeness and its insistence on the threefold duty of prayer, study and manual work. The Benedictine monastery was essentially a community, originally a self-sufficient rural community like the Roman villa. It combined an oratory, a library, a guest house, a novitiate, an in-

---

[4] Much controversy has taken place in recent years over the relation of this Rule to the possibly older *Regula Magistri* which contains a large common element. The date and place of origin of this Rule are still very uncertain.

firmary, as well as refectories, kitchens, dormitories and workshops and, if possible, a well, a mill and a garden, all within a walled enclosure.

It was a little self-contained world, "a school of the service of the Lord," in which it was possible to live a completely Christian life without any surrender to the lower standards of secular culture. But this isolation was only relative. It presupposed the existence of some kind of social code. And this condition was lacking in the age of barbarian invasions. Thus, during the Lombard invasions which caused such immense suffering to the Christian population of Italy, Monte Cassino itself was destroyed about the year 580 and the monks were forced to take refuge in Rome, bringing with them the "Book of the Holy Rule, some other books, the weight for bread and the measure for wine." At Rome they established themselves in a monastery by the Lateran Basilica. Here they became known to St. Gregory, who was then living as a monk on the Caelian Hill, and it is probable that he adopted the Benedictine Rule for his own foundation of St. Andrew's on the Caelian.

We know from the *Dialogues* of St. Gregory what importance he attached to the life and work of St. Benedict, and it is this association of the Benedictine tradition with St. Gregory the Great that explains the immense diffusion of the Benedictine Rule in the following century. For it was from St. Andrew's in 596 that St. Augustine, the prior, and his fellow monks were sent by the Pope on his mission to England, taking the rule with them to the monastery they established at Canterbury.

The advance of this Roman mission from Kent to Northumbria brought the knowledge of the Rule to Northern England, where it was apparently accepted by St. Wilfred, St. Benedict Biscop, and their great foundations at Hexham, Jarrow and Wearmouth. This has sometimes been disputed, but it seems to me clear that as Wilfred and Benedict Biscop and Ceolfrid were the great propagators of Roman against Irish influence—the Roman chant, Roman church architecture and Roman usages—they would naturally have also followed the monastic rule, so closely associated with Rome and with St. Gregory. In fact, Bede expressly states that St. Wilfred, while still a young monk at Lindisfarne, gradually came to realize that the way of life taught by the Irish was very imperfect, so he decided to visit Rome and see what ecclesiastical and monastic customs were in use in the apostolic see.

In any case, it is certain that the Benedictine Rule was the standard for the non-Celtic monasteries in England in the seventh century and that it was brought from there by St. Boniface and the other Anglo-Saxon missionaries to the Continent, where it became the Rule at Fulda and the other German monasteries they founded. It had already spread into Gaul from the South, and in the reign of Louis the Pious, the Council of Aix-la-Chapelle in 817 decreed that the Rule of St. Benedict should be observed in all the monasteries of the Empire.

Every monastery formed a self-contained society, both spiritually and economically, and thus provided an oasis of peace in a land of war, a cell of Christian culture in a barbarous and semi-pagan world. It is relatively easy for us to study the life, the ideals and the culture of Western monasticism, since, at least in Northern Europe, it possessed a monopoly of literary culture, and all the literature of the period was produced in the monasteries. We have the monastic rules, such as St. Benedict's; above all, the *Codex regularum* of Benedict of Aniane. We have the lives of the monastic founders, St. Benedict, St. Columban, St. Columba, Bede's Lives of the Abbots, and hundreds more. We have their theological and spiritual writings and, finally, enough of their educational treatises to form a clear idea of the nature of monastic education.

Thus, one side of early medieval culture—the specifically Christian side—is clearly visible and we can study it in detail. But the other side—the barbarian and secular side—lies in shadow; it is impossible to know it in full, and our partial knowledge is often deceptive. For example, the ship discovered in 1939 at Sutton Hoo was the cenotaph of a nominally Christian king, Aethelhere, who nevertheless allied himself with the pagan Penda of Mercia to expel from his throne his sincerely Christian brother King Anna, destroyed the Irish monastery established at Burgh Castle and held its monks for ransom.[5] His cenotaph at Sutton Hoo has the pagan magnificence of the heroic age of the Scandinavian world. Though his body was buried elsewhere, in Christian ground, his royal dignity must be honored by the archaic ceremonies of the old pagan ritual.

Here we have the dualism of early medieval culture exhibited on the grand scale. But it is much harder to discover its workings on the popular level among the peasants and the serfs. Men from this level might become totally integrated in the new Christian culture, as we see in the case of Caedmon, the illiterate founder of the new Christian Anglo-Saxon poetry, but the mind of the peasant, even more than that of the king, was divided between two traditions, and he still remained bound to the old pagan customs of peasant culture long after he had become a nominal or even a devout member of the Christian society.

It is therefore easy enough to understand why the great historians of the period of the Enlightenment, Gibbon above all, regarded early medieval culture with contempt and aversion, as a dark age— or an age of "Gothic" barbarism. For it was a very barbarous age from the material point of view, and all those things which Gibbon admired in the Roman Empire of the Antonine period were entirely missing. The Pax Romana had given place to a state of endless and meaningless warfare, the cities, villas and aqueducts had been destroyed. The cultivated society of men of letters like Pliny and Lucian and Marcus Aurelius had been replaced by uncouth warriors or pious monks.

Similarly, it was natural that the Protestant historians of the past should have had little sympathy for this period. To them it was an

[5] The identification with Aethelhere is accepted by Sir Frank Stenton ("The East Anglian Kings of the Seventh Century" in *The Anglo-Saxon*, London, 1959) and is endorsed by Grosjean, who quotes a passage from a contemporary Nivelles chronicler who relates Aethelhere's usurpation. In his view Anna is "a most Christian king." *Analecta Bollandiana*, Vol. LXXVIII, Fasc. iii-iv.

age of superstition and ignorance, when all the things that they most disapproved of in Catholicism were most evident—image worship and the veneration of relics, the growth of the Papacy and the power of the clergy, the cult of the saints and the pilgrimages to holy places. In fact, this was the central theme of the great Reformation Church History of the Magdeburg Centuriators which formed the basis of Protestant historiography for centuries.

But today we approach the history of these ages in a very different spirit. As Christians we cherish—or ought to cherish—a genuine *pietas* towards the institutions and the men who laid the foundations of Christianity in the West and from whom our own ancestors first received the Catholic Faith. And secondly, as modern historians and students of culture, we have travelled a long way from Gibbon and the other historians of the Enlightenment. We have been taught by the great nineteenth-century historians and sociologists that every age must be judged by its own cultural standards and achievements, and that we have no right to expect the Anglo-Saxons of the seventh century to conform to the standard of eighteenth-century French philosophers or nineteenth-century liberals. We now realize the importance of the dynamic creative periods in history when a new start is made from small beginnings, since for an historian the seed time is more important and more deserving of study than the time of harvest. From this point of view these ages, which have not unjustly been called *dark*, are the most interesting of all, since they contain the germ of a thousand years of cultural development—a development which perhaps has not yet been completed.

From the religious point of view, this was pre-eminently a missionary period. Even if it is not the greatest missionary age in the Church's history, it is the greatest for us, because it saw the conversion of our own parent stocks—the Celtic and Germanic peoples of the West, the Franks, the Anglo-Saxons, the Lombards and the Saxons, and later on the Scandinavians, the Poles and the Hungarians, and in Eastern Europe, the Russians, the Bulgars and the Yugoslavs.

Moreover, this is pre-eminently the age of *Christian history*, since almost all the history we have is Christian, and it was during this period that a new pattern of Western historiography was developed in which the tribal or national traditions which had hitherto been oral were first given literary form and integrated with, or at least related to, the Christian pattern of world history, derived from Eusebius and Orosius. This process was started in the sixth century by the last of the Romans, men who still preserved the old tradition of culture, though they were subjects of the new barbarian kingdoms, like Cassiodorus, whose history of the Goths has not survived, and St. Gregory of Tours, whose *History of the Franks* gives us such a vivid picture of conditions in Christian Gaul under its barbarous Merovingian rulers, whose native savagery was curbed but not cured by their respect for the Church and their fear of the power of the Saints.

But the real father of medieval history, St. Bede (673–735), *semper venerabilis*, was no Roman but a man of pure English stock, a typical representative of the new Christian culture which had been planted in Northumbria by the convergent efforts of the Roman mission of St. Gregory and St. Augustine, and the Irish mission of St. Columba and St. Aidan. Bede's *Ecclesiastical History of the English People* is a classic in its own right, but a miracle when one considers that it was the work of a man whose immediate ancestors were illiterate barbarians. For what strikes one about the book is not merely that it is well written, in a Latin incomparably better than that of St. Gregory of Tours, but that it shows such a singularly civilized and mature intelligence. The culture that produced this remarkable work must have been genuinely and profoundly Christian, and its appearance marks a new starting point for Western culture. No doubt it did not spring out of nothing: it had a long history of religious achievement behind it. On the one hand, there was the Roman mission and the monastic tradition of St. Benedict and of the monasteries of Gaul. And, on the other hand, there was the Christian culture of Ireland and the Celtic West which had already reached its full development by the sixth and the beginning of the seventh century. Witness the life and work of the great Irish missionary saints, like St. Columba of Iona and Columban of Luxeuil. Unfortunately, we know far less than one might have expected about this golden age of Ireland's saints and scholars, owing to the lack of contemporary historians and biographers, since most of the Irish monastic annals date from a much later period.

The one great exception is Adamnan's *Life of St. Columba,* which at least gives us an insight into the spirit of Celtic monasticism. And it was Columba's monastery of Iona which was the great source of the conversion of Northumbria. It was the coming together of this tradition, as represented by the Columban monastery of Lindisfarne, the home of St. Aidan (–651) and his successors St. Finan (–661) and St. Cuthbert (–687), with the Roman mission, represented by the twin Benedictine abbeys of Jarrow and Wearmouth, the foundations of St. Benedict Biscop and the home of St. Ceolfrid and St. Bede, that explains the richness and fertility of the new Christian Northumbrian culture. In the course of the eighth century, this new culture extended its influence to continental Europe, first by its missions to the heathen Frisians and Saxons, later by the help that it gave to the rulers of the Franks, Pepin and Charlemagne, in their reconstruction of Western Christendom.

Thus St. Boniface (680–754) was not only the apostle of Germany but also the reformer of the Frankish Church, while Alcuin of York (c. 735–804) acted as a kind of minister of education and ecclesiastical affairs to Charlemagne during the critical years when the new Christian Empire of the West was being established. It was the Anglo-Saxon monks, Boniface above all, who were the chief agents in bringing about that alliance between the Papacy, the Frankish monarchy and Benedictine monasticism which was the keystone not only of the Carolingian Empire but of the order of medieval Christendom in the West. They were the chief authors of the liturgical reform which established a unified Roman or Roman-Gallican rite for Western Europe, and they were the educationalists

whose schools at the royal court at Aachen and at the great Benedictine abbeys like Fulda, Tours and Corbie set the standards for
medieval education down to the coming of the universities four
hundred years later. Thus, while the Carolingian Empire itself was
very short-lived, the Carolingian culture, which was predominantly
monastic and episcopal, was of fundamental importance for the
whole of Western Christendom. For unlike the Empire, which was
simply the Frankish monarchy in a new dress, Carolingian culture
was genuinely international in character.

I have dwelt on this subject at some length because there is no
other factor that had so profound an influence on the development
of Christian culture in the West. The monastery in the age of St.
Benedict is nothing but a simple and modest pattern of Christian
culture. It has a defined social form or constitution, a high spiritual
end and an independent economic foundation. It is true that it is
based on the denial of the three most powerful instincts that govern
society—that is to say, the sexual impulse, the economic impulse
and the power impulse, which are excluded by the threefold vow
of Poverty, Chastity and Obedience. Yet, in spite of this radical
refusal to compromise with human nature, the monastic community
proved to be highly successful as an efficient social institution. In
the course of time, it produced all the fruits of higher culture—art,
music and learning—and passed them on through its educational
activity to the society that surrounded it. Indeed, from the seventh
to the tenth century, the monasteries were the only effective educational force that survived in the Western world.

Perhaps the most remarkable thing about the Benedictine Rule
has been its extraordinary power of survival. The Benedictine form
of community life has travelled down the centuries virtually unchanged through all the vicissitudes of history, and it is still flourishing today here in America,[6] so that we can still find men living the
same life under the same Rule in twentieth-century America as they

---

[6] Notably, for example, at Collegeville in Minnesota.

did in Italy fourteen centuries ago under the Gothic and Byzantine emperors.

It has been my aim to show how Christian culture has changed through the ages and how in each successive age it produces new forms adapted to new circumstances. But one must also remember the existence of some elements that do not change, but retain the same form throughout the ages. When the Christian way of life, which is the center of Christian culture, is reduced to its simplest elements and organized on the basis of first principles, it is practically indestructible and can preserve its institutional form indefinitely. This has proved to be the case with the Benedictine way of life, and it is thus perhaps the most remarkable instance of the indestructible element in Christian culture. And it is especially remarkable because it was created in the sixth century, in an age when everything else was being violently destroyed or was breaking to pieces; when even such a stout-hearted leader as Gregory the Great despaired of the future of Rome and Italy and believed that the end of all things was at hand.

No one in those years saw any future for Western Europe or for its Christian civilization. No doubt the Christian civilization of the Eastern Empire still seemed flourishing in the age of Justinian. But his attempts to recover Italy and Africa seriously overstrained the resources of the Empire, and his reign terminated in a series of disasters, with the Lombards invading Italy, the Huns laying waste the Balkans up to the walls of Constantinople, while the Eastern provinces were continually threatened by fresh Persian invasions.

But meanwhile the foundations of Christian culture in the West were being laid by the monks of the West.

XII. THE CAROLINGIAN AGE

I.

In the eighth century the new civilization of Western Christendom began to take shape under the dynasty which replaced the Merovingians in the government of the Frankish kingdom. Charles Martel (714-742), the natural son of Pepin the Younger, mayor of the palace from 681 to 714, had restored the unity of the Frankish kingdom by the defeat of his rivals and of the neighboring peoples— Frisians, Bavarians and Saxons—who threatened its independence. Above all Charles' defeat, in 732, of the Saracens, who had extended their conquests into Central France, made him appear the outstanding champion of the culture of Western Christendom in the eyes of the Roman Papacy, which was being hard pressed by the Lombard kingdom and, owing to the anti-clerical policy of the Iconoclast emperors, could no longer look to its traditional support, the Byzantine Empire. Yet Charles has little to commend him to the party of ecclesiastical reform. He was a successful warrior, and nothing more. He used the wealth of the Frankish Church to reward his supporters and carried out a wholesale secularization of Church property.

It was at this point that the influence of St. Boniface and his Anglo-Saxon missionaries made itself felt. From the first Boniface had regarded himself as bound by a special bond to the See of St. Peter. This personal link with the Holy See, fortified by his visits to Rome in the pontificate of Popes Gregory II and III, was recognized when Gregory II consecrated him as Apostolic Legate in Germany and organizer of the Church in this mission field. At the

same time the Pope commended him to the protection of Charles
Martel, thus inaugurating the relations between the Papacy and the
Frankish monarchy which became the cornerstone of Carolingian
polity henceforward. Under Charles Martel's successors, Carloman
and Pepin, St. Boniface was encouraged to carry out a far-reaching
reform of the Frankish Church and a restoration of canonical Roman
discipline.

In a letter to Pope Zachary, he explains how "Carloman, Emperor
of the Franks, summoned me to his presence and desired me to
convoke a Synod in that part of the Frankish kingdom which is
under his jurisdiction. He promised me that he would reform and
re-establish ecclesiastical discipline, which for the last sixty or seventy
years has been completely disregarded and denied. If he is truly
willing under divine inspiration to put this plan into execution, I
should like to have the advice and the instructions of the Holy See.
According to their elders, the Franks have not held a council for
more than eighty years; they have had no archbishop, nor have they
established or restored in any place the canon law of the Church.
The episcopal sees which are in the cities have been given for the
most part into the possession of avaricious laymen, or exploited by
adulterers and unworthy clerics for worldly uses. If I am to undertake this task at your bidding and on the invitation of the ruler,
I must have at once, with the appropriate ecclesiastical sanctions,
both the counsel and the decision of the Apostolic See."

The series of reforming councils which followed, first in Germany,
Carloman's kingdom of Austrasia, afterwards in Pepin's kingdom
of Neustria, laid the foundation of the Carolingian work of canonical reform, and secured the co-operation of the Papacy and the
Carolingian monarchy which was the climax of St. Boniface's life
work.

It found its first realization in 751, when papal approval was given
to the change of dynasty. The solemn consecration and anointing of
Pepin by St. Boniface at the national assembly of Soissons emphasized the religious character of the new regime, which distinguished

it from the Merovingian monarchy. Henceforward King Pepin and his successors insisted on the sacred character of their authority, clearly manifested by their action as leaders of the movement of ecclesiastical reform.

But it was the Papacy which took the decisive step in the transformation of the Frankish monarchy into a new world power. Gregory II was not only responsible for entrusting St. Boniface with his life-long mission as the representative of Apostolic authority in Germany. He was also the first to recognize the epoch-making revolution in the relations between East and West which resulted from the policy of the Iconoclast emperors. In his letters to the Emperor Leo III, the Pope appeals to the new Christian world coming into existence in the West and announces his intention of leaving Rome on a journey "to the uttermost bounds of the West" to baptize the newly converted rulers and peoples.

This journey did not take place. But from this time forward the Popes began to direct their appeals to the kings of the Franks. From Gregory III onwards they sought their support against the Lombards, who had taken the place of the Byzantine Emperors in the Western provinces of the Empire. Finally in 753, after a final appeal to the Lombard king Aistulf, Pope Stephen II crossed the Alps and threw in his lot with the new power. In 754 he repeated, at St. Denis, St. Boniface's solemn act of consecration, by consecrating Pepin as king. He concluded an agreement with him at Quierzy and Ponthieu in the same year, by which he recognized Pepin as protector of the Holy See. In turn the king of the Franks bound himself to compel the Lombards to restore the conquered Byzantine territory to the Pope. This agreement was put into effect by Pepin's Italian campaigns in 754 and 755, and confirmed by the famous "Donation of Pepin" which conferred upon St. Peter as a perpetual gift the towns and territories wrested from the Lombards. Consequently, Fulrad, abbot of St. Denis, received the submission of Ravenna and the other towns of the former Byzantine exarchate in the name of St. Peter.

It is possible, though it cannot be proved, that Pope Stephen had brought with him to France, to influence Pepin, a document certainly forged in Italy at this time. This was the famous Donation of Constantine in which the first Christian Emperor, in his devotion to the Holy See, withdrew his seat of empire to Byzantium and left the government of the Western Empire in the hands of Pope Sylvester and his successors: as Dante has expressed it, "to make room for the Shepherd, he made himself a Greek."

Such was the foundation of the States of the Church, which were to remain a cornerstone of the political order of Western Christendom for more than a thousand years. But it was not until after the death of Pepin and the accession of his son Charles the Great, who finally destroyed the Lombard kingdom in 774, that the new regime was completely established. Charles was now much more than the King of the Franks. He had acquired a universal authority over the whole of Western Christendom, and his ecclesiastical advisers, notably the Anglo-Saxon Alcuin, constantly insist on his duty as the leader of the whole Christian people.

In a letter to Charlemagne written in June 799, Alcuin lists the three persons who were at the summit of the world's hierarchy. First the Vicar of St. Peter, Prince of the Apostles; second the holder of the imperial dignity who exercises the secular government of the Second Rome (Byzantium); "finally, in the third place, the royal dignity that Our Lord Jesus Christ has reserved for you who govern the Christian People. It raises you above the other two . . . and surpasses their sovereignty. It is now on you alone that the Churches of Christ depend, to you alone that they look for safety—to you avenger of crime, guide of those who err, comforter of the afflicted and support of the good."

This conviction of Charles' imperial mission was recognized by Pope Leo III when he crowned Charles as Roman Emperor at Rome on Christmas Day 800, thus uniting the new Western ideal of an *Imperium Christianum* with the old Roman Byzantine tradition of a Christian Roman Empire. Most modern historians believe

Pope minted this coronation to show it to be a papal gift

that the initiative came from the Pope, not the Emperor, and that Charles himself was surprised and taken aback. That he would later crown his son suggests that he disliked the implication that his imperial dignity was a papal gift. Moreover, he already possessed the reality of empire over Western Europe thanks to his own and his father's victories, completed by the conquest of the most formidable pagan power, that of the Avars, whose Khagan (Khan) accepted baptism in 805.

From a territorial point of view, Charles' empire was not unworthy to be compared with the Western Roman Empire, especially after his conquest of the Avar robber state. His rule extended from the Danish frontier to Catalonia, and from the Atlantic to the Adriatic and the middle Danube. From its center in Austrasia between the lower Rhine and the Seine he was able to make his authority obeyed without question throughout the whole of this vast territory. But the character of the government and the administration was entirely different from anything the Romans had conceived. The Roman Empire had been essentially a civilization of cities. Every city had its territory and they were bound together by a network of solidly engineered roads. In so far as it was not civic, it was military. But its military organization was that of a professional army, firmly established on a system of permanent fortifications, like the Roman Wall or the Limes Germanicus.

The Carolingian Empire, on the other hand, was essentially a rural society based on a natural economy which centered in the abbeys, the bishoprics and the royal and noble estates. The unit of government throughout the Empire was the *county*, which had been the local unit of the Frankish kingdom from the beginning and had originally corresponded to the old territory of the Roman city—the *pagus*—but which was now extended to the whole territory of the Empire and no longer had any necessary connection with a city. Like the comparable institution of the later Anglo-Saxon kingdom—the shire—which also became known as a county in Norman times, it might represent an old tribal territory, the German *gau,* or an ancient city territory in more civilized regions. As with the English counties, which have remained almost unchanged since Saxon times, there was no attempt to regulate their size or population. They might be large or small, and there was no distinction in official rank between their governors, although there was a great difference between the wealth and influence of the noble families from whom the Counts were recruited. The whole Empire was divided into about three hundred counties, and over all the Counts was the King of the Franks.

To make his authority obeyed, Charles the Great made use of an institution which had already existed as an exceptional instrument of government in the earliest times of the Frankish monarchy. It was the institution of travelling *missi dominici,* representatives of the central government, who conducted annual tours of inspection and supervision through a group of about half a dozen counties. These *missi* were two in number, one lay and the other clerical, a bishop or an abbot, whose post was often more important than that of the lay *missus,* since so much of Charles' legislation was concerned with ecclesiastical reform. This is proved by the long series of *capitularies* which emanated from Charles himself and his son Louis the Pious, which it was the business of the *missi* to put into effect and which, to a considerable extent, represent a conscious effort to carry on St. Boniface's reforming activities.

It is indeed evident already in the first capitulary of 769, promulgated soon after Charles' accession, in which he lays down the basic principles which were to guide his action—the assertion of the authority of the bishops, the moral reform of the people and the raising of intellectual culture among the clergy. These principles were reasserted in the great capitulary of 789 in which Charles explains his theocratic conception of his mission as ruler and guide of the Christian people, prescribes the precise duties which were to be fulfilled by the clergy and repeats the canons of the great Councils contained in the canonical collection—the *Codex Hadriana*—which had been sent to him by the Pope. The whole document resembles the encyclical of a Pope rather than the law of a secular prince, so that the activities of the *missi dominici* were often more like an episcopal visitation than a government inspection.

   This religious or ecclesiastical character of the Carolingian government provided the principle of unity so necessary for the very existence of the Empire. Viewed politically, the Empire was a society of many different tribes and peoples, each possessing its own code of laws and united only by the authority and military power of the King of the Franks from whom all the three hundred Counts of the Empire derived their authority. But from the religious point of view Charles was the leader of the Christian people, who were united by their common faith, their common baptism and the common laws which were those of the whole Church. It was the great, outstanding virtue of Charles that he realized this and devoted so large a part of his legislative activity to the reform of the Church and the promotion of Christian culture.

   It is not clear who were the ecclesiastics who first instilled these ideas into his mind. Fulrad, the abbot of St. Denis, who had played such a great part in the reign of Pepin, was still a leading counsellor. But he was already an old man and died in 784. During the central period of the reign there is no doubt that the most influential figure was the Anglo-Saxon Alcuin, who had been the head of the School of York, which from the time of Archbishop Egbert had succeeded the monastic school of Jarrow in the leadership of Northumbrian culture.

   Alcuin was not an original mind, but he had been thoroughly trained in the traditions of Bede and Egbert. He was an excellent teacher, a man of wide learning and of genial disposition. Charles found in him exactly the qualities that he needed, so that he became in effect a Minister of Culture for the whole Empire. One of Charles' most remarkable characteristics was his conviction that Frankish culture could not be built up unless there was a sound and authentic written tradition on which it could be based, and he used Alcuin as his instrument to provide authentic texts of the Scriptures, the liturgical books and the collection of canons, as well as a reform of the script without which the exact reproduction of these fundamental documents could not be secured.

In estimating the importance of Charles' work for Western culture, we cannot but be impressed by the way in which the king found time to concern himself with such details as the legibility of the script and the authenticity of the liturgical books, even while he was carrying on campaigns almost simultaneously in Spain and Saxony, in Italy and on the Danube. And at the same time he was working incessantly through councils, laws and instructions to the *missi* for the unification and reform of the Church throughout his dominions. No doubt these reforms did not always go very deep. But they were by no means superficial. To the diverse peoples of the Empire they brought home the reality of Christendom as a living society of Christian peoples united by a common religious faith and a common political allegiance.

At the same time Charles' genuine concern for culture made possible the work of Alcuin and his fellow scholars in raising the level of clerical education. In addition to the Anglo-Saxon teachers, whose influence was strongest at Fulda and the other German monasteries, the Carolingian Empire employed Irish scholars from the West, like Clement and Dungal and Smaragdus, Lombards from Italy like Paul the Deacon and Paulinus of Aquileia, and Spaniards or Visigoths, like Theodulf of Orléans and Agobard of Lyons. All these men shared a common Latin Christian culture which they communicated to their Frankish pupils, such as Einhard, Rabanus Maurus and Walafrid Strabo.

Of all these educational centers, the most important (after the School of the Palace, which had exceptional advantages) was undoubtedly the great Anglo-Saxon abbey of Fulda which St. Boniface had founded and where his body had finally been laid to rest. Thanks chiefly to the work of St. Rabanus Maurus, the *"praeceptor Germaniae,"* who was himself a pupil of Fulda and was afterwards successively head of the School and abbot for forty years (in all from c. 807 to 847), Fulda produced most of the leading scholars, at least those who were Franks, such as Einhard, the biographer of Charles the Great, Servatus Lupus, afterwards abbot of Ferrières, and Walafrid Strabo from Reichenau, who afterwards became the tutor of Charles the Bald.

But all the great monasteries and many of the bishoprics also took a leading part in this educational work—notably Tours under the rule of Alcuin, St. Riquier under Angilbert, Corbie under Adalhard, the great South German monasteries of St. Gall and Reichenau, the bishoprics of Orléans under Theodolph, Lyons under Agobard, and Liège, which became a center for Irish scholars like Sedulius Scotus.

The most remarkable Irishman, however, was John the Scot, "Erigena," who taught at the Palace School of Charles the Bald and is outstanding not only for his knowledge of Greek, but for his originality as a philosopher at a time when philosophy was almost forgotten in the West, for his distinctive version of Neo-Platonism, and his translation of Dionysius the Areopagite.

II.

The Carolingian Empire represented an ambitious but premature attempt to realize the unity of Western Christendom. It consequently had to reconcile two fundamentally conflicting ideals. On the one hand was the ideal of the Frankish Imperialism founded on the wars and conquests of Charles Martel, Pepin and Charlemagne, which had brought together Saxons and Lombards, Avars and Huns, under Frankish rule. On the other hand, it represented the ideal unity of the whole Christian people, united in a common Faith and in obedience to a common religious law.

Charlemagne embodied both these aspects. He was a great warrior king and emperor, but at the same time he was the leader of the Christian people who presided over the assemblies of bishops and abbots and issued the capitularies which laid down the duties of Christian life and the order of Christian society.

The accession of his son Louis laid even greater emphasis upon ecclesiastical responsibilities of the government. With the help of St. Benedict of Aniane, the Emperor embarked on a program of reform directed against the moral laxity of the Carolingian court and towards the restoration of a strict standard of regular observance in the monasteries. The Emperor himself took the lead in this movement by an act of public penance which he performed at Attigny in 822. The general effect of this new policy was to increase the influence of the clergy in the shaping of imperial policy. They became increasingly responsible for maintaining the cause of unity. Thus as soon as the strong hand of the Emperor Charles had been removed, the bishops and abbots, like Adalhard, Walafrid Strabo and Agobard of Lyons stood forth as the champions of the theocratic ideal of imperial unity against the somewhat vacillating policy of Louis. And when Lothair and his brother revolted against their father, it was the support of the Pope and the bishops that led to the deposition of Louis at Colmar in 833 in the name of Christian unity.

Nevertheless this was a fatal blow to the existence of the Empire as an effective unity. For it depended on the personal authority of the Emperor, who was the actual representative of the principle of unity and the leader of the whole society. But with the division of the Carolingian inheritance among the sons of Louis, this ceased to be the case, and the episcopate became the one guardian of Christian unity, arbitrator and judge between the rival princes. The bishops continued to insist on the need for a regime of "fraternal concord" which would unite the separate kingdoms against the common enemy of the Christian name.

Unfortunately the imperial claims which were inherited by Louis's eldest son, Lothair, proved fatal to the ideal of fraternal concord. While his brother Louis's inheritance was identified with the German provinces of the Empire, and the youngest son, Charles, laid claim to the West Frankish territories, Lothair was not content with his kingdom of Italy. He strove to assert authority over the Central

Austrasian territories of the original Frankish dominion—the lands between the Rhine and the Seine. Hence the Civil War of 840, which culminated in the disastrous battle of Fontenoy in 841. Lothair was defeated by Louis and Charles, who ratified their alliance in the following year by the famous bilingual Oath of Strasbourg, sworn in German and Romance by the two kings in the presence of their armies.

But Lothair continued to maintain his imperial claim, and the war of the brothers was finally concluded by the treaty of Verdun in 843. This divided the Frankish Empire of Charlemagne among three kingdoms—that of Louis the German in the East, that of Charles the Bald in the West, Lothair retaining the central territory which ran from Friesia to Italy through the old Frankish lands between the Rhine and the Scheldt and southwest to the Rhone and the Alps. This was the kingdom of Lotharingia or Lorraine, which remained in possession of the Emperor.[1]

The Partition of Verdun was of fundamental importance for the future of Europe. The Carolingian Empire ceased to exist; France and Germany never came together again under a common authority. But the memory of the Carolingian Empire lived on in each of the three kingdoms; and the Church continued to maintain the ideal of a common Christian society, divided between three kingdoms whose policies should be controlled by a regime of fraternal concord.

But the Empire of Charles was close to breakdown. Its collapse at the end of the ninth century left Western Christendom in a perilous condition, and in some ways the tenth century was the darkest age of all—even darker than that which followed the fall of the Roman Empire in the West. But this was not due only to the failure of the Carolingian Empire. It was also an age of decline for the Papacy. Conditions at Rome were even worse during the tenth century than in the age of the Borgias. Consequently there was no center of light or spiritual leadership left in the West. Indeed Western Christendom had shrunk to a mere island between the

[1] Later, however, Charles the Bald secured the imperial title.

pagan Northmen on the one side and the Moslem pirates who controlled the Western Mediterranean on the other. The Byzantine Empire still maintained its power and prestige, but it was separated from the West by another barbarian people, the Magyars, who had recently settled on the Danube and who were as great a scourge of Central Europe and North Italy as the Vikings were of the West. Nevertheless the spiritual power of Christianity was still strong enough to make an impression on its barbarous enemies.

The turning point came about the year 1000 when the Danes and the Norwegians, the Magyars and the Poles became Christian, while in Eastern Europe the Viking princes of Kievan Russia also received Christianity from the Byzantine Empire. After this crisis had been surmounted there was no longer any possibility of Christianity being destroyed, and the recovery of Western culture was extraordinarily rapid and complete.

Throughout this dark age, it was the monasteries that were the saviors of Christian culture and of the Christian way of life. The abbey was a microcosm of Christian culture, an island which preserved the tradition of Christian culture—education and learning, books and writing, music and liturgy, art and architecture. It was able to survive because it did not seek to impose itself on the barbarous warrior societies that surrounded it. It demanded no more than what St. Benedict had proposed in his Rule—a withdrawal from secular business and a life of continuous prayer and work; and study also, if this was possible. Hundreds of monasteries were swept away by the violence of the barbarian invaders and the greed of the lawless feudal nobility, and the richer they were the more likely they were to attract the attention of the spoilers; but every monastery was an independent organism, and so long as the tradition of the Holy Rule remained, every new foundation provided a new opportunity for a fresh start, for a return to the elementary simplicity of Christian communal life.

XIII. FEUDAL EUROPE
AND THE AGE OF ANARCHY

1.

The external menace of pagan attack had been steadily increasing since the breakdown of imperial unity. The most formidable of these new enemies were the Vikings from Scandinavia. From the beginning of the ninth century they had entered on an extraordinary period of expansion which lasted for two centuries and extended from the British Isles in the West to Russia and Byzantium and the Moslem emirates of the Caspian in the East. In spite of their barbarism and destructive activity, they possessed remarkable gifts of organization and construction which were manifested in the trading principalities they established among the Slav and Finnish tribes of Russia in the ninth century, and the purely Nordic commonwealth that they founded at a later period in Iceland, which in spite of its remoteness was to become the great center of Scandinavian literary culture.

It is, however, impossible to exaggerate the destructiveness of the Viking attacks on the West in the ninth century. They began by destroying the flourishing cultures of Ireland and Northumbria, the monastic centers of which were especially vulnerable to the pirate raids of the Viking fleets. With the weakening of the Carolingian Empire through disunity and civil war, they extended their raids, which steadily increased in violence until civilization was destroyed. As the chronicler of St. Vedast writes in 884: "The

190

Northmen cease not to slay and to carry into captivity the Christian people, to destroy the churches and burn the towns. Everywhere there is nothing but dead bodies—of clergy and laity, nobles and common folk, women and children. There is no road or place where the ground is not covered with corpses. We live in distress and anguish before the spectacle of the Christian people."

The Carolingian Empire was too large to be devastated completely. In the Southeast the great monasteries of Switzerland and Bavaria were hardly touched by the Vikings, though they faced other enemies from elsewhere. It was, however, through these monasteries that the great cultural achievements of the Carolingian age were preserved and handed on to a new age.

In England the course of events was somewhat different, since the destruction of the monasteries by the new barbarian invasions was almost complete, and Northumbria, which had hitherto been the center of Anglo-Saxon culture, now became an independent Danish colonial territory, as Normandy did on the Continent somewhat later. But in Southern England the situation was saved by the personal action of a very remarkable character—King Alfred. Amidst the terrible crisis of the Viking invasions Alfred found time to think out afresh the problems of Christian education and to lay with his own hands the foundations of a Christian vernacular culture.

In the preface to his translation of Pope Gregory's *Pastoral Care* (which is, I suppose, the earliest relic of English prose) he gives his diagnosis of what was wrong with English culture and what steps must be taken to remedy it. Comparing the England he knew with the great days of the past—the golden age of the Anglo-Saxon Church—he finds the source of the evil in the neglect of Christian education. "Thinking of this," he says, "I remember also how before they were all plundered and burnt, the churches stood around all England filled with treasures and books and a great company of God's servants, and how little the English profited by them, because they could not understand what was not written in our own tongue. As though they said 'our elders who held these places before us loved wisdom, and through it they got wealth and left it to us. Here we see their traces but we cannot follow them, and for that reason we have lost both the wealth and the wisdom, because we are not willing to turn our minds to the pursuit of wisdom.'" "In the past," he says, "the Greeks translated the Scriptures from the Hebrew into their own tongue, and so did the Romans and the other Christian peoples. So it seems well to me that we too turn into the tongue that we all know these books that all men need to know. And I think that we will bring it about very easily with God's help, if we have peace, that all the youth of England who are of free birth and have the opportunity to give themselves to it, be set to learning until they all know how to read English books. Then let those who desire to learn more and rise to a higher estate study Latin also."

To carry out these ideas he devoted himself "in the midst of the various and manifold troubles of the kingdom" to translate and get translated the books which seemed to him most useful. His selection consists of St. Gregory's *Pastoral Care* and the *Dialogues* (which contains the life of St. Benedict), the *World History* of Orosius, Bede's *Ecclesiastical History of the English People*, Boethius' *Consolation of Philosophy* and an anthology based on the first book of St. Augustine's *Soliloquies* and including some other extracts from St. Augustine and St. Jerome and some reflections of his own. Taken as a whole, this is a remarkable choice for a warrior king and suggests an original conception of a liberal education based on Christian history and Natural Theology rather than on the grammar and rhetoric which had been usual hitherto.

It is also probable that King Alfred was responsible for the compilation of the first great vernacular chronicle—the *Anglo-Saxon Chronicle*—for it gives an especially full account of his reign and shows some resemblances in style and wording to his translation of Orosius. Unfortunately he left no one capable of carrying on his work. He never possessed a tithe of the resources and opportunities of Charlemagne. Yet it is possible that his modest plans for the diffusion of a vernacular Christian culture were more suited to the real needs of the age than the ambitious theocratic universalism of the Carolingian Empire.

Of the Carolingian territories, it was the West Frankish realm that suffered most. Here the great abbeys were practically all destroyed, or survived only because the monks took refuge in some fortified town. But most of the towns were destroyed too. The Carolingian Empire was ill fitted to cope with an emergency of this kind. It was a cumbrous territorial power which depended for its defense on the annual levy of free men who were summoned to attend the "grand plea"—*plaidum magnum*—serving at their own expense for two or three months. But under the constant attacks of the Vikings and the constant civil wars, the Carolingian state tended to lose its centralized unity, and to regroup itself round the local centers of resistance represented by the Counts and the holders of feudal benefices. Thus Charles the Bald entrusted the defense of Northern France against the Vikings to Robert the Strong (852–866), whom he created "Duke" of the territories between the Seine and the Loire. At the same time he created the March of Flanders in favor of his son-in-law, Balduin, to guard the coast from the Scheldt to the Somme. In this way there grew up a series of great fiefs, each of which possessed its own army of armored horsemen who were bound to their lord by a personal link of honor and piety.

But the outstanding creation of this age of anarchy was the great fief of Normandy, which arose from the settlement of Rollo's Viking army in consequence of an agreement with the Carolingian king, Charles the Simple. By the treaty of Saint-Clair-sur-Epte in 911 the Vikings accepted baptism and promised to abstain from their depredations on neighboring territories. The Norman settlers rapidly assimilated Frankish culture, and their dukes remained dependable allies of the French kings.

Thus a new feudal society grew up under the later Carolingian

Emperors. It succeeded to a great extent in warding off the invasions of the Vikings, as in the stubborn defense of Paris in 855 and 866 by the elder Hugh Capet, the son of Robert the Strong, which marks a turning point in the struggle with the invaders.

On the other hand, the higher civilization of the Carolingian court and the great monasteries broke down into a mass of feudal states founded by successful warriors and maintaining themselves by perpetual war and violence. Thus the deliquescence of the Carolingian society and culture brought society back to a state of barbarism. The only social bond was the barbaric relation of the warrior to his lord.

All over the coastal regions of France, the monasteries were destroyed and the bishoprics deserted. Very many of the sees of Normandy, Brittany and Gascony were left vacant for years during the latter part of the ninth century and the early part of the tenth. It was the same in Southern France, where the Saracens established on the Riviera made it almost impossible for the bishoprics and abbeys to survive. Where they did survive, they were apt to become wholly or partially secularized. The bishop or abbot became assimilated to the holder of a feudal benefice. These feudal abbots often replaced their monks by canons, who were able to hold property, so that the abbot was not obliged to support them. The bishops of the province of Rheims in their synod at Troslé in 909 sum up the situation as follows:

"The cities are depopulated, the monasteries ruined and burned, the land is reduced to a solitude. As the first men lived without law or constraint, abandoned to their passions, so now every man does what pleases him, despising the laws of God and man and the ordinances of the Church. The powerful oppress the weak, the land is full of violence against the poor and the plunder of the goods of the Church. Men devour one another like the fishes in the sea. Of the monasteries some have been destroyed by the heathen, others have been deprived of their property and reduced to nothing. In those that remain there is no longer any observance of the rule. They no longer have legitimate superiors, owing to the abuse of submitting to secular domination. We see in the monasteries lay abbots with their wives and their children, their soldiers and their dogs. . . .

"God's flock perishes through our fault. In consequence of negligence, and the ignorance of ourselves and our brethren, there is in the Church an innumerable multitude of both sexes and every condition who reach old age without instruction, so that they are ignorant even of the words of the Creed and the Lord's Prayer."

II.

The beginnings of a new order were, however, laid by the very class who were the chief source of the disorder—the feudal princes and nobles. It is typical of the confusion which prevailed in this age that the great hero of the war against the Saracens, who had established themselves in Southern France in 888, the man who was the chief figure in the great feudal epic of the *Chansons de Geste*—William Short Nose, William of Gellone—himself became a monk and a saint, the founder of the monastery of Gellone which carried on the reforming tradition of St. Benedict of Aniane. His great-grandson, the Duke of Aquitaine, William the Pious, became in turn the founder of Cluny in Burgundy (910), which was to become the center of the reforming movement and the most famous abbey in Christendom. For abbot he chose Berno, who had himself founded two monasteries at Cigny and Baume in which the reform tradition of Aniane was kept alive. But the great novelty of the new abbey was that its founder made it exempt from all external authority save that of the Papacy and at the same time secured the rights of free election which had become so utterly disregarded at the time.

It was the second abbot, Odo (927–942), who first made Cluny famous, since he developed the original link between Cluny and the Papacy and became the reformer of the great abbey of St. Paul's Outside the Walls and of many other Italian monasteries.

In France, there were many among the lay nobles who had got control of monasteries, whose consciences were ill-at-ease and who preferred to pass on their power to St. Odo, whom they knew to be genuinely devoted to the monastic ideal, rather than to the bishops who for the most part had become feudal princes like themselves. In this way St. Odo before his death had become the reformer of very large numbers of monasteries, of which the most important was the great abbey of Fleury, or Saint-Benoît-sur-Loire, which had become secularized in consequence of the Norman invasions. Fleury in turn became associated through St. Oswald with the great movement of the restoration of the monastic life in England at the time of St. Dunstan, so that the work of St. Odo and the Cluniac reform continued to spread through many different channels for more than a century.

But this was not the only reforming movement. For almost contemporary with St. Odo, a number of monastic reformers, representing the same social class and the same spiritual ideals, arose in Lorraine, notably St. Gérard of Brogne, who founded the monastery there in 937, St. John of Vandières, who refounded the ancient monastery of Gorze in 933 and was its abbot from 960 to 975. In Lorraine the movement of reform found more support from the bishops than it had found in France. This was important because Lorraine contained some of the greatest ecclesiastical centers of the Carolingian empire, such as Liège and Metz and Toul, so that it was favorably situated as a center for the diffusion of reforming ideas eastward into Germany and west to Flanders and England.

In fact it was in Lorraine that most of the leading figures in the eleventh century had their origin, above all, the first of the reforming Popes, Leo IX, Bruno of Toul. But no less important was the political connection of Lorraine with Germany, which was an essential factor in this extension of the influence of the Lorraine reformers.

For it was in Eastern Europe that the tradition of Carolingian culture and of the Empire itself was strongest. The East Frankish kingdom had never fallen to pieces in feudal anarchy to the same extent as the Western kingdom. The prestige of the monarchy and the Empire had survived down to the death of the Emperor Arnulf in 899 and his son Lewis the Child in 911, and the revival of the royal power by the kings of the Saxon house, Henry I (919–936) and Otto I (936–973), had been justified by their success in warding off the attacks of the heathen Magyars and of the Slavs in the Northeast.

This new monarchy found its chief support, as the Carolingians had done, in an alliance with the Church, first with the bishops and secondly with the great monasteries, the so-called "royal abbeys," which numbered about eighty-five by the end of the tenth century.

These German rulers went even further than the Carolingians in associating the bishops with the royal power. They allowed no lay authority to intervene between them and even went so far as to transfer to them a large measure of secular power by making them counts and using them as their chief agents in administering the kingdom. Finally Otto I followed the example of Pepin II and Charles the Great by his repeated intervention in Italian politics and finally by his consecration as Roman Emperor by Pope John XII in 962.

It was not only in these respects that the new German kingdom resembled the old Frankish monarchy. It also devoted itself to the expansion of Christendom in Northern and Eastern Europe by its conquests of Slavs and Magyars and by the creation of new bishoprics and settlements in the conquered territories. Here the establishment of the new archbishopric of Magdeburg, and the episcopal sees that were dependent on it, was especially important for the Christianization of Northeast Germany.

As patrons of education and culture the German emperors did not equal their Carolingian predecessors. They rather resembled the Anglo-Saxon kings by the way in which they established monasteries under the rule of princesses of the royal house, such as Quedlinburg and Gandersheim, which became important centers of culture. The outstanding example of this is the writing of the nun Hrotswitha of Gandersheim. This is an almost unique case of a woman of this period who was both a scholar and a poet. The comedies she wrote in rhymed prose were based on her studies of Terence.

But the continuity of tenth-century culture with that of the Carolingian age is to be seen most clearly in the great German abbeys, especially those of the Southwest—St. Gall and Reichenau. For St. Gall holds a somewhat similar place in the new age to that which Fulda had occupied in the past. As Fulda represented the traditions of Anglo-Saxon culture, so did St. Gall those of the Irish scholars. And as Rabanus Maurus of Fulda had been the great educator of the Carolingian period, so was Notker Balbulus (the Stammerer) of St. Gall (840–912) the greatest teacher of the following period and a poet whose name has always been associated with the creation of the liturgical sequence which had such great importance for the history of medieval music.

Equally important was the second Notker. Notker Labeo (950–1022) was almost the creator of the Old High German as a literary language, by his numerous translations from Latin of classics and school books, such as Boethius and Martianus Capella, which he translated for his pupils, *"propter caritatem discipulorum."*

III.

But the greatest importance of the new Empire was undoubtedly the part it played in the reform of the Papacy. After the decline of the Carolingian Empire, Rome had fallen prey to the feuds of Italian princes and factions, and though a great Pope like John

VIII might for a few years (872–882) vindicate the independence and international authority of the Holy See, he was powerless to prevent his successors from becoming the puppet of these Italian nobles. Eventually Rome fell into the hands of the family of the papal chamberlain Theophylact and his wife Theodora, who founded a dynasty which survived for sixty years. Marozia, the daughter of Theophylact, controlled Rome and the Papacy from 916 to 932. In 932 she was defeated and her son, Pope John XI, was deposed by her second son, Alberic, who ruled Rome and the Papacy from 932 to 954. On his death he was succeeded by his son, Octavian, who himself became Pope John XII (955–964). But his power was less stable than that of his father, Alberic, and his fear of Berengar, the pretender to the crown of Italy, led him unwisely to make an appeal to Otto of Germany, as former popes had appealed to the Franks against the king of the Lombards. Otto at once answered his appeal, but in return he demanded to be crowned Emperor (in February 962) and the recognition by the Pope of his right to require future popes to take an oath of fidelity to him. But it was not easy to enforce this provision, and for the remainder of the tenth century there was a continual succession of Roman revolts and German acts of repression, which kept the papal succession in a state of uncertainty and disorder.

Meanwhile in Germany the party of ecclesiastical reform was growing steadily stronger. In this the Emperors Otto I and II played little part. They were fully occupied with their campaign against the Arabs and the Greeks in South Italy. But the Empress Adelaide, who was the heiress of the Burgundian kingdom, was a close friend of the reformers—of the two great abbots of Cluny, St. Mayeul and St. Odilo, of St. Adalbert, the archbishop of Magdeburg, and of St. Bernard, the great bishop of Hildesheim; while the younger Empress, Theophano, who was a Byzantine princess, was also a woman of strong character with a high idea of the imperial mission.

Consequently when Otto II died prematurely in Italy in 983,

aged only eighteen, leaving the Empire to his infant son, Otto III, aged three, the long regency, which was to last for thirteen years, left the power in the hands of this reforming group, which now also included that remarkable figure Gerbert of Aurillac, soon to be made Archbishop of Ravenna and afterwards Pope (999–1003) under the title of Sylvester II. The first Sylvester had been Pope while Constantine was Roman Emperor.

The brief reign of Otto III, who attained his majority in 996 at the age of sixteen, was revolutionary. On arriving in Italy in the spring of 996, he made his cousin Bruno, who was also his chaplain, Gregory V, the first of the non-Italian popes who were to be so numerous and important in the next two centuries.

But the moment Otto returned to Germany, the Romans reasserted themselves by driving out the new German Pope and consecrating an Italian Greek as John XVI. He did not last long. For Otto returned two years later, deposed John XVI and restored his cousin. But the latter died almost immediately and Otto now appointed his adviser, Gerbert, as Sylvester II. Gerbert, who was the greatest scholar of his time, acquired a strong influence over the young Emperor, who was himself highly educated by his Byzantine mother and who had a very exalted idea of his mission as Roman Emperor and head of Christendom. In the year 1000, he made a pilgrimage to the tomb of Charlemagne at Aachen, but he made Rome his headquarters and permanent residence and did all he could to reassert the imperial tradition in Italy. He was a young man, and it is interesting to speculate what would have happened if he and Gerbert had reigned for many years.

XIV. THE PAPACY
AND MEDIEVAL EUROPE

*Monasticism
+
Papacy* = *medieval culture*

If monasticism was one of the main formative influences in medieval religion, the Papacy was the other; and it was the alliance of these two forces from the time of St. Gregory the Great onwards which did more than anything else to create medieval culture. Nevertheless, Rome itself was far from being the center of that culture. It had developed on the basis of the Frankish monarchy and the Carolingian Empire. Its center was in the North, in the lands between the Rhine and the Loire, while Rome remained for many centuries in closer touch with the Byzantine East than with the Frankish North.

During the Dark Ages, as we have seen, the Papacy underwent a gradual reorientation. The turning point came in the eighth century with the conversion of Germany by St. Boniface, acting as the legate of the Holy See, and with the breach between Rome and the Byzantine Empire in the Iconoclast controversy.

The result of this change was that alliance between the Papacy and the Frankish kingdom which was sealed in 754, on the one hand by the solemn anointing of Pepin by Pope Stephen II as King of the Franks and, on the other, by "the donation of Pepin," which placed the remnants of Roman territory in Italy under the papal sovereignty and thus laid the foundation of the States of the Church. But this did not in fact secure the independence of the Holy See. For the growth of the Frankish power threatened it with fresh dangers, and the new Christian Empire of Charles the Great was inspired by the same Caesaropapist ideal as the

Byzantine. Nevertheless, the situation in the West was essentially different from that in the East. There the Empire stood, so to speak, on its own feet, and was able to incorporate the Church in the fixed *cadres* of its bureaucratic organization. In the West, on the other hand, the Church was older and more firmly organized than the new Christian State. In fact the latter was itself the product of the pre-existing ecclesiastical unity.

Consequently, when the Carolingian Empire began to decline, the Papacy naturally stepped into its place as the leader of the Christian people and the supreme authority of Christendom. Thus the pontificate of Nicholas I (858–867) already foreshadows the great age of the medieval Papacy, when the Holy See acquired a theocratic character which involved the subordination to it of the temporal power.

The age of Nicholas I was, however, separated from the age of Gregory VII and his successors by a dark period of almost two hundred years, during which the Papacy fell a victim to the ambition of the Roman nobles and was used as a pawn in the party struggles of the local oligarchy. It was not until the Christian Empire had been revived by the German emperors and the morale of the Church restored by the work of the monastic reformers that it was possible for the Papacy to realize the ideals of Nicholas I, to secure the independence of the Holy See and its effective supremacy in Western Christendom.

In the North, as we saw in the preceding chapter, the Carolingian tradition of the union of Church and State reached its climax in the tenth century in the restored Empire of Otto I and his successors. The German emperors made the bishops the cornerstone of their system of government, so that the latter combined with their episcopal office the secular office of the count and the secular privileges that went with it. Thus there arose the anomalous figure of the prince-bishop who governed his territories and made peace and war like any other feudal noble, and whose dual position and functions were an endless source of difficulty and friction alike to the medieval Church and the medieval State.

This state of things was felt to be intolerable by the more spiritually-minded element in the Church, which looked back with longing to the golden age of the Fathers and the primitive Church. Thus there arose a reforming movement which, beginning in the monasteries of Burgundy and Lorraine in the tenth century, gradually spread throughout the Western Church.

The Lorraine movement was exceptionally important, for Lorraine formed part of the Empire, and when the Emperor Henry III intervened at Rome to take the Papacy out of the hands of the Roman factions which had been exploiting it, it was to the Lorraine reformers that he turned. The greatest of the new popes from the North, St. Leo IX, had been bishop of Toul and for twenty years had been in close touch with the monastic reformers. When he came to Rome in 1049 he brought with him as his advisers and helpers some of the leading figures of the reforming movement—Humbert, Abbot of Moyenmoutier, Hugh, Abbot of Remiremont, and Frederick of Lorraine, who was to become Abbot of Monte Cassino and finally Pope Stephen II.

From this moment the Papacy became identified with the reforming movement and devoted all its powers to the restoration of canonical discipline. This involved the liberation of the Church from the control of the secular ruler, who had acquired the power to appoint bishops and abbots, or at least to demand an act of homage from them before they exercised their jurisdiction.

This was a revolutionary change, especially in the lands of the Empire where Church and State were inextricably mingled and the bishops had been for centuries the vital organs of the imperial government. Thus arose the great conflict between the Empire and the Papacy, known as the struggle of the Investitures, which lasted from 1076 to 1122, but which attained its climax during the pontificate of Pope St. Gregory VII (1073 to 1085), who was the creator of the theocratic ideal of the medieval Papacy. It was due to him that this rather limited question of lay investiture became

[margin notes in handwriting:] Henry III · Pope Leo IX 1049 · Papacy becomes reform · Investiture Struggle 1076-1122 · Gregory VII 1073-1085

the first great ideological conflict in the history of Western culture. It was not so much a conflict between Church and State as between two different parties in both Church and State, each of which was supported by powerful interests and able writers; and in the course of the controversies the most fundamental problems were raised, such as the origin of political power, the right of resistance to unjust power, the nature of the social contract: problems which were destined to acquire increasing importance in later periods of Western history.

The full program of the reforming party is to be found in the *Dictatus Papae*, a memorandum drawn up by Gregory VII in May, 1075. In addition to the classical doctrines of the divine origin and authority of the Holy See, its infallibility and its rights as the supreme court of appeal and the final authority in jurisdiction and doctrine, there is a novel assertion of the political rights of the Pope—the right to depose emperors and release subjects from their allegiance to unjust princes. These were the claims that had emerged in the course of the struggle with the Empire, and their assertion is one of the most characteristic features of the later medieval Papacy, above all in the period between Gregory VII and Boniface VIII. We cannot understand them unless we remember the peculiar character of the medieval state, which had its origin with Charles the Great, and which had been restored and continued by the Germanic emperors. It was not so much a secular state, in our sense of the word, as the temporal organ of a spiritual society. As the canonist Stephan of Tournai remarks: "In the same city, and under the same King, there are two peoples and two authorities. The city is the Church, the King is Christ, the two peoples are the clergy and the laity, and the two authorities are the priesthood and the monarchy."[1] Now if we regard Christian society in this way as an undivided unity, it is clear that the ultimate authority will be the spiritual one, and that the temporal

---

[1] Stephan of Tournai, cited by Carlyle, *A History of Mediaeval Political Theory in the West*, Vol. II, p. 198, and Vol. IV, p. 166.

power will be regarded as its minister in earthly matters and will possess only a delegated authority.

The imperialist partisans, it is true, contested this, since they regarded the Emperor as the true head of Christendom. Nevertheless, they accepted the same unitary conception of Christian society—indeed it is with them rather than with the Popes that this idea originated—and consequently their claims on behalf of the State amounted not to the independence of the secular power in its own province but to the right of the Emperor as the anointed ruler of the Christian people to control the Church as well as the State and to be, like the Byzantine Emperor, the head of the two hierarchies of the civil and ecclesiastical orders. It is obvious that these conceptions both involve a certain confusion between the functions of the temporal and spiritual powers. It is indeed inaccurate to describe the resultant conflicts as due to the theocratic claims of the Papacy, since the Imperialist position is equally theocratic. Nor was it a struggle between Church and State in the modern sense, since both parties assumed the existence of a common social unity—a Church-State of the Christian people.

If we accept these premises, it is clear that the Papacy was far better equipped for the task of common leadership, even in temporal matters, than was the Holy Roman Empire which, for all its universal claims, remained a local Central European power. Consequently, so long as the unitary conception of medieval society endured—that is to say, from the time of Gregory VII to Boniface VIII—the Papacy fulfilled a dual task as head of the Church and as leader and judge of Christian society in its widest aspect; and the greatest of the medieval Popes—men such as Gregory VII, Urban II, and Innocent III—were not unequal to the immense burden laid upon them, as is evident from the record of their many-sided activities that is contained in the papal registers.

No doubt the Emperor still claimed the leadership of Christendom, and was to continue to do so down to the time of Dante; but as a matter of fact he was no longer able to fulfill even formally the universal functions that had been performed by the Empire of Charlemagne. He had become merely the head of an unwieldy feudal state.

The Papacy, on the other hand, was a genuinely international power that made its authority felt in every corner of Christendom. For the medieval Church was not only a much more universal and comprehensive body than the Empire or the feudal state, it exercised many functions which we regard as essentially political. It was a sovereign power which imposed its own laws and enforced them in its own courts by its own judges and lawyers. It possessed an elaborate system of appellate jurisdiction, an organized bureaucracy and an efficient system of centralized control carried out by permanent officials and supervised by the visits and reports of the papal legates who played such a prominent part in the international life of Christendom.

This new order of Western Christendom was primarily due to a succession of great Popes in the eleventh century—St. Leo IX, St. Gregory VII and Bl. Urban II—who carried out the work of ecclesiastical and social reform. But their achievements would have been impossible if they had not been preceded and supported by the monastic reforming movement which provided the dynamic spiritual force behind the new order. The reformed Papacy was in fact mainly a monastic creation, and it continued to find its ablest and most disinterested helpers in the monastic orders from the time of St. Peter Damian and St. Hugh of Cluny down to St. Bernard of Clairvaux in the twelfth century.

It is true that this involved a certain change in the original ideals of monasticism as expressed by St. Benedict. For the monastic popes, cardinals and legates were obliged to leave the solitude of the cloister to take the lead in the government of the Church and the Christian republic. And in the same way the monastic order ceased to be an end in itself but became part of a larger unity and devoted itself as a corporate entity to the service of the Christian people.

This, we may note, is one of the most striking differences between Eastern and Western Christendom. Monasticism is equally important in both, but in the East the monk is a monk and nothing else, whereas in the West since the Middle Ages he is essentially the member of a religious order which is set apart to perform some definite function in the service of the Church, such as preaching or teaching or engaging in missionary work.

This change first begins at the close of the eleventh century with the formation of the Cistercian Order, which spread all over Christendom from Spain to Poland during the twelfth century. But an even more striking example of this functional principle is the foundation of the military orders such as the Order of the Temple founded under the inspiration of St. Bernard in 1118–1128. This was a lay order, a society of fighting monks living under a strict rule composed by St. Bernard himself. Thus it formed a bridge between lay and ecclesiastical society and brought the ideals of the monastic reformers into relation with those of chivalry. It marks the culmination of the reformers' attempt to introduce a Christian element into the barbaric traditions of Western feudalism.

The first attempt in this direction early in the eleventh century was the movement of the Peace of God, which sought to limit the evils of private war by the protection of noncombatants. Far more important, however, was the Crusading movement, which was one of the most characteristic expressions alike of the reviving energies of Western society and of the new international spirit of loyalty to the common cause of Christendom which had been generated by the reforming movement. At the Council of Clermont in 1095 the great Cluniac Pope Urban II put himself at the head of the movement which was intended to divert the energies of feudal society from internecine warfare by turning them against the external enemies of Christendom and which united Western society in a common enterprise under the leadership of the Papacy. For it was the Crusade more than any other single factor which

brought the unity of Christendom home to lay society as a fact of
daily experience: so that the age of the Crusades—the two centuries from 1095 onwards—was also the great age of medieval
unity and the period during which the moral and social authority
of the Papacy was greatest.

As E. G. Passant wrote in the fifth volume of the *Cambridge
Mediaeval History*: "There can be little doubt that this moral enthusiasm of Europe for the Crusade proved in the twelfth century
an almost incalculable assistance to the Papacy in its struggle with
the Empire. To this force of a united Christendom behind them
the successors of Gregory VII, who died in exile, owed much of
the great advance which they were able to make in the century
after his death. For the Crusades were a living parable of the doctrine of the spiritual sword. They were organized by the Popes
and directed by their legates and, what was more, all those who
took the Cross became by that act the subjects of the Papacy in a
new and special sense. Their goods during their absence, themselves, before they departed and until they returned with their
vows fulfilled, were removed from secular and placed under ec-
celesiastical jurisdiction. The Kings of France and England, of
Hungary or Naples, even the very Emperors themselves were, as
Crusaders, at the orders of the Pope. . . . It is difficult except
by this explanation to account for the amazing differences between
the position of the Papacy at the accession of Urban II. . . . and
the position of almost undisputed supremacy occupied by Innocent III."[2]

Moreover, in the Crusades the warlike energies of European society found an explicitly religious outlet. The very idea of a
religious war is apt to shock the modern mind, but we cannot understand medieval religion, at least in its more popular aspects,
unless we realize the strength of the religious emotion which
drove so many myriads of Christians to take the Cross, leave their

[2] *Cambridge Mediaeval History*, Vol. V, p. 322.

bones on the long road through Asia Minor, or rot in the prisons
of Egypt and Syria. The significant thing about the Crusading
movement is that it was an attempt to Christianize medieval society in its most vital but least Christian aspect, and thus it de-
notes a real fusion between the native tradition of the warrior
peoples of Western Europe and the ideals of the Church and the
Christian tradition. We see in early medieval literature—for example, in the *Chansons de Geste*—how wide was the gulf between
these two traditions and how much of the leaven of pagan barbarism still remained in the feudal society of the twelfth century.
Yet in the following century the Crusading ideal finds expression
in the life of St. Louis, which is one of the noblest examples of
medieval religion.[3] Here the leaven of paganism is entirely purged
away, while the characteristic heroic idealism of the northern warrior tradition remains.

But in addition to these moral effects on the internal economy
of Christendom, the Crusades also had a profound influence on
the development of Western culture. The establishment of the
Crusading States in Syria and Palestine, and the almost contemporary reconquest by the Christians of Sicily and the greater part
of Moslem Spain, brought the West back into contact with the
higher civilization of the Near East and reopened the channels of
trade between Italy and the Levant. This intercourse with the
Arab world brought with it new ideas as well as new wealth.
Arabic science, which was mainly Greek science in Arab dress,
reached Western Europe through the translators of Toledo and
Palermo, most of whom were Jews or Jewish converts, and enlarged the horizon of Western learning, thus preparing the way
for the great advance of Western philosophy in the thirteenth
century.

But even without this external stimulus, a remarkable intellect-

---

[3] There is an English translation of the Life of St. Louis by Joinville in Every-
man's Library. The same volume contains Villehardouin's chronicle of the Fourth
Crusade, which shows the reverse side of the movement.

ual, literary and artistic revival was already taking place during the latter eleventh and early twelfth centuries. Guibert de Nogent, the historian of the First Crusade, writing at the beginning of the twelfth century, describes how completely the conditions of education had changed during his lifetime, and the fruits of this change were apparent not only in theology and religious studies, but also in literature and poetry and in the number and quality of the historians who flourished in the twelfth century all over Christendom, but most of all in Britain.

This revival was not, however, confined to the intellectual sphere. This central period of the Middle Ages, from 1060 to 1260, witnessed an extraordinary outpouring of social energy in every field. In spite of all the oppression and lawlessness of feudalism, it was an age of freedom and enterprise. Above all the rise of the medieval city, with its intense communal and religious activity, marks the emergence of the West from barbarism to a new civilization which differed alike from those of classical antiquity and from the contemporary oriental world. Thus the original social dualism of warrior-noble and peasant-serf was transcended and replaced by a complex corporative order based on status and function and maintaining a balance between authority and freedom.

For although Christendom was a hierarchical society, its constituent members possessed a considerable degree of autonomy; nor were these corporate unities closed societies, since they interpenetrated one another, while the greater common institutions of Christendom—the religious and military orders and the most influential universities—were international societies which drew their members from all parts of Europe and from different social classes.

The most remarkable of these international institutions, those that had the widest impact on society, were the Orders of Friars —the Franciscans, the Dominicans and others—who were vowed to poverty and were free to travel wherever their mission required. Their activities as preachers in the cities, as teachers in the universities, as missionaries, writers and spiritual reformers made them one of the leading forces in Western culture during the thirteenth century, at the time when the influence of the monastic order was beginning to decline.

At the same time the international unity of the Church under the authority of the Holy See was transformed from a theory into a reality. The loose federation of provinces and national churches which had existed in the tenth century gave place to a centralization of authority and jurisdiction which left little power to the Metropolitans and brought every part of Christendom into immediate relations with Rome. Above all, the new system of canon law, created by the movement of reform and by the great Popes of the eleventh and twelfth centuries, supplied a firm juridical basis for the international order of the reformed Church. This development of canon law and scientific jurisprudence, which had its center in the University of Bologna, was hardly less important for the history of the medieval Church than the philosophical and theological movement which had its center in the University of Paris. Indeed, as de Ghellinck has shown, it was not without its influence on the latter. For in the twelfth century, the age of Gratian and Peter Lombard, theology and canon law still overlapped one another, and dealt to some extent with the same subject matter.[4]

All this work of constitutional and juridical organization was, however, only one side—the external side—of the movement of reform. To those who concentrate their attention on this aspect alone medieval religion must inevitably appear external and legalistic, an affair of obligations and sanctions.[5] But there is also the interior aspect of the movement, which the reformers themselves regarded as its true end and *raison d'être*.

[4] See P. Fournier and G. le Bras, *Histoire des collections canoniques depuis les Fausses Décrétales jusqu'au Décret de Gratien*, 2 vols., 1931–1932.

[5] Cf., for example, the generalization of the editors of the *Cambridge Mediaeval History*, Vol. VII, p. 20: "Christian doctrine from 1100 to 1300 had grown steadily legalized."

If, however, we regard medieval religion from this point of view, we shall see that its dominant tendency was not to exteriorize religion, but just the opposite—to humanize and interiorize it. Byzantine religion had developed the transcendent side of Christianity. It had emphasized the divine nature of Christ, the Uncreated Word, rather than the Divine Humanity. That is why the greater part of Oriental Christendom, Syria and Egypt, Armenia and Abyssinia, fell away from orthodoxy by a denial of the Human Nature of Christ and adopted the errors of Monophysitism. Medieval Catholicism, on the other hand, concentrated its attention on the Humanity of Jesus, on the contemplation of his Life and Passion, and on the practice of the Imitation of Christ. These are the characteristic notes of medieval devotion from the time of the reforming movement down to the Protestant Reformation, from St. Anselm and St. Bernard to St. Francis and St. Bonaventure, down to the Yorkshire hermit Richard Rolle and Thomas à Kempis. St. Bernard is perhaps the greatest of these "doctors of the Sacred Humanity," and no single personality is more characteristic of medieval religion, both in thought and action. It is, however, in St. Francis that medieval religion finds its most sublime expression, and one which makes a unique appeal not only to the medieval mind but also to modern men. And the secret of this appeal is not to be found precisely in the Christocentric character of St. Francis' life and doctrine. What impressed his contemporaries and still impresses us today is the "conformity" of St. Francis to the pattern of the Divine Humanity, so that, in the words of a medieval writer,[6] "St. Francis became as it were the picture of Christ, and was transformed at all points into Jesus, the Lord Himself, completing and finishing this work by the impression of the stigmata."

But St. Francis was not only a master of the spiritual life, he was also among the greatest of the leaders of the reforming move-

[6] The author of the *Meditationes vitae Christi*, which were falsely attributed to St. Bonaventure (John de Caulibus?).

ment, and his order, together with that of St. Dominic, was the most efficient and devoted agent of the Papacy in its universal mission.

For the coming of the Franciscans and the other mendicant orders of the thirteenth century involved an entirely new form of life for the religious community. In contrast to the Cluniac and Cistercian reforms, St. Francis went back behind the whole monastic movement to the New Testament, and substituted the apostolic life of preaching and teaching for the ascetic and liturgical ideals of the older monastic orders. The new orders could devote themselves to the service of the Church and the poor without the rules which restricted the external activities of the monk to his cloister. This principle of the socialization of the religious life in the service of the Church marks an epoch in the history of Christendom, since it is typical not only of the Franciscans and the Dominicans, but also of the post-Reformation orders, such as the Jesuits, which have played such an important part in the history of the modern Church. If the early Middle Ages are the age of the monks, the later Middle Ages are the age of the friars. Their action is to be seen not only in their missionary activity, but also intellectually in the universities and in the development of Scholasticism, and spiritually in their influence on the great mystical movement of the fourteenth century, and on the new forms of piety and popular devotion. Their influence was especially strong in Italy during the period of the early Renaissance, through such saints and religious leaders as St. Catherine and St. Bernardino of Siena, St. Antoninus of Florence, and Savonarola. In fact, their action did much to save the religious life of Italy from the secularizing influence of the Renaissance culture, and thus to prepare the way for the religious revival of the Counter-Reformation.

XV. THE UNITY
OF WESTERN CHRISTENDOM

The achievement of the later Middle Ages from the eleventh to the fifteenth century deserves the name of a "renaissance" better than the more limited movement to which the name has been appropriated. These centuries, especially the twelfth and the thirteenth, witnessed a most remarkable revival of cultural activity in every field, intellectual, political, and economic. It saw the building of the great cathedrals and monastic houses, the foundation of the new medieval cities, the development of canon law, Scholastic philosophy, and vernacular literature.

For six hundred years Western society had been slowly emerging from barbarism and attempting to create a new Christian order out of the ruins of the Roman Empire and the chaos of warring tribes. The foundations had been laid in the eighth and ninth centuries, when the Frankish kingdom in alliance with the Papacy and the Anglo-Saxon missionaries created a new Christian Empire which extended from its center in North France and Belgium and Western Germany to the rest of France and Germany as well as to Northern and Central Italy and to Northeastern Spain. This achievement was interrupted and almost destroyed by the new barbarian invasions of the Vikings and the Magyars in the ninth and tenth centuries. But the conversion of Scandinavia and of the peoples of Eastern Europe—the Czechs, the Poles and the Magyars—marked the turn of the tide, and from the beginning of the eleventh century a period of progress and expansion began which was to continue for three centuries.

But this movement was no longer identified with a great state, as in the Carolingian period. Although the Carolingian Christian tradition was still maintained by the restored Christian Empire in Germany, the real center of the movement of advance was to be found in the new feudal society which had grown up on the ruins of the Frankish kingdom in France. The greatest of these feudal states was the duchy of Normandy, and it was the Normans who led the victorious advance of Christendom in the eleventh century and created the new kingdom and principalities in England, Sicily and Antioch.

At first sight the spirit of this turbulent and predatory feudal society seems incompatible with the tradition of Christian culture and the ideal of the unity of Christendom. But it was fully aware of the evils of its own violence and disorder, and it looked outside itself for a principle of spiritual order and unity. Thus it was that the reform of the Church and the revival of Western monasticism developed in the same region and at the same period as the feudal society. As the Carolingian culture owed its origin to the collaboration of the Frankish monarchy with the Anglo-Saxon monks and the Roman Papacy, so the culture of medieval Christendom was the result of the co-operation of the feudal society with the monastic reformers and the reformed Papacy.

By the end of the eleventh century, when Urban II proclaimed the Crusade at the Council of Clermont, the Papacy had taken the place of the Empire in the leadership of Christendom; and thenceforward for two centuries a succession of great Popes, supported by the monastic reformers and the founders of the new religious orders, built up the elaborate organization of ecclesiastical government and law which served the unity of Western Christendom more effectively than any political system could have done.

In the thirteenth century this work of unification was almost complete, at the time when the external expansion of feudal society had reached its full development. Almost the whole of Europe and a considerable part of the Eastern Mediterranean formed one great society, united by a common faith, a common law and common institutions. A man could travel the pilgrimage routes from England and Ireland or Scandinavia to Rome, Compostella and Jerusalem and find everywhere men who shared the same way of life, the same standards of thought and behavior. The religious orders, the orders of knighthood and the universities were international institutions with members and contacts in every land, so that a monk who left his abbey in the far North, at Alvastra or Rievaulx, would find his brethren a thousand miles away at Alcobaca or in Cyprus, living precisely the same life, in the same kind of building, saying the same prayers in the same language, and perhaps even thinking the same thoughts.

This combination of the unity of social institutions with the unity of religious faith and ecclesiastical order explains the achievements of medieval culture in so many different fields, and in particular in the field of art. The pilgrimage routes were channels through which the new artistic influences of Romanesque architecture and sculpture had been disseminated through Western Europe, and it is at Durham Cathedral in 1093 that we find the highest development of vaulted stone architecture in the North in the eleventh century. From the Southeast the influence of the art of Moslem Spain penetrated into France along the line of these routes, and through the Cluniac priories, as is seen in the appearance of the horseshoe and cusped forms of arch, not only at St. Paul's at Barcelona, but as far north as Burgundy.

The most important, however, of all the French contributions to Romanesque art was the renaissance of statuary which took place at the Cluniac priories of Moissac and Daurode in Languedoc at the beginning of the twelfth century. For almost six centuries the statue had disappeared from European art, and its rediscovery and application to architecture dominated all the subsequent medieval development. The plastic architecture of Western Europe with its statue columns and its great porches and friezes with their thousands of figures is unparalleled save in the almost contemporary art of medieval India, as at Bhwanesvar, and both arts owe their origin to a somewhat similar process of fusion between an oriental and an Hellenistic tradition. But whereas the Indian figure sculpture is derived by direct tradition from the Graeco-Buddhist art of Northwest India, that of medieval France was created anew from the imitation of painted ornaments and manuscripts, such as the famous Spanish Apocalypse of the Abbot Beatus, which inspired the carving of the portal of Moissac. This explains the marked orientalism of the eleventh-century sculpture—the strange beasts with interlocked necks or with many heads, derived through the works of Syrian and Sassanian artists from the ancient iconography of Sumerian Mesopotamia. This influence was reinforced by the direct contact with the Moslem art of Spain and Syria in the age of the Crusades, so that we find the figure of Gilgamesh between his lions on the capital of a Norman abbey (Jumièges at Boscherville) and degraded Arabic inscriptions on the doors of churches in Auvergne.

It was the same age which saw the rise of the splendid Arab-Byzantine art of Palermo and Monreale in Sicily.

In Northern France, however, these influences were combined by the French genius into a new and original style. The birth of Gothic art took place in the Ile de France in 1140 with the Abbot Suger's rebuilding of Saint-Denis, where the new sculpture of the school of Moissac was united with the new principle of the cross vault, which, by concentrating the strain upon the piers and buttresses, made it possible to dispense with the massive walls and ponderous roof of the older Romanesque style. The perfect Gothic church is no longer a building, solidly planted upon the soil. It has become an exquisitely balanced machine, every member of which is engaged in constant activity of stress and counterstress, while the walls vanish to a mere veil of masonry ultimately to be replaced, as at the Sainte-Chapelle, by a series of vast painted windows. But while a Roman building is as indestructible as a rock, a Gothic structure will collapse like a pack of cards if a single stress gives way, as occurred in the most daring masterpiece of all—the Cathedral of Beauvais.

This new school of architecture reached its full development early in the thirteenth century with the great cathedrals of Northern France—above all Chartres, Rheims and Amiens, and spread through Europe with extraordinary rapidity, until it became the universal medieval style—the French style, as it was often called. And it was everywhere accompanied by the new Gothic sculpture, which had developed after Saint-Denis, particularly at Chartres and Paris. In the latter part of the twelfth century the oriental influence was on the wane. St. Bernard had already protested against the fantastic oriental imagery of Romanesque art, alike on the score of religion and taste. A reaction towards classical models is clearly to be seen in the art of Provence, with its Corinthian columns and fluted pilasters, its sculptured architraves, its statues in niches and its purely classical decoration such as volutes and acanthus leaves.

The new art of the North, however, drew its inspiration from nature. The plants of the field and the daily tasks of peasant life replace the monstrous beasts of the oriental tradition. Above all, the human figure reappears in forms of ideal beauty. If the majestic figures of the portals of Chartres have all the stiffness of archaic Greek art, those of Rheims in their flowing draperies have the liberty and perfection of the classical age. And at Auxerre even the Greek gods themselves return.

Nevertheless all this freedom and perfection of form are subordinated to a great scheme of religious symbolism.[1] The Gothic cathedral, like the culture which produced it, is a profound unity. The whole medieval cosmic order—the life of nature and the drama of redemption—is represented in symbol and image, in type and

[1] For an examination of the details of this scheme, Emile Mâle's *The Gothic Image* (Harper Torchbook edition, 1958) is invaluable.

antitype upon its walls. But there is nothing redundant or extraneous. Everything is related alike to the structural and the intellectual unity of the whole. If there is a fault, it is that the whole scheme is too logical and too intellectualized—the very opposite of that confused and disorderly spirit which the post-Renaissance mind conceived to be characteristically "Gothic." Nevertheless it is one of the great arts of the world, the expression of one of those rare moments in the life of humanity when the inner and outer worlds are united in vital rhythm and intelligible harmony.

Alike in the art of the Gothic cathedrals, the thought of the great thirteenth-century philosophers and the institutions of the medieval city and kingdom, the same power of co-ordination and comprehension is at work, the same spirit of hierarchical order and the same sense of transcendent spiritual values which make the thirteenth century one of those ages which "vindicate the greatness of the human spirit and compensate the historian for the barren prospect of a thousand years of stupidity and barbarism."

When Voltaire wrote these lines he was thinking of the ages of Louis XIV and Leo X and Pericles, and he regarded the thirteenth century as an age of barbarism and superstition, unworthy of the attention of a man of taste and good sense. Indeed it was not until the nineteenth century that the achievements of thirteenth-century culture were understood and accepted as equal or even comparable to those of the other great ages of civilization. Even today there are many who would regard such a view as that of Henry Adams in *Mont-Saint-Michel and Chartres* as a romantic idealization of the past which ignored the realities of history. They would say that the unity of thirteenth-century Christendom was superficial and partial, and that the achievements of a small aristocratic and clerical minority bore little relation to the lives of the anonymous masses which carried the feudal and ecclesiastical structure on their backs. Nor is this view without some justification, inasmuch as our knowledge of medieval culture is inevitably biased by the fact that the clergy was the only element in medieval society that was fully literate and articulate, so that all the historians, philosophers and legists were drawn from the same class and represent the same point of view. And, above all, there was the Inquisition.

The revival of Western culture had been accompanied from the eleventh century onwards by a new heretical movement which, in the twelfth and thirteenth centuries, became a serious danger to Catholicism. This was the Catharist movement. It should perhaps be regarded not so much as a heresy as a rival religion, since it was rooted in the non-Christian and perhaps pre-Christian dualism of the ancient East, which was transmitted to the West, through the Balkan peninsula, by the Paulicians and the Bogomils. In any case, it is of the greatest importance for the history of medieval religion, and we cannot understand the latter unless we realize that Catholicism's most dangerous foe was not some form of simplified or rationalized Christianity, but a religion which regarded the body and the whole material world as the creation of Satan, condemned marriage and child-bearing as essentially sinful. It was forbidden for the Catharist not only to marry, but to kill any living thing, or to eat anything that was the fruit of sexual generation. But this life of strict asceticism belonged only to the "perfect," who had received the *consolamentum*, "the baptism with the spirit and with fire," which was the sacrament of the Catharist religion. The ordinary Catharist was merely a "believer" who shared neither the privileges nor the privations of the "perfect," through whom alone he could hope to attain contact with the spiritual world. Thus Catharism combined extreme asceticism with considerable laxity, and even antinomianism, in practice.

It is not surprising that a heresy of so fundamental a nature, which regarded the God of the Catholics as an evil power and the Church itself as the creation of Satan, should have been met with remorseless repression. Indeed, the rise of Catharism in Western

Europe seems to have been largely responsible for the new attitude to heresy and persecution which marked the later medieval Church. Hitherto, it is true, the Church had regarded the suppression of heresy as part of the duty of the State, but it had shown itself averse from extreme measures, and the sentence *"Ecclesia abhorret a sanguine"*—"The Church abominates bloodshed"—had been accepted as an established maxim. But the Catharists were in an entirely different category to other heretics. Manichees, and such the Catharists substantially were, were regarded alike by pagans and Christians as enemies of the human race. Even before the advent of Christianity, Manicheanism had been treated as a capital offence by Roman law, and the Byzantine Empire had attempted to exterminate the Paulicians with fire and sword. Though isolated rulers or bishops from the eleventh century onwards had executed heretics, the Church had given no official sanction to their capital punishment, and the leaders of orthodox opinion, such as St. Bernard and Gerhoh of Reichersberg, continued to condemn it. When, however, the Church had taken the lead in preaching the Crusade against the infidel abroad, it seemed inconsistent to condemn the use of the sword against the heretic at home, above all in face of a heresy so radically subversive as Catharism. Accordingly, in the second half of the twelfth century we find a growing movement in favor of a Crusade against the Albigenses and the Crusade was in fact declared in 1208. Nevertheless, though Innocent III, under the influence of Roman law, assimilated heresy to the crime of high treason (*laesae majestatis*), for which the penalty was death, he still stopped short of the death penalty, and decreed only exile and confiscation in the anti-heretical legislation of the Fourth Lateran Council.

The final step seems to have been taken in consequence of the action of that brilliant and sinister figure, Frederick II, who covered his own doubtful orthodoxy by the zeal with which he persecuted heretics and the ruthlessness of his anti-heretical legislation. In 1224 he made heresy punishable by burning. It is probable that his action was due to a desire to assert his authority in religious matters at the expense of the ecclesiastical authority. In any case the Pope (Gregory IX) was unwilling to leave the "inquisition" of heretics to the civil power, and he accordingly appointed special commissioners for the purpose in 1231, which may be regarded as the date of the official foundation of the Inquisition.

The very name Inquisition has become so highly charged with emotion that we are disposed to see in its operation nothing but cruelty and injustice. The excesses of two of the earliest Inquisitors, the Dominican Robert le Bougre and his contemporary, the Premonstratensian Conrad of Marburg, are indeed deserving of such condemnation. Even so, the former was removed from his office by Pope Gregory IX and condemned to lifelong imprisonment; and the latter combined with his fanatical intolerance, zeal for social justice in defense of the poor against noble or princely oppressors.

Far more representative was the fourteenth-century inquisitor Bernard Gui, whose manual of procedure (*Practica*) is a serious attempt, however defective by our judicial standards, to secure justice. Out of 930 sentences passed by Gui only 42 delivered the accused to the secular arm for capital punishment. At Pamiers and Toulouse about the same period the proportion was respectively one in fifteen, one in twenty-two. Lea, the Protestant historian of the Inquisition, concludes: "The stake consumed few victims."

Both the legislation of Frederick and that of the Popes were affected by the influence of the revived Roman Law as, for example, in the use of judicial torture, introduced into the Inquisition in 1251 and one of its worst features. This was a serious breach with the older medieval tradition, for the Church had opposed the use of torture not only in patristic times, but in the darkest period of the Dark Ages, when Pope Nicholas I had insisted on its essential folly and injustice in his letter to the converted Bulgarians. Here the attitude of the Dark Ages seems more enlightened than that of the later medieval and Renaissance periods. The same is true of the belief in witchcraft: belief in its reality was opposed as a relic of pagan superstition by Nicholas I and Agobard, and the ecclesiastical advisers of Charlemagne.[2] Witch-burning, however, spread like a contagion throughout Europe at the close of the Middle Ages and reached its height in the post-Reformation period.

It is easy to exaggerate these negative aspects of medieval culture. The life of the medieval Church with its feasts and fasts, its pilgrimages and its devotion to the saints in whom every locality and every occupation had its appropriate patron, was the common possession of the whole Christian people, and it was in his membership of the Church rather than the state that medieval man found his true citizenship. No man was too poor or wretched to be included in this community—even the beggars and the lepers possessed their own spiritual dignity which was solemnly recognized by the powers of the world when the king washed the feet of the poor on Maundy Thursday and fed them at his own table.

This ideal of Christian democracy or fraternity found its highest expression in the Franciscan movement with its cult of poverty and its apostolate of the poor. The influence of the Friars was all-pervading in the thirteenth century: it affected every level of society and culture, and was especially strong in the case of St. Louis IX, who took the Friars as his advisers and ministers as well as his friends. But it was in the cities that the influence of the Friars was most important. For the spirit of the new religious institutions was peculiarly adapted to the needs of the new civic society and the new social classes.

Indeed the great communal movement which began in Northern Italy in the eleventh century and spread through France and the neighboring lands in the following centuries was itself an expression of the new spirit of Christian fraternity as well as the product of

---

[2] So, too, Gregory VII had warned King Haakon of Denmark against the persecution of witches. "Learn rather," he writes, "to turn away the wrath of God by worthy penance, than to provoke His anger yet further by useless savagery against these innocents." *Register*, ed. Caspar, ii.498.

new economic forces. The constituent principle of the medieval commune was the common oath, by which all the members of the town swore to establish a common peace and brotherhood and defend the rights of each member against all comers. "It has been established and confirmed by the bond of the oath that each will give his fellow faith, strength, aid and counsel, so far as justice shall determine," says the charter of Abbeville.[3]

Thus the oath of the commune was a kind of social contract which gave the medieval city a genuinely democratic character. For the medieval city was essentially a community of free men, and whatever a man's origin might be, he became free after he had lived for a year within the city walls. In the words of the *Etablissements de St. Quentin* (c. 1151), "The gate is open to all. Whoever wills, whence so ever he comes, so long as he is not a thief, shall be able to live in the commune, and after he shall enter the town, no man shall be able to lay hands on him or do him violence."[4]

When men of every class, inspired by the new communal spirit, began to form associations, confraternities and guilds, communes and sworn leagues of peace, all these had their basis and sanction in religion. It is often difficult to draw the line between the religious and the economic functions. For instance, in the case of the "Charity of St. Christopher" at Tournai, we find a guild of merchants, which undoubtedly originated as a religious confraternity, but which had come in time to be charged with the whole administration of the city finances.

This religious character was revealed with equal clarity in the case of those communes and leagues of peace which were in opposition to the established order of feudal society, such as the great confraternity of the Capuchonnes which waged war on the brigands and nobles of Central France in 1182–1183, and which was founded by a carpenter in Le Puy in obedience, as he declared, to the com-

[3] Petit-Dutaillis, *Les Communes Françaises*, p. 100.
[4] *Ibid.*, p. 71.

mands of Our Lady in a vision. The same energy that produced the Crusades was at work also in these little-known social movements which did so much to transform the life of Europe in the twelfth and thirteenth centuries.

When the medieval economic development was complete, every economic and social function possessed its corporate organization, and the medieval city became a federation of self-governing societies, each of which had its own statutes, its own meeting place and chapel and its special patron saint. There was, it is true, rivalry enough between the different classes and factions in the cities, between the aristocracy of merchants and the democracy of craftsmen, but nevertheless the economic theories of the theologians and the canonists were implicitly accepted by all parties as the foundations of industrial and commercial life.

They taught that the economic order must be dominated not by the shifting forces of competition and self-interest, but by a fixed law in justice. Every individual and every corporation had its special office to fulfill in the Commonwealth, and each was entitled to a just reward. The non-economic functions, whether political or religious, had their fiefs or benefices to enable them to fulfill their office. The economic occupations, though they also might possess their corporate endowments, were supported primarily by selling the products of their labor. The "just price" was that which was a true recompense for the labor expended, whereas a price raised by scarcity and the buyer's need, or lowered by the seller's economic weakness, was unjust and illegitimate.

The most honorable economic functions were those that were most productive; hence the medieval preference for the husbandman and the craftsman to the merchant. The true end of labor was not pecuniary profit, but the service of others. To work for profit alone was to turn honest work into usury, and all occupations which looked for excessive profit, or in which the profit was unrelated to the expenditure of labor, were looked upon with disfavor. Medieval life and literature are full of this ideal of disinterested labor. We see it in *Piers Plowman*, and in the Plowman of Chaucer, who

> . . . wolde thresshe, and therto dyke and delve,
> For Cristes sake, for every povre wight,
> Withouten hire, if it lay in his myght.

And the Church has raised it to her altars in the person of St. Isidore Agricola.

The ideal for craftsmen was no less high. "It is good and true work," says a medieval writer, "when craftsmen by the skill and cunning of their hands in beautiful buildings and sculptures spread the glory of God, and make men gentle in their spirits, so that they find delight in all beautiful things, and look reverently on all art and handicraft, as a gift of God for the use, enjoyment and edification of mankind."[5]

These theories and ideals found practical expression in the economic regulations of the cities and the guilds.

Membership of the latter was compulsory, so that each guild possessed a monopoly of its own craft. It represented the principle of corporate responsibility, both towards the community by guaranteeing the quality of the wares produced, and toward its members by ensuring to all equal opportunity and mutual assistance in need.

The city, for its part, aimed at safeguarding the supply of necessaries at a just price. All goods had to be sold by retail in the open market, and numerous laws against "engrossing, forestalling, and regrating," were directed against any attempts on the part of individuals or rings to dominate the market or control supply. This was looked on in the Middle Ages as the essential economic function of the state.

Outside the towns these co-operative economic ideals had less scope, for feudal society always rested to a great extent on the rule of force. But even there the same tendencies were at work. The influ-

---

[5] Jansen, *History of the German People*, Vol. II, p. 97.

ence of the Church tended to transform the right of the stronger into an office of honor and service in the Christian commonwealth. As medieval royalty was consecrated into a semi-religious function, so too the military ruling class was spiritualized by the ideals of Christian knighthood into an order for the maintenance of justice and the defense of the weak and the oppressed.

Moreover, throughout the Middle Ages, the agricultural population made steady progress in communal rights and economic independence, and this in spite of the failure of their attempts (as in 1381) to shake off the feudal yoke altogether. By the fifteenth century their condition in most countries was even superior to that of the organized craftsmen of the free cities, as is shown, for instance, by the parish churches and guild chantries of rural England.

The coming of the communes changed the character of medieval society by opening the gate to social advance and creating a new free population between the privileged orders of the nobles and the clergy and the unenfranchised peasantry. In the course of the thirteenth century this new class came to hold an increasingly important place not only in the economic order, but also in the life of the medieval state. First in Spain and Italy, and later in the North, the cities were called to send their representatives to the royal curia to take counsel for the good of the realm and the service of God, and it was the addition of this new element which transformed the old feudal council into a representative assembly of the "estates of the realm."

Moreover, it was in the medieval city that the thirteenth-century ideal of unity found its highest political expression. The feudal state retained to the end the mark of the disunity out of which it had arisen. It was based not on common citizenship but on the bond of personal fidelity and loyalty that bound a man to his lord. But the medieval city was a true commonwealth—an organic community with an exceptionally rich communal life and a highly organized political life. The civic life of the great Italian communes in the thirteenth century and of the Flemish communes in the following century is something entirely different from the political life of the feudal state of the early Middle Ages. It has far more in common with the traditions of the Greek city-state. In both we see the same active participation of the citizen in public affairs, elaborate devices for the popular supervision and control of the magistrates and the same tendency to party conflict and sudden revolutionary change. In this, as in many other respects, the culture of the thirteenth century represents not so much the culmination of the older medieval development as the emergence of a new social principle in the life of Western Europe.

XVI. THE ACHIEVEMENT OF
MEDIEVAL THOUGHT

1.

The almost complete discredit and oblivion into which medieval thought fell during so long a period is one of the most curious phenomena in history. It was due to the simultaneous convergence of a number of hostile influences of various orders—religious, literary and scientific. Of all these, probably the most powerful was the change that accompanied the Renaissance and caused the humanists to look upon the old learning as a mass of barbarism and pedantry. It was, in fact, not the Reformers, but Catholic scholars of the type of Vives and Erasmus, the Italian humanists, and Pascal and Boileau, who did most to bring the name of the Schoolmen into contempt. The mockery of Rabelais was more deadly than all the invectives of Luther. And it is impossible to deny that the decadent Scholasticism of the sixteenth century deserved much of the ridicule that was levelled at it. The high metaphysical speculation of the thirteenth century had degenerated into a sterile logic-chopping.

But whatever view men may take of the objective philosophical value of Scholasticism, there can be no question of the importance of its influence on the development of European thought. The Schoolmen were the schoolmasters of our civilization and they were largely responsible for the training and formation of the Western mind. During the early Middle Ages the conditions in Western Europe were not unlike those that obtained in the old Russia. It

was a peasant culture in which the only element of higher civilization was represented by the monasteries and the intellectual heritage
of the patristic tradition. These were the true Dark Ages, in spite
of the real achievements of the Carolingian period. But there is no
excuse for applying the expression to the later part of the Middle
Ages, from the eleventh century onwards. It can be justified only
by the absurd idea that the world stopped thinking at the end of the
classical period and began again abruptly at the time of the Reformation. So far from being a blank page in the intellectual history of
Europe, the age of Scholasticism has left a more indelible imprint
on the Western mind than any other period. As Professor Whitehead has said, it was the age that laid the foundations for the
scientific achievements of the modern world. For we owe to it that
confidence in the power of reason and that faith in the rationality
of the universe without which science would be impossible. It
destroyed the old magical view of nature which our ancestors shared
with every other primitive people and which still lingers on, not
only in remote corners of Europe, but under the surface of our
modern urban civilization.

This achievement was due above all to the recovery of the
Hellenistic scientific tradition which Western Europe had lost for
nearly a thousand years. In fact, Western Europe can hardly be said
to have ever possessed it, since it had been very imperfectly assimilated by the Roman mind even during the golden age of Latin
culture. Cicero, Varro and Seneca had indeed provided the Roman
world with a popular version of Greek philosophical ideas; but it
was the philosophy of a cultivated man of the world, rather than
of a scientist or a metaphysician. And it was this tradition, deepened
by the spiritual genius of Augustine and by the infusion of some
Neo-Platonic elements but not sensibly widened, which became the
sole intellectual patrimony of Western Christendom.

Now, however, in the twelfth and thirteenth centuries, the Western mind at last came into contact with the main tradition of
Hellenic thought, and acquired for the first time a knowledge of

strict scientific method and an interest in ultimate metaphysical problems. This is an epoch-making event in the history of European thought. No doubt the Renaissance would in any case have discovered Greek philosophy and science; but it would have discovered them in a different way—as part of the tradition of classical culture received from the Byzantines, that is, in a literary and antiquarian spirit.

The Schoolmen, on the other hand, received them from the Arabs as part of a living scientific movement, and their attention was concentrated not on the form but on the content of the newly discovered literature. Moreover, if the contact with Greek thought had been delayed until the sixteenth century, there can be little doubt that the conflict between the new knowledge and the orthodox tradition—between theology and science—would have been far more acute than that which actually occurred. In the sixteenth century the centrifugal forces in our civilization were predominant, and the conditions were unfavorable to the creation of a synthesis such as the thirteenth century achieved. If Greek science and metaphysics had made their first appearance in the West under the auspices of men like Pomponazzi, Telesio and Giordano Bruno, instead of Albertus Magnus and St. Thomas, the resistance of the theologians and the traditionalists, alike in Catholic and in Protestant Europe, would have been far more uncompromising and the consequent break in the intellectual continuity of Western culture have been much more complete.

We must not, however, exaggerate the importance of the Hellenic or even the Hellenic-Arabic element in medieval thought. The awakening of the medieval mind was due to two causes, not one: on the one hand, to the contact with the higher culture of the Moslem world from which it received the intellectual heritage of Greek philosophy; on the other, to the revival of the native Western tradition of Latin culture which had already made itself felt as early as the Carolingian period. When we speak of Scholasticism or of the Schoolmen, it is usually in reference to the later development of medieval thought following the recovery of Aristotle. But in its strict etymological sense Scholasticism is nothing else but the educational tradition of the medieval schools—the curriculum of the seven liberal arts, the *Trivium* and the *Quadrivium*; above all those of the *Trivium*—Grammar, Rhetoric and Dialectic (Logic).

This tradition goes back to the schools of rhetoric in the later Empire, and to the teaching of such writers as Macrobius, Martianus Capella, Boethius and Cassiodorus. Although it had been adapted to the needs of the ecclesiastical and monastic culture by the Irish and Anglo-Saxon monks who were the great educators of the Dark Ages, it retained something of the literary humanism of the classical tradition as well as the logical subtlety and the passion for argument which had characterized the schools of rhetoric in antiquity.

The awakening of the Western mind in the eleventh century manifested itself first and above all in the revival of the schools and in the renewal of classical studies, as embodied in the three arts of the *Trivium*. The eleventh and twelfth centuries were the great age of the episcopal schools in the West. The earliest centers were Liège, which had preserved the tradition of learning since Carolingian times, and still more Chartres, where the new movement was inaugurated by Fulbert (c. 960–1028), a pupil of the famous Pope Sylvester II; but it soon spread to all the principal ecclesiastical centers of Northern France and Belgium—Orléans, Tours, Rheims, Laon, Tournai, and especially Paris, which was destined to eclipse them all. By the middle of the twelfth century Chartres and Paris had become educational centers of international importance which attracted students from every part of the West and especially from England.

The characteristic feature of this phase of the medieval revival is its humanism. This is particularly evident in the school of Chartres under the direction of Bernard of Chartres (c. 1130) and William of Conches, and it finds its supreme representative in John of Salisbury (1110–1180). But it was far from being confined to the members of that school. It characterized the whole twelfth-century development.

Nevertheless, even in the earlier phase of the medieval development, the influence of Aristotle was far from negligible. Aristotelian logic formed an essential part of the scholastic program of studies. It was the most prized of the seven liberal arts, and it benefited no less than grammar and rhetoric from the awakening of intellectual life in the eleventh century. Owing, however, to the absence of any real body of scientific material on which it could be exercised, logic tended either to degenerate into barren sophistry, as with Anselm the Peripatician and Adam Parvipontanus, or else to be used in theological discussion, as in the case of the Berengarian controversy on Eucharistic doctrine, or Roscelin's argument on the Trinity.

Both these tendencies provoked the indignation of the rigorists, who were inclined to regard the liberal arts as vain superfluities with which the devout Christian had little business to concern himself. "The disciples of Christ have no need of strange doctrines," writes Gregory of Czanad, and Peter Damian attacks the grammarians and dialecticians after the fashion of Tertullian—that is to say, with all the exaggerations of a converted rhetorician. But the resistance of the traditionalists was powerless to prevent the application of dialectic to theology, for it found its justification in the theological tradition itself.

The one great patristic philosopher of Latin Christendom had been St. Augustine, and in his thought there is no abrupt line of division between the sphere of theology and that of metaphysics. His philosophy is not a philosophy of nature. It seeks to know God and the human soul and nothing else, and consequently its *raison d'être* is not to explain the nature of things, but to serve as the metaphysical foundation of his religious doctrines. Consequently when St. Anselm, the disciple of St. Augustine and the first original philosopher of the Middle Ages since the days of Erigena, produces his system, his philosophy is not an autonomous construction of pure reason but has its beginning and end in the Christian faith. For him, as for St. Augustine and the Fathers, Christianity is the one true philosophy and without faith there can be no understanding. Nevertheless, within this common unity he recognizes the distinctive character of the philosophic method—the use of rational demonstration in contrast to the appeal to authority.

Above all in the *Monologion* he attempts to establish his theology on purely rational grounds. Avoiding even the use of the word God, he establishes the absolute and spiritual character of true being, the *summa natura* which alone exists of itself, and on which the secondary and semi-real semi-being of all other things is dependent. But Anselm is not satisfied with this purely metaphysical concept of the divine nature. He goes further and attempts to establish by pure deduction the doctrine of the Trinity and even the rudiments of that of the Incarnation. Here he is nearer to Erigena than to St. Thomas. Yet it is not without reason that Anselm has been named the Father of Scholasticism. For he is the founder of the scholastic ideal of a strictly philosophical proof of the fundamental truths of religion which was to bear its final fruit in the *Summa contra Gentiles* of St. Thomas.

The most typical figure of the earlier phase of medieval thought is, however, that of Abelard, since in him all the tendencies of contemporary thought are represented. He was at once a humanist, a theologian and a dialectician, while he contributed—more, perhaps, than any other thinker—to the progress of the scholastic method by his thorough assimilation of Aristotelian logic. Nevertheless, he was no nearer than St. Anselm to constituting philosophy as an autonomous discipline distinct from theology, and hence, though he was no rationalist, his application of dialectic to theological problems continually brought him into conflict with traditionalists such as St. Bernard. A natural philosophy is in fact impossible without some science of nature, but on the other hand an experimental science could not be developed without a philosophical background. The purely religious philosophy of an Erigena or an Anselm sees in nature only the symbol and shadow of spiritual reality, and consequently leaves no room for a science of things; while the thoroughgoing theologism of a Peter Damian, like that of the Moslem Motekalim, rejects even the principles of causality and the uniformity of nature in the interests of the divine omnipotence.

From this *impasse* Western thought was delivered, not by a gradual process of criticism and experiment, but by the importation *en bloc* of the scientific and philosophical tradition of the Moslem world. This was the great intellectual event of the twelfth century.

Already some small infiltration of oriental science had taken place in the tenth century, through Barcelona,[1] and in the eleventh through the school of Salerno, where Constantine the African had translated Arabic and Syrian medical works: but it was not until the twelfth century, after the Crusades and the Christian reconquest of Toledo, Saragossa and Sicily, that a genuine intellectual contact was established between Arabian and Western culture. This contact took place in the regions of mixed culture and mixed speech, the Christian kingdom of Spain, the Norman kingdom of Sicily, the Crusading states of Syria and the cities of Southern France. Of these Spain was by far the most important, since the Moslem States of the Peninsula were during this period at the height of their intellectual productivity; indeed, the center in Southern France was merely an extension of this area.

But Sicily was also of importance owing to the enlightened policy of the Norman kings, Roger and William I, and to the existence of a Greek as well as an Arabic element in the population. One might have supposed that this opportunity for a direct contact with the Hellenic tradition would have had more importance for Western culture than the roundabout method of communication by way of second-hand (and often third- or fourth-hand) translations from the Arabic. But though a number of direct translations from the Greek were made (notably that of the *Almagest* of Ptolemy, c. 1160), they

---

[1] Where Gerbert (Sylvester II) studied and his friend Lupitus translated an Arabic work on astronomy.

never attained the popularity of the versions from the Arabic, and often remained unknown outside Southern Italy. The reason for this was that it was the Arabs and not the Greeks who were the leaders of the thought of the age, and it was only in so far as it formed a part of this living tradition that Greek thought was appropriated by the new scientific movement of the Christian West.

The scholars responsible for the introduction of the new knowledge to Europe came from many different nations, including several from Italy, England and Spain. In the work of translation, the Spanish Christians of Arab speech played an important part; but the majority of the translators were either Jews or converts from Judaism. Moreover, it must be remembered that there was an independent Jewish movement of translation from Arabic into Hebrew; also an independent movement of Jewish philosophical thought which preceded the similar movement in Christendom and influenced its development. The great Jewish thinker Moses Maimonides of Cordova (1135-1204) was occupied with essentially the same problem as the great Schoolmen of the thirteenth century—that is, the reconciliation of Aristotelian science with the revealed religion of the Scriptures—and his conclusions in some respects anticipate those of St. Thomas himself.

Despite the derivative character of the work of the scholars and translators of the eleventh century, and the eccentricity of the scientific ideas they proposed, the ideal which inspired their activity was genuinely scientific. They belong to the same line of succession as Leonardo da Vinci and Copernicus, Bacon and Descartes and the other forerunners of the modern scientific movement. For there is only one scientific tradition—that of the Greeks—and it was recovered for Europe by the men of the twelfth century.

Nor were they unconscious of the importance of their task or the backwardness of Western culture in the field of science. One of them, Adelard of Bath, that remarkable English scholar who visited Southern Italy, Syria and Cilicia in the pursuit of knowledge, contrasts the scientific method of his Arabic teachers with the blind reliance on the authority of tradition which characterized the Western schools. "I have learnt one thing from the Arabs under the guidance of reason," he writes; "you follow a halter, caught by the appearance of authority, for what is authority but a halter? For as brute beasts are led by a halter and know not where nor why they are led, but only follow the rope that holds them, so written authority leads not a few of you into danger, bound captive by bestial credulity."[2]

It is obvious that such an attitude was more likely to arouse the hostility of the traditionalists than even the theological rationalism of a Roscelin or an Abelard. Nor was their distrust unjustified. For, as the theologians of Islam had long before realized, Hellenic science was not the obedient servant of revealed religion, but an independent and rival power. It was a danger alike to Christianity, to Judaism, and to Islam since it challenged the fundamental dogmas common to the three religions—the doctrine of creation, the doctrine of personal immortality, and the belief in a personal deity who governed the world by his providence and the free exercise of his omnipotent will.

Nevertheless, when the Western mind had been awakened by the translators of the twelfth century to a consciousness of the intellectual riches of the Greek tradition, it was impossible to prevent the gradual infiltration of the new knowledge. Even William of Auvergne, in spite of his complete orthodoxy and his loyalty to the Augustinian tradition, was himself deeply influenced by Graeco-Arabic thought, and it was generally recognized that the orthodox tradition must come to terms with the new knowledge by separating its positive elements from the heterodox theories with which they had been associated.

The ground was already prepared by the university movement which had made Paris the intellectual capital of Christendom. Here and still more at Oxford, the new learning became the basis of the university curriculum in the Faculty of Arts. The Faculty of

2 *Questiones Naturales* c. vi, in Haskins, *Studies in Medieval Science*, p. 40.

Theology remained faithful to the old tradition of Peter Lombard and St. Augustine and tended to adopt a hostile attitude to the new learning. But it was impossible for either party to acquiesce in this division. Medieval science was not an independent discipline, it was part of an organic whole, embodied in the Aristotelian corpus, and the theologians could not remain indifferent to the theological implications of Aristotelian metaphysics. Thus the situation was ripe for the battle of ideas—a conflict of opposing world views—which was fought out during the second half of the thirteenth century. On the one side there was the theologians' view of the universe based on the teachings of the Fathers and colored by the tradition of Christian Platonism. On the other, there was the scientific cosmology of Aristotle, as developed by his Arabic disciples and commentators.

In the eyes of the theologians, there was no room for an independent science or philosophy which based itself on human reason and could dispense with the light of revelation. The true wisdom was essentially theocentric. It sought the explanation of all things in God and related every fact of experience, every form of art and science, to its divine source and center. For the universe is nothing but a reflection or image of the glory of God. From the sphere of pure light and fire that lies beyond the stars down through the nine heavens to the earth and depths below, the whole creation glows and burns with the light of divine wisdom and the strength of divine power. *"Totus mundus est sicut unam speculum plenum laminibus praesentantibus divinam sapientiam, et sicut carbo effundens lucem."*[3]

Man stands on the lowest steps of this divine ladder poised dizzily between heaven and the abyss, and yet he possesses a unique function which even the pure intelligences which rule the heavens cannot share. He is the mediator between the two worlds of spirit and matter, the high priest of the sublunary world whose mission it is to bring spiritual life and light into the sensible world. This hieratic function can be fulfilled only through the ecclesiastical hierarchy

[3] St. Bonaventure, *In Hexaemeron* ii.27.

which is the earthly counterpart of the angelic hierarchy of the heavens and which builds and organizes mankind into a spiritual society which is the living temple of God on earth. Thus human existence is dependent at every stage on the spiritual order which surrounds and transcends it. The visible world is a shadow, and the importance of man is not to be found in this shadow existence, but in the place he occupies on the ladder of being which rises from nothingness to God and in his actual and potential participation in the spiritual world on the frontier of which he is situated.

This theological view of the universe had a natural affinity with the Christian Platonism of St. Augustine and the Christian Neo-Platonism of Dionysius the Areopagite. The only elements which it found acceptable in the new Graeco-Arabic learning were those which were thoroughly Neo-Platonic, such as the treatise *de Causis*, or were deeply impregnated by Neo-Platonic elements, such as the writings of the eleventh-century Spanish Rabbi Ibn Gebirol of Malaga and the Jewish Christian Domingo Gondisalvi, or Gundasallinus, who was archdeacon of Segovia in the twelfth century.

On the other hand the Aristotelian elements in the new learning, including the very idea of autonomous rational science which embraced the whole of reality and found its expression in the Aristotelian cosmology, appeared to the theologians as a revolutionary innovation which ran counter to the whole tradition of Christian thought.

From the Christian point of view, the most objectionable features in the new philosophy were its tendency to determinism and to the denial of free will and divine providence, its belief in the eternity of the world, and above all, its theory of "the unicity of the active intellect"—in other words, that the higher principle of thought was external to the human mind, the individual soul corruptible and mortal. Nothing could be more irreconcilable with the basic Christian doctrine of creation, incarnation and personal salvation than this complex of ideas which was commonly, though inaccurately, called Averroism.

But it had behind it the authority of Aristotle and the prestige of the newly discovered science of nature, and the two elements were so completely integrated in the Aristotelian system that it was difficult for its orthodox critics to dispute its theological errors without becoming involved in a controversy which covered the whole field of philosophy.

Thus the great task of thirteenth-century Scholasticism was to subject the whole body of new knowledge to a searching and systematic process of criticism, so as to rethink Aristotle in Christian terms. To this task all the great thinkers of the century devoted themselves—St. Albert and St. Thomas, Robert Grosseteste and Roger Bacon, Siger of Brabant and Duns Scotus, as well as a whole host of lesser men, such as Thomas of York, Richard of Middleton and Giles of Rome. The result was an outburst of metaphysical speculation which has never been equalled save in the creative century of Greek thought and perhaps in modern times in the century of Kant and Hegel.

II.

The thirteenth century has been regarded, not without reason, as the culminating point of the Middle Ages—the crown of the preceding six centuries of development of Christian civilization. Nevertheless if it was a culmination it was also a turning point: it was the age when the old tradition of the unity of Christendom under the double headship of Pope and Emperor passed away forever, and when the centrifugal forces which became dominant in the later Middle Ages were already asserting their power. The century that opens with Innocent III closes with Boniface VIII and Philip IV.

It is especially important to remember this aspect of the thirteenth century when we are dealing with its intellectual history. For St. Thomas has become so complete a representative of medieval thought that we are apt to simplify the whole process of development and interpret it from an exclusively Thomist point of view.

In reality St. Thomas was far less representative of medieval thought than is usually supposed. His philosophy is not the mature fruit of the old medieval tradition but the first fruits of the new scientific thought. He was a bold innovator, who, as Professor Gilson has said, always chose the line of greatest resistance and made a decisive break in the continuity of the medieval tradition.

If we wish to find a typical representative of the older tradition, we should look not to St. Thomas but to St. Bonaventure. It is he who summed up with a master's genius the intellectual heritage of Western Christendom and created a synthesis which incorporates all the vital elements of medieval thought. It was the work of St. Thomas to launch the Western mind on a path it had not known hitherto: to vindicate the autonomous rights of reason and to create a scientific philosophy which rested on purely rational foundations and was not, like the earlier Scholasticism, a philosophical superstructure superimposed on a basis of Christian dogma. Thus St. Thomas looks forward to the Renaissance rather than back to the Middle Ages, and it was not until the sixteenth century that he was recognized as the official doctor of the Church and found worthy disciples in men like Cajetan, Vittoria and Suarez, who freed Scholasticism from the sophistry and barbarism of the later medieval Schoolmen.

The inaugurator of the new Christian attitude to philosophy was the German Albertus Magnus, the most learned man of the thirteenth century. His greatest achievement was to put the whole corpus of Graeco-Arabic thought at the disposal of Western Scholasticism through an encyclopaedic series of commentaries and expositions. Nor was he merely a passive intermediary between two intellectual traditions, but it is in science rather than in philosophy that his originality is to be found. As a philosopher he tended rather to syncretism than to synthesis, and his philosophical works form a kind of metaphysical museum in which theories of diverse origin and of inconsistent character find themselves side by side.

The true creator of the new synthesis was not the German

encyclopaedist but his Neapolitan pupil, St. Thomas. His philosophy marks a complete break with the old Augustinian-Neoplatonic idealism which had hitherto dominated the intellectual development of the West. Not only did St. Thomas accept the cardinal principles of Aristotelian physics, he applied them resolutely to the nature of man, teaching that matter is the principle of human individuation and that the soul is the form of the body. Hence the human intelligence is not that of a pure spirit which exists only for the contemplation of absolute reality. It is consubstantial with matter, subject to the conditions of space and time, and it can construct an intelligible order only out of the data of sensible experience, systematized by the scientific activity of reason. And thus while, on the one hand, human reason is distinctly animal, the lowest and most obscured form of intelligence, on the other hand it is the one principle of spiritual order in nature, and it is its essential function to reduce the unintelligible chaos of the material world to reason and order.

Moreover, man is not entirely confined to the inevitable cycle of generation and corruption. As an intelligent being his nature partakes of the spiritual and the eternal. The spiritual side of his nature demands its satisfaction, and since he is incapable of finding it in an immediate contact with spiritual reality, God has opened a channel by which he reveals and communicates himself to man. Thus St. Thomas finds room for the whole economy of Christian redemption, as a second order, a spiritual creation with its own laws and its own principle of activity. This new order does not destroy or supersede nature; it is analogous and complementary to it; nor is it antirational, since it possesses a higher divine rationality of its own. The whole Thomist synthesis is governed by this principle of the concordance in difference of the two orders—of Nature and Grace, of Reason and Faith, of the temporal and the spiritual powers. This is the essential significance of Thomism in the history of European culture.

St. Thomas, however, did more than integrate Aristotelian metaphysics into a comprehensive theological vision of truth. He gave Aristotelianism a new orientation, a deeper significance. For he distinguished, as Aristotle had not, between the essence, the nature of an object, and its existence. The latter he conceived dynamically as the act which imparts being to essence, which of itself is but the possibility of existing. Existence actualizes this possibility within the limits imposed by the distinctive nature of the essence thus made actual. "This distinction," writes Professor Knowles, "between essence and existence is vital, it is the shibboleth of Thomism."

In God, however, there is no distinction between essence and existence. For God's essence, his nature, is precisely to exist; his nature is existence in its plenitude. "God," writes Gilson, "is the being whose whole nature it is to be such an existential act: this is the reason why his most proper name is, He is."

This metaphysical existentialism, as Gilson has emphasized, derives its origin not from any pagan philosophy, concerned rather with essence, but from the Christian understanding of God's words to Moses: "I am that I am": I am the self-subsistent Being, Existence pure and simple, and therefore the source of all created existence.

It was in fact this distinctively Jewish-Christian existentialism which enabled St. Thomas to complete Aristotle's philosophy of essence and impart to it a novel dynamism. It was not, however, that he added a revealed doctrine to the insights of philosophic speculation. Rather his Christian theology, his Christian experience, enabled his intelligence to perceive a metaphysical truth, to advance further along Aristotle's road than the philosopher himself. A revealed truth was for St. Thomas a lens focusing his philosophic vision on a metaphysical truth otherwise unseen.[4]

The boldness and originality of the thirteenth-century thinkers is

---

[4] Note: For this Thomist existentialism see Frederick Copleston, S.J., *A History of Philosophy*, Vol. II, pp. 332., sqq., 424; David Knowles, *The Evolution of Medieval Thought*, p. 262; Etienne Gilson, *History of Christian Philosophy in the Middle Ages*, pp. 368–369.

the more remarkable when we remember that it was carried on under a strongly authoritarian regime; as it were, under the shadow of the Inquisition. The great condemnation of philosophical errors promulgated in the University of Paris by Archbishop Tempier in 1277, within a few years of St. Thomas's death, did not confine itself to banning Averroistic theories and in particular the teaching of Siger of Brabant. It also extended to some of the central principles of St. Thomas and Giles of Rome, as well as to Roger Bacon and other more obscure thinkers.

The strength of the traditionalist opposition must not be underestimated, and it would be a great mistake to suppose that the Thomist synthesis of Christianity and Aristotelianism was accepted in the thirteenth century as the final expression of Christian thought. Nevertheless the work of St. Thomas and his contemporaries did succeed in averting a catastrophic conflict between Christianity and the new learning. Thanks to the work of St. Thomas and his master St. Albert, the West was able to recover the tradition of Greek thought without destroying the unity and integrity of the Christian world view.

This synthesis was of incalculable importance for the future of Western culture. For the reception of Aristotle and the new learning brought Western Christendom once more into living contact with the great tradition of Hellenism which was to stimulate and fertilize the intellectual life of the West. And at the same time the Thomist synthesis enriched Greek thought by the deeper spiritual insight of the Christian tradition.

The Thomist doctrine of the unity of the human personality and the individuality of the human intelligence freed Greek thought from the cosmic determinism that had such a fatal influence on Hellenistic and Arabic philosophy and provided a metaphysical foundation for the ethical humanism of Aristotle's thought. Thus the philosophy of St. Thomas is more profoundly humanist than that of the secular humanists, since it is a metaphysical humanism which transcends man's superficial activities and bases itself on the structure of the human soul and on man's place in the hierarchy of being on the frontier between the two worlds of spiritual and sensible reality.

Thus the Thomist version of Aristotelian ethics and politics transformed the character of Greek humanism. As the latter had maintained, man is essentially a social being who finds his good in the life of the city; he is not, however, merely the citizen of the earthly city, but a member of a universal supertemporal society, and the laws which man makes for the good of the state are subject to and dependent on the universal divine law by which all things are ruled. For "man is not subordinated to the political community totally and in all that he has. But all that a man is and has and is able to do is ordered towards God."[5]

But while St. Thomas was the creator of the most enduring and complete synthesis between Greek philosophy and Christian theology, his influence on the scientific thought of his age was comparatively small. The recovery and assimilation of the new learning was a collective work in which all the leading minds of the age took part, and to which Oxford contributed no less than Paris, and the Franciscans no less than the Dominicans. The English Franciscan school in particular attempted to solve the problem of the new learning in quite a different way from that of St. Thomas. It was more conservative in its attitude to the Augustinian tradition but more adventurous and original in the field of science. In this it followed the line laid down by Robert Grosseteste, who was the dominant figure at Oxford in the first half of the thirteenth century, and though himself a secular, the founder and organizer of the Oxford Franciscan school.

Unlike the great dialecticians who dominated the tradition of teaching at Paris, Grosseteste was interested primarily in positive theology and positive science. He was the first man to attempt to introduce the study of Greek into the West, and his own work as a translator included not only Aristotle's *Ethics* but also patristic and

[5] *S. Theol.* 1–2ae, XXI, a 4 ad 3.

Byzantine works. But though he was one of the chief pioneers of Aristotelian studies in the thirteenth century, his scientific interests were far wider than those of St. Thomas and had a profound effect on the philosophical tradition of Oxford and of the Franciscan school.

In his scientific views he shows a striking originality which at times seems to transcend the limits of his age and point the way towards the path which Western science was to follow in future centuries. He saw the material universe as a dynamic process, the radiation of the cosmic energy which he calls light, *lux*, as distinguished from *lumen*, which is its visible embodied reflection. This primary light is by its nature auto-diffusive, and its infinite multiplication produces the finite gradations of the material universe. It is also the principle of action, the source of all movement and difference, "since the things which are many are many through the multiplication of light itself in different degrees."[6] To understand physical reality, it is therefore necessary to study above all the laws of the diffusion of light, as found in the science of optics, and the laws that govern the transmission of force from one body to another. And since these studies are essentially mathematical, mathematics is the key to the understanding of nature. "All causes of natural effects," he writes, "can be stated by lines, angles and figures. Without them it is impossible to understand natural philosophy. For they hold good in the whole universe and in its parts, absolutely."[7]

Grosseteste's theory of light and his interest in mathematics had an immense influence on the new learning in the thirteenth and fourteenth centuries. They affected Dominicans like William of Moerbeke, the translator of Aristotle, and Dietrich of Freiburg, as well as isolated thinkers like Wildo the Pole and the unknown author of the treatise *De Intelligentiis*. Grosseteste's influence, however, was naturally strongest among the Franciscans at Oxford, such as Adam Marsh and Thomas of York, whence it was transmitted

---

6 *De Luce.*
7 L. Baur, *Die Philosophie des Robert Grosseteste,* pp. 92–93.

to the Franciscans at Paris, above all to the great St. Bonaventure himself.

But the most remarkable of all the representatives of the Oxford Franciscan tradition was Roger Bacon, who is never tired of singing the praises of the great bishop of Lincoln as the one man in modern times worthy to be compared with the sages of antiquity and the Fathers of the Church.

Although he was himself one of the first to introduce the study of Aristotle's *Physics* and *Metaphysics* in the faculty of Arts at Paris, Bacon's whole approach to philosophy is dominated by strictly religious and theological interests. He saw all knowledge—theological, philosophical and scientific—as forming an organic whole which has been revealed in diverse ways by the one God for one end—the salvation of mankind. But this teleological conception of science made him critical of the sterile intellectualism of the metaphysicians and the blind traditionalisms of the theologians. He was intensely aware of the immense possibilities of physical science, and like his namesake three centuries later, he dreamed of a *magna instauratio* which would transform the world by the application of science to practical ends.

But what distinguished Bacon from all the other thinkers of his age was the practical and experimental character of his work. He related the new studies directly to the needs of humanity and regarded science as the predestined instrument by which, and by which alone, the Church could fulfill its mission of uniting the human race and guiding it in the way of salvation. All knowledge was one, given by one God to one humanity for one end, but although the whole of this divine revelation was contained in principle in the Scriptures, it was impossible to understand it without the subordinate sciences of grammar and philosophy and the scientific study of texts. In the same way, although "the end of all true philosophy is to arrive at a knowledge of the Creator through the knowledge of the created world," it is impossible to do this without the study of the mathematical sciences, "for he who knows not mathematics cannot know any other sciences, and what is more, he cannot discover his own ignorance or find its proper remedies."

Finally to perfect the work of science and to apply it to its proper end—the guidance of the world—we need another and a novel kind of science—experimental science—which is the most perfect of them all. For without this science there is a gap between theory and practice, between philosophy and life, which prevents the sciences from producing their full fruit. Experimental science not only gives man a more certain knowledge, it also gives him power to change his life and to control the world. Armed with this weapon, the Church will be the mistress of the world in fact and not merely in principle. She will no longer have to fear the attacks of the infidels nor rely on the bloody and uncertain methods of the Crusades. By the reform of studies and the application of science to life, the world will be made one and the unity of true science will bear fruit in the unity of a truly universal Christian society.

All this is to be found in the vast yet incomplete program for the reform of Christian learning which he dedicated to his patron, Clement IV, during the latter's brief pontificate (1265-1268). The foundations of this reform were to be laid by philology and textual criticism for the knowledge of the Scriptures, and by mathematics and experimental science for the knowledge of nature. When this was accomplished the Church would be scientifically equipped to fulfill its world mission. The schismatic Greeks would be reunited and the pagans would be converted, while those who resisted would be subdued by the secret weapons which science would put at the disposal of the Papacy.

In spite of his extravagance, Roger Bacon was profoundly conscious of the universal mission of the Church to humanity and of the function of the Papacy as the center and leader of the work of unity. Moreover, he had a prophetic sense of the urgency of the situation and of the perils which threatened Christendom if this opportunity was lost.

In the light of these principles and ideals, Bacon's impatience with the one-sided intellectualism of Parisian Scholasticism and his violent and unjust criticism of the great Dominicans are readily understandable. He had the vision of a new world of knowledge and power which was ripe for conquest, and he was exasperated at seeing the intellectual energies needed for this essential task being squandered on the endless cycle of dialectical controversy. Against the purely logical and metaphysical culture of the school of Paris, Bacon appealed to what seemed to him the wider and deeper learning of his own people, and above all to their two greatest representatives, Robert Grosseteste and Adam Marsh.

Both these elements contributed to the formation of the European scientific tradition. The pragmatic experimentation of the Baconian ideal could have borne no fruit apart from the intellectual training and discipline provided by Aristotelian Scholasticism. And the latter might have smothered the initiative of scientific thought under the weight of its traditional authority had it not been for the independent criticism of Bacon and the experimentalists. St. Thomas vindicated the autonomous rights of reason and scientific enquiry against the theological absolutism of the early Middle Ages. Bacon in turn intervened to safeguard the independence of science from the metaphysical absolutism of the philosophers.

Pierre Duhem has shown that the teaching of Bacon was by no means so sterile and lacking in influence as it has usually been supposed. His followers included some of the leading writers on astronomy in the next generation—Bernard of Verdun, William of St. Cloud and John of Sicily, not to mention Pierre d'Ailly at a much later period. And apart from this direct influence, the spirit of his teaching and of his appeal from authority to experience survives in the tradition of critical and scientific Nominalism which became the dominant force in the intellectual life of the following century. In the Schoolmen of the fourteenth century, who belong rather to the tradition of Bacon than to that of St. Thomas—William of Ockham, John Buridan, Albert of Saxony, and Nicholas Oresme —we find not only a critical reaction against the authority of the Aristotelian and Arabic tradition, but also a movement of original scientific research, which prepares the way for the coming of Copernicus and the new European science of the Renaissance.

XVII. EAST AND
WEST IN THE MIDDLE AGES

Our attention has hitherto been fixed on the development of
Christian culture in the West, and this is undoubtedly the most
important subject for our consideration. For it is the historic source
not only of Western Catholicism, but of the whole Western Christian tradition, both Catholic and Protestant, and of what we call
European civilization in general. I do not mean that it is the ultimate source of these, but that it is the channel and the social tradition through which all of them have come down to us. Nevertheless we must not forget the existence of that parallel stream of
Christian culture which continued to flow in Eastern Christendom
throughout these periods, during the thousand years from the
Council of Chalcedon to the Council of Florence and the fall of
Constantinople.

During the first half of this period—down to the year 1000—
Eastern Christendom was far more important than Western in
civilization, in wealth and population and in political power. During the second half, from 1000 to 1453, it was gradually declining
and Western culture was gradually advancing, until by the end of
the period, Western Christendom had become one of the great
world civilizations, while the Christian East, with the exception of
Russia, had been almost completely swallowed up by the new
Moslem Empire of the Ottoman Turks.

All through these thousand years Eastern and Western Christendom had been gradually drifting apart, until their growing alienation from one another was manifested in a final schism between Rome and Constantinople—between the Catholic and Orthodox Churches. There is considerable difference of opinion between historians as to the date at which this schism became complete, as well as with regard to the real and apparent causes of it. But there can be no question of its importance: for its results are still with us, and it constitutes the most difficult obstacle to remove in the way of the modern movement towards Christian unity. And it deserves to be studied with care, since apart from its historical interest it affords most valuable insights into the whole nature of the problem of disunity.

In the first place it is a remarkable fact that the division between East and West is not a result of the great heresies that imperilled the unity of the Church in the patristic period. It was only after these fundamental dogmatic issues had been finally settled and when East and West had become agreed on the articles of the Creed that this schism took place, and this absence of real theological motive is shown by the equivocal terms by which the two parties are distinguished. The Western Church is Catholic, but it is also orthodox; the Eastern Church is Orthodox, but it also claims to be Catholic. The real causes of division lie elsewhere.

To understand the causes of the schism we must go back to the very beginning of the Middle Ages to the Age of Justinian, when the unity of the Christian Empire was still a reality. To Justinian, Church and Empire formed an organic unity, as he explains in his famous *Sixth Novellum*, issued on March 16, 535. He still regarded Rome and the West as a part of the Empire, though temporarily occupied by barbarians, and he regarded the Pope as the great bulwark of this Christian-Roman unity in the West. Similarly, the Pope looked to him for support against the Arian Goths who were the *de facto* rulers of Italy. Yet in spite of this concordance in external matters, Rome and the Western

Church in general found it difficult to accept Justinian's role as defender of the faith when it went beyond the edifying generalities of the *Fifth Novellum* and prescribed what this Faith should be.

This, in effect, was what Justinian did in his *Edict of the Three Chapters*, which condemned the three former leaders of the School of Antioch—Theodore, Theodoret and Ibas—as Nestorians in order to placate the Monophysites. The Western Churches regarded this edict as an implicit condemnation of the Council of Chalcedon. They regarded it as another example of that policy of compromise represented by the *Henoticon* of the Emperor Zeno which had caused the long Acacian Schism between East and West (484–518). And no doubt they were right, since Monophysite influence was strong at the court of Justinian, where the heresy was patronized by the Empress Theodora herself, who in fact was the chief agent in the organization of a Monophysite hierarchy. Justinian was determined to impose his condemnation of the *Three Chapters* on the universal Church by means of a General Council. But if this was to be effective, the consent of Rome was necessary, and to obtain it the Pope was brought to Constantinople in 547, where he was kept a prisoner for seven years until he had given his full adhesion. In spite of this he refused to attend the Council, which met in 553, and issued his own decision, the *Constitutum*, which he declared to be final. This, however, was ignored by the Emperor and by the Council, which accepted the Emperor's policy and excommunicated the Pope. Vigilius was not strong enough to maintain his resistance: in the following year he withdrew his *Constitutum* and accepted the decrees of the Council.

But the West refused to follow his example. The Churches of Africa, Illyricum and Gaul rejected its decisions, and there was danger that a schism might develop dividing Western Christendom not only from the Emperor and the Byzantine Church but from the Pope as well.

The issue here was not that of the rival claims of Rome and

Constantinople, but the resistance of the Western Church to the royal supremacy, which was understood by Justinian to extend not only to ecclesiastical matters, but even to the most abstruse theological issues. As Msgr. Duchesne writes, whenever such a question arose, "he called it before him, and studied it with his theological advisers. In due time an imperial edict appeared in which the question was carefully discussed and finally decided in definite terms. The document was then sent to the patriarchs, who expressed their views in conformity with it and repeated the imperial anathamas. After which the faithful had only to obey."[1]

No doubt Justinian's conception of the royal supremacy differed from that of Henry VIII. He was a traditionalist who professed to follow the rule of the canons and the Holy Fathers. Yet he adds that "nothing escapes the monarch to whom God has entrusted the care of all men."[2]

This system of all-embracing theocratic authoritarianism is what has traditionally been called *Caesaropapism*, and though modern scholars disapprove of the use of the word, there is no better term to describe the system by which the Emperor attempted to rule the universal Church in matters of dogma as well as discipline, using the patriarchs and the councils as instruments to impose his policy. No doubt the Orthodox in the East, as well as the Catholics in the West, realized the dangers of this system. In fact it was the Patriarch of Antioch, Anastasius, rather than the Pope, who in 565 made the strongest resistance to Justinian's theological dictatorship.

The widespread opposition to this Byzantine Caesaropapism in the East was one of the main causes of the success of the Moslem invasion. And the fact that the Orthodox are still known as Melkites or Royalists shows how closely Orthodoxy has become associated with the State in the minds of the subject peoples.

[1] L. Duchesne, *L'Eglise au sixième siècle* (Paris, 1925), p. 266.
[2] *Justinian Novella* 123, 133.

But effective opposition by the bishops of the State Church, as opposed to the schismatic bodies, was almost impossible in the Eastern provinces where the Emperor's word was law. The situation was different in the West, which was becoming progressively detached from the Empire, even though Ravenna and Rome still remained outposts of the Empire, and consequently the Western Church retained a much larger measure of independence and never fully accepted the ecclesiastical control of Constantinople. This is apparent, we have just seen, in the reign of Justinian in the case of the schism of the *Three Chapters*, and the same situation is repeated in the following century when Heraclius and his successors attempted to impose the new theological *via media* of Monothelitism in order to make a union with the Monophysites possible.

In the beginning Pope Honorius I (625-638) gave a favorable reply to the first Byzantine proposals, but the Western Churches rejected the new doctrine, which was condemned by all the popes who succeeded Honorius. In the final stage of the controversy the orthodox resistance was led by the Pope, St. Martin (649-655), who died in exile in South Russia and is reckoned a martyr in both East and West, and by the Byzantine monk and theologian St. Maximus, who also suffered for his faith.

None of these early schisms, however, caused a permanent division between East and West, since the Eastern and Western Churches were both fundamentally orthodox in dogma, and union was restored as soon as political pressure was removed by a change of emperors or of imperial policy. But the situation became more difficult when the Emperor Justinian II attempted to impose a common code of canon law on the Western as well as the Eastern Church, on the basis of the canons of the Council of Trullo (the Quinisext Council) held at Constantinople in 692.

Here no theological question was at stake, but only matters of law and ritual order. Nevertheless the divergence was very serious, since Rome would never submit to Constantinople in such matters as the celibacy of the clergy and still more the primacy of the Roman See, while Justinian II, the most autocratic of all the Byzantine emperors, was not a man with whom it was possible to argue. Eventually some kind of settlement was reached, but we do not know what exactly occurred when the Pope finally met the Emperor, since Justinian II was murdered in the same year and the Empire entered on a period of revolutionary crisis from which it was rescued only by the coming of the Isaurian dynasty.

But though the Isaurian Emperors saved the Empire, they exercised their authority over the Church more ruthlessly than ever. In the course of their reforms they came into violent conflict with orthodox piety by their prohibition of image worship, and the Iconoclastic controversy which resulted was no less bitter than the dogmatic disputes of the previous age. It led, on the one hand, to a revolt against the principle of Caesaropapism by the leaders of the orthodox party such as St. John of Damascus and St. Theodore of Studium, and on the other to a breach with the Papacy and the revolt of the Byzantine provinces in Italy. This marks a further step in the separation between East and West, abandonment of the traditional political bond between Rome and the Byzantine Empire in favor of a new alliance of the Papacy with the Christian peoples of Northern Europe.

Pope Gregory II was fully conscious of the momentous character of his decision, as is clear from his letter, cited in an earlier chapter, to the Emperor Leo III, the genuineness of which has recently been vindicated by Professor Caspar. He appeals from the verdict of the Emperor and the civilized Byzantine world to the new Christian world that was coming into existence in the West, and to show his independence of the former, he announced his intention of leaving Rome on a journey "to the uttermost bounds of the West" in order to baptize the princes of the newly converted nations that were bringing the first fruits of their faith to the See of Peter.

"The whole West," he writes, "has its eyes fixed on our poor person, and though we are unworthy of it, yet they have great confidence in us and in him whose image you would destroy and abolish, the Holy Apostle Peter whom all the kingdoms of the West reverence as a god upon earth. . . . You know your empire cannot insure control of Rome, apart from the city itself, on account of the nearness of the sea and the ships, but the Pope has only to depart three miles from Rome and he has no more to fear from you. It grieves us that the savages and barbarians are becoming tame while you, the civilized, are becoming barbarous. The whole of the West brings the fruits of its faith to the Prince of the Apostles, and if you send troops to destroy the images of St. Peter, look to it, we warn you beforehand that we are innocent of the blood that you will shed. Be it on your own head."[3]

As an act of reprisal the Emperor removed all the sees of the Roman patriarchate that still formed part of the Byzantine Empire—Illyricum, Greece, Sicily and Calabria—and annexed them to the See of Constantinople, which thus became the universal patriarchate of the Byzantine world, so that it was able to enforce canonical and liturgical conformity to the decrees of the Quinisext council against the Roman and Western canons, even in Southern Italy itself. Even when the Iconoclast Schism was ended by the Second Council of Nicaea in 789 and communion was restored between Rome and Constantinople, there was no restoration of the lost ecclesiastical provinces. The Papacy acquired a new authority in Northern Europe by St. Boniface's conversion of Germany and the reorganization of the Frankish Church, but it never recovered Illyricum, which remained a part of the Byzantine patriarchate.

This tendency towards the separation and autonomy of Latin and Greek Christendom was accentuated by the foundation of the Western Empire under papal auspices in 800. Henceforward there were to be two empires, each with its own center of ecclesiastical jurisdiction. More and more these two empires became separate

[3] Cf. E. Caspar, *Geschichte des Papsttums*, Vol. II, pp. 656–662, and more fully in *Zeitschrift für Kirchengeschichte*, Vol. 52, pp. 29 ff. (1933).

cultural worlds, each revolving in its own orbit. The situation seemed ripe for schism, and the occasion soon occurred (in the second half of the ninth century), when the Papacy and the Byzantine Patriarchate were each represented by an outstanding and masterful character—Pope St. Nicholas I, on the one hand, and the Patriarch Photius on the other. The immediate cause of dispute was the deposition of Photius' predecessor, St. Ignatius, and the legitimacy of his own appointment. But it quickly developed into a general controversy which involved all the differences in ritual, canon law and jurisdiction between the two Churches.

The rival claims to jurisdiction over Illyricum had once more become a live issue, owing to the fact that the power which now ruled the Balkans, the Khan of Bulgaria, had just become Christian and was negotiating simultaneously with Rome and Constantinople. But Photius raised the controversy to a theological level by denouncing the Papacy for its heresy in adding the *Filioque* to the Creed (a Carolingian rather than a Roman addition) and by teaching the Dual Procession of the Holy Spirit from both the Father and the Son, as well as for its manifold errors in practice— allowing its converts to eat milk and cheese in the first week of Lent, making them fast on Saturday, and forbidding priests to marry.

These errors were condemned and Pope Nicholas excommunicated by the council which Photius held at Constantinople in 867 —an event which was formerly regarded as the beginning of the great schism—"the Photian Schism"—between Eastern and Western Churches. In fact it was nothing of the kind, since less than a month after the council was held, the Emperor Michael was assassinated and his successor Basil, the founder of the great Macedonian dynasty, promptly deposed Photius and restored Ignatius, who in due course held a new council—the council of 869-870, which excommunicated Photius and restored communion with Rome.

The schism, however, had been extinguished not by an agreement between the Churches but by the will of the Emperor, who imposed his own decision on the rival factions with a strong hand. His attitude of contemptuous impartiality towards these *querelles de sacristie* is brought out very strongly by his son, Leo VI, in his brief and unsympathetic account of the episode: "An absurd conflict and schism had broken out some time before Basil's accession among the ministers of God. Those who should have been preachers of peace waged a merciless war against one another: those who should set their flock an example of peace and unity, bred hatred. He who struck hardest was considered the best priest. The whole thing was absurd—pontiffs and priests fighting with priests and pontiffs. And the evil seemed to defy every cure until the Emperor took matters into his own hands and restored peace by recalling the banished patriarch and forcing the two parties to make peace with one another."[4]

This passage refers primarily to the local Byzantine schism between Photius and Ignatius, but the imposed settlement also involved a reconciliation between Constantinople and Rome. There was a very realistic element in Byzantine policy, and though the Emperor was ready to support the Patriarch against the Pope in the matter of Bulgaria, so long as the Empire hoped to regain its hold on Italy it was a key point of imperial policy to remain on good terms with Rome, and the Emperor was not prepared to jeopardize these practical interests to satisfy the scruples of theologians.

But this political opportunism was no adequate foundation for genuine spiritual unity. The East and West continued to drift apart all through the tenth century and became divided by an almost insurmountable wall of mutual prejudice, evident in Liutprand of Cremona's mordant account of his visit to Constantinople in 968. Only the political link remained, and consequently it was

[4] Quoted by Dvornik, *The Photian Schism*, pp. 169–170, from Vogt.

no accident that the loss of the Byzantine provinces in Italy to the Normans coincided with the final separation of the Churches in the eleventh century.

The patriarch, Michael Cerularius, who was the instrument of the schism, was the personal rival of Argyrus, the Byzantine viceroy in Italy, who was the chief partisan of the alliance with the Papacy against the Normans. The patriarch was an arrogant and domineering character who was determined to assert himself by enforcing a strict conformity with Byzantine usage against both the Latins and the Armenians, who were no subjects of the Empire and who had certain ritual practices in common with the Latins, notably the use of unleavened bread—"the azymes"—in the Eucharist. Accordingly he refused communion to Argyrus, who was an Italian of the Latin rite, and finally ordered all the Latin churches in Constantinople to be closed.

This occurred at the very moment when Argyrus had succeeded in bringing about his alliance with the Pope against the Normans and when Pope Leo was preparing to send an embassy to Constantinople to restore friendly relations both with the Emperor and the Byzantine Church.

From this point, however, everything went wrong with their plans. The Normans defeated the forces of both Argyrus and Leo IX and made the Pope himself a prisoner. The legation, which was led by the most fiery protagonist of the reforming party, Cardinal Humbert, arrived at Constantinople only to find their credentials questioned and their orthodoxy impugned. In face of this, Humbert showed neither tact nor moderation. On July 24th, 1054, the legates departed abruptly from Constantinople, leaving behind them a Bull of Excommunication against the patriarch listing a whole series of his errors and heresies. Nevertheless this was not intended to cause a final break between the Churches, since it was expressly declared that nothing was to be said against the orthodoxy of "the honorable and wise men of this most orthodox and Christian city," but only against Michael Cerularius and his immediate supporters.

In the same way, though the Emperor and the synod ordered the Bulls to be burnt and the legates excommunicated, they were declared to be false envoys whose letters had been forged by Argyrus, so that their own condemnation did not involve either the Papacy or the Western Church. Michael Cerularius himself went much further, for in his letter to the other patriarchs he declared that the Latin Church was heretical and the Orthodox could have no communion with it. Nor was this anything new, for he held that the Churches had been in schism ever since the Sixth General Council and that no pope had been recognized by the Church of Constantinople since Vigilius.

This was not the view of the patriarch of Antioch, who in a reply pointed out the mistakes and exaggerations of Cerularius's letter. Nor was it the view of the Emperor, who still hoped for a restoration of the old alliance with Rome and who regarded the patriarch with increasing displeasure until he was ultimately deposed in 1058 in favor of Isaac Comnenus. It was, however, the view of the majority of the Greek people, who were becoming increasingly anti-Latin and who readily adopted all Cerularius's theories on the origin and nature of the schism. Most of all they agreed with him in making the minor issue concerning the use of unleavened bread the touchstone of orthodoxy. Henceforward the Latins were known as Azymites, and no word in the Greek language became more heavily charged with religious and national prejudice.

Meanwhile the balance of power in the Eastern Mediterranean was being profoundly altered, and the Byzantine Empire was faced with catastrophe. The rising power of the Normans had destroyed its position in Southern Italy and the Adriatic, and the Turkish Conquest of Asia Minor had reached the Aegean and threatened the heart of the Empire. Eastern Christendom now found itself in the same predicament as Western Christendom in the previous century—an island of Christian culture surrounded by a rising tide of barbarian invasion. The founder of the new dynasty, Alexius Comnenus, now sent envoys to the West—to Pope Urban II at the Council of Piacenza in 1094, asking for Western aid. And the Pope in the following year launched his appeal for a general Crusade for the liberation of Eastern Christendom—a project which went far beyond anything the Emperor had conceived or asked.

Henceforward the history of the Byzantine Empire and the Greek Orthodox Church was conditioned by these two opposing forces, the pressure of the Turkish invasions in Asia Minor and the Balkans and the coming of the Crusading armies from the West. Had the Byzantine Emperors and the leaders of the Crusades been able to understand one another and work together against their common enemies, the Empire might have been saved. But though the statesmanship and patience of Alexius Comnenus almost achieved this end, it was ultimately defeated by the mutual antipathy of Greeks and Franks—above all, by the way in which differences of culture and economic interest were continually exacerbated by the deep-seated feud between the Churches.

We possess an admirable witness to the Byzantine reaction to the West at this time in Anna Comnena's famous biography of her father, the Emperor Alexius. It shows more clearly than any modern historical work how the cultural issue determined the Byzantine attitude. To Anna Comnena, Byzantine civilization, identified with Hellenism and with Orthodoxy, was the only civilization, and the Latins were either subjects in revolt, like the Italians, or warlike barbarians, like the Franks and the Normans. Consequently, in spite of her interest in theological questions, she says nothing of the religious issues that divided the Churches. She dismisses the claims of the Papacy as a characteristic example of Latin impertinence, and merely points out that the transference of the capital of the Empire to Constantinople naturally involved the transference of the ecclesiastical primacy and that the Emperors had given the supremacy to the bishop of Constantinople.

This somewhat naive simplification of the issues probably represents the point of view of Byzantine court circles and of the government, which was never inclined to stress dogmatic issues. On the other hand, the clergy and the monks saw the problem in strictly theological terms and were always suspicious lest the Emperor should sacrifice their jealously guarded principles to the political expediency of an alliance with the West.

All through the Comnenian period—from 1087 to 1180—the Emperors were constantly making approaches to Rome and putting forward plans for reunion. In 1166-1169, the Emperor Manuel and Pope Alexander III even went so far as to discuss a plan by which the two Empires and the Churches should be united by the recognition of Manuel as sole Emperor and the election of the Pope as Patriarch of Constantinople also!

But it is not surprising that all these negotiations between Pope and Emperor greatly increased the suspicion and hostility of the Greek clergy. Especially striking is the *Dialogue* in which the next patriarch, Michael of Anchialus, answers the Emperor Manuel. For this protest is directed not, as hitherto, against the doctrinal and ritual errors of the Latins, but against the fundamental principle of papal supremacy. He concludes his argument by saying that rather than submit to the Pope it would be better to accept the Turkish yoke. "Let the Saracen," he writes, "be my lord in outward things and let not the Italian run with me in the things of the soul, for I do not become of one mind with the first if I obey him, but if I accept harmony of faith with the second, I shall have deserted my God."

This was the fatal preference that would be expressed by Luke Notaras when the union of the Churches was proclaimed by the Emperor and the Patriarch in St. Sophia in December 1452 while the Turks were actually at the gates of the city—"Better the Turkish turban than the Latin mitre," and the people responded with the cry of "Death to the Azymites." For the politico-religious entente between East and West which was the official policy of the Comneni had been made impossible by the events which followed the fall of the dynasty. Only two years after the death of Emperor Manuel, the usurper Andronicus had won power by appealing to the anti-Latin sentiment of the mob, which massacred the papal legate and the Italian colony and destroyed the Latin churches. This led to the war with the Normans and the Venetians which revealed the nakedness of the land to determined aggression.

This opportunity was exploited by the Venetians and their allies in the Fourth Crusade when Constantinople was captured for the first time in its history and a Latin emperor and patriarch installed in the sacred city. After this outrage there could no longer be any hope for a genuine reconciliation of East and West.

After they had recovered the city in 1261, the later Byzantine Emperors continued intermittently to follow the old policy of the Comneni and the Macedonians, reunion and co-operation with the West. It found expression in the Council of Lyons, the Union of 1274, and the nominal union effected by Michael VIII in 1369. Reunion was achieved by the Emperor John Palaeologus at the Council of Florence in 1439. But what was the value of a formal union, however illustrious its adherents, if the heart of the people was unchanged, their hatred of the Azymites greater than their fear of the Turks? Ever since the eleventh century there had been an unofficial alliance between the national prejudices of the Greek people and the traditionalism of the theologians who were bent on preserving every jot and tittle of Orthodox belief and practice and who magnified the smallest deviation into a major cause of offense. Thus the root of the great schism between the East and the West was not theological. It was cultural estrangement, mutual misunderstanding and the hoarded memories of unforgotten feuds.

From the beginning of its decline in the eleventh century, the Byzantine Empire was a closed world, as the Chinese empire became during the nineteenth century. It was rich in its tradition of theological wisdom and former greatness, still possessing a magnificent heritage of Christian art and a high standard of civilized behavior, but weak from a military and economic point of view— no longer possessing any power of expansion and with little understanding of the new forces that were changing the course of history.

XVIII. THE DECLINE OF THE
MEDIEVAL UNITY

1.

The remarkable unity of culture achieved in the thirteenth century was not destined to be permanent, nor was it so complete as we might suppose from the spectacle of its great achievements in art, philosophy and ecclesiastical organization. It was the result of a great conscious spiritual effort which involved so high a degree of tension that it was followed by an inevitable reaction in which repressed or ignored elements in Western culture reasserted themselves.

The Pope under whom the movement of medieval unity reached its climax, but also its turning point, was Gregory X (1271-1276). In many respects he seemed the great Pope whose coming Roger Bacon had foretold. He was an apostle of peace who did all in his power to put an end to the feuds of Guelfs and Ghibellines which had ravaged Italy and the Empire during the previous fifty years. He was the restorer of the unity of Christendom who achieved reunion of the West and the East at the Second Council of Lyons in 1274. Finally he did more than any other medieval Pope to revive the original ideal of the Crusade as the common task of the whole Christian people. During his short pontificate he succeeded in gaining the support of all the princes of the Christian world for this end. Both the Emperors, Michael Palaeologus and Rudolf of Hapsburg, took the Cross, as well as the kings of France, England, Sicily and Aragon. And he also gained the support of the Mongol Khan, Abaka, one of whose envoys was solemnly baptized at the Council of Lyons. But the pontificate of Gregory X and the Second Council of Lyons were the final expression of the international unity of medieval Christendom.

The opportunity was lost, and after the death of Gregory X, the forces of disunity and reaction gained the upper hand. As we have seen, the sweeping condemnation of the new philosophy at Paris in 1277 involved not only the so-called Averroists like Siger of Brabant and Boethius of Dacia, but also Roger Bacon, Giles of Rome and even St. Thomas himself. At the same time the ambitions of Charles of Anjou undid the work of Gregory X. Pope Martin IV allowed himself to become the tool of Angevin power politics by excommunicating the Byzantine Emperor who had stood almost alone with the Patriarch John Veccos in support of the Union, and gave his blessing to the pseudo-Crusade planned by Charles of Anjou for the conquest of Constantinople. When this project failed, owing to the revolt of Sicily and the intervention of Aragon, the Papacy once more misused the Crusade by turning it against Christians and Catholics in the disastrous Crusade of Aragon in 1291, and this at the very moment when the last of the Crusaders were making their last stand against overwhelming odds in Palestine.

A few years before, Rutebeuf had written the complaint of Jofroi de Sergines, the good knight whom St. Louis had left to defend Acre:

> *Qu'ils faisent large cimitière*
> *Ceux d'Acre, ils en auront besoin.*
> *Tout est plein d'herbes le sentier*
> *Qu'on battait jadis volentier*

Pour offrir l'ame au lieu de cire
Messire Jofroi de Sergines
Je ne vois plus, deca, nul signe
Que l'on desormais vous secoure.[1]

For two hundred years the armies of Christendom had thronged that path, which was at once a way of pilgrimage and a way of conquest. The blood and wealth of Europe had flowed out through it like an open vein. No one can measure the good and the evil, the heroism and the cruelty, of that long-drawn-out struggle. Now the path was closed, the account ended. Nothing remained but the ruins of the Crusaders' castles, stranded on the slopes of Lebanon and on the shores of the Mediterranean like the skeletons of extinct monsters.

But though the Crusade was ended, the struggle with Islam was by no means at an end, and the late Middle Ages witnessed the gradual retreat of Christendom not only from the Levant but from Southeastern Europe as well. Ten years after the Fall of Acre in 1291, the Ottoman Turks began their career of conquest in the Byzantine Empire, and thenceforward for more than three centuries a new movement of Moslem expansion continued which did not stop until it had reached the walls of Vienna and the frontiers of Italy. The unity of Western Christendom, which had been painfully achieved from the eleventh to the thirteenth centuries, was now threatened by internal division and external defeat.

II.

Thus from the close of the thirteenth century the unity and prosperity of medieval Europe gradually declined. The destruction of the Order of the Temple and the defeat of the Papacy by Philip

---

[1] "Let the men of Acre enlarge their cemetery. They will need it. Overgrown now with weeds is the path erewhile men trod so eagerly to offer their lives like wax for holy candles. My Lord Jofroi de Sergines, I see no sign of reinforcement."

IV of France weakened the supernational unity of Christendom. At about the same time the economic progress of Western Europe was checked and population began to decrease, and this seems to have occurred before the coming of the Black Death, the most lethal epidemic of which we have record, the effects of which were as disastrous to Western Europe as the Famine of 1845–1846 was to Ireland. This was followed by a series of further disasters —the repeated devastation of France in the Hundred Years' War, the conquest of the Christian kingdoms of Southeastern Europe by the Turks, the Great Schism of the Papacy and the growth of heresy.

Nevertheless it is from this period of social decline that most people derive their ideas of medieval culture, owing perhaps to their greater familiarity with its literature. For it was in spite of everything an age of great writers—of Dante, Petrarch and Boccaccio in Italy, of Chaucer and Langland in England, and of Jean Froissart in France.

Dante, the most classical of these writers, united in his work both the traditions of medieval culture and those which looked forward to the Renaissance, both the exotic knightly culture of the Provençal troubadours and the classical learning and positive scientific spirit which characterized the Italian bourgeoisie.

But to the expression of these in the *Divine Comedy*, Dante added a third element—the mystical apocalypticism of Joachim of Flora and the Franciscans—which had never before attained to literary expression. The *Divine Comedy* owes its inspiration and also its unity to Dante's philosophy of history, to his conception of a mysterious parallelism and harmony between the Christian world and that of pagan antiquity, between the Empire and the Church, nature and grace, Virgil and Beatrice. Thus Dante's apocalypse of the Holy Roman Empire, which has so often been regarded as the swan song of a dying medievalism, was in fact a kind of mystical humanism which had a formative influence on the new Italian culture. In Vosller's words, "As natural science sprang from the mystical symbolism of numbers, so humanism arose out of a mystical philosophy of history."

Dante, it is true, even in his philosophy of history, is not an entirely original thinker. He built upon the foundations laid by the thirteenth-century Schoolmen—above all on the Thomistic ethics. His idealization of natural reason in the person of Virgil and of natural virtue in that of Cato was rendered possible only by St. Thomas' demonstration of the independent and autonomous existence of the natural order, of the distinction between reason and faith, nature and grace, yet of their harmony in difference.

It is in his theory of ethics that Dante is most indebted to St. Thomas, and the *Divine Comedy* is hardly conceivable apart from this ethical framework. Even the discussions of technical points of ethical theory contain some of the finest passages in the *Commedia*.[2] One may even go so far, I think, as to assert in general that it is the ethical and religious element in the *Divine Comedy* which is the easiest for us to understand and the least affected by the passing of time, whereas the secular element is responsible for our chief difficulties in the understanding and appreciation of Dante. This is true above all of the scientific element, which is intolerably wearisome to the ordinary reader.

Moreover, to Dante the religious element in his poem is not sim-

---

[2] For example, the discussion of free will in *Purgatorio* XVI, 85 ff.:

> *Esce di mano a lui, che la vagheggia,*
> *Prima che sia, a guisa di fanciulla,*
> *Che Piangendo e ridendo pargoleggia*
> *l'anima semplicetta.*

> "Forth from his hand, who yearns to her in thought
> Ere she exists, comes, like a little maid
> All tears and smiles, eager to play with aught
> The little, simple soul."—(Trs. Geoffrey Bickersteth)

Also the passage in *Paradiso* III, 70 ff., which describes the acquiescence of the soul in its appointed share of beatitude: *E'n la sua volontade è nostra pace*—"His will is our peace."

ply an allegory. It represents the fundamental structure of reality. It is impossible for us to understand Dante, unless we understand his spiritual realism. There is nothing subjective or ideal in his world, everything has its profound ontological basis in an objective spiritual order. The intelligible and the real are one. As the moral order of the visible world has its cosmic foundation in the celestial, so too all moral disorder and evil naturally gravitate to a lower plane of being in which nature becomes distorted and unintelligible. Consequently the cruelty and ugliness of the *Inferno* are not, as the romantics suppose, the fruit of a grotesque imagination. Still less are they the relics of a barbarous superstition which is incongruous with the rest of Dante's thought. In his philosophy they are the inevitable destiny of a nature which turns away from the principle of intelligible reality—the Sun of spirits—and plunges itself in darkness and disorder. Filippo Argenti, the brutal and arrogant man, finds his last home in the black mud of the fifth circle. "Sullen were we in the sweet air that is gladdened by the sun, carrying gloomy smoke in our hearts; now we lie sullen here in the black mire."

Now just as Dante's thought involved two elements, the religious world-view of the Middle Ages and the humanist structure of the Renaissance, the Middle Ages themselves can be considered from two different points of view. If we wish to study them as the source of later Western developments, then nothing can be more important than these later centuries, from 1300 to 1500; for they witnessed the development of the European national kingdoms and the Western vernacular literatures, and disclose the reasons for the coming of the Reformation and the roots of the religious changes which produced the later divisions of Christendom.

On the other hand, if we are studying medieval Europe as a type of Christian culture—the greatest example in history of the influence of Christianity on social life and institutions—then it is to the earlier centuries that we must direct our attention. During this period there was a continuous progress towards the expansion and unification of Christendom, and this was accompanied by an internal movement of religious reform, a revival of learning and the creation of a great religious art. Medieval Christendom, at least in this its greatest period, was not a static, unchangeable, hierarchic order, like the civilizations of the ancient East. It was a dynamic movement, continually changing, which hardly achieved completion before it began to pass away. Modern writers have frequently been so impressed by the logical completeness of the medieval synthesis, as revealed in the works of St. Thomas and Dante, that they have failed to realize its dynamic character. Thus Bertrand Russell in his *Impact of Science on Society*[3] describes Dante's universe as "tidy and small." "Everything is contrived in relation to man: to punish sin and reward virtue. There are no mysteries, no abysses, no secrets; the whole thing is like a child's dolls' house, with people as the dolls. But although the people were dolls they were important, because they interested the Owner of the dolls' house."

In reality medieval man lived precariously between two abysses with hell beneath his feet and the heavens filled with the mysteries of a succession of spiritual worlds above his head. And in the same way medieval civilization itself was a precarious achievement, like a great arch thrown over the abyss of barbarism.

If we want an image of the medieval world, it is not a dolls' house but a Gothic cathedral, as Henry Adams described it in the last pages of *Mont-Saint-Michel and Chartres*:

"Knowing by an enormous experience precisely where the strains were to come, they enlarged their scale to the utmost point of material endurance, lightening the load and distributing the burden until the gutters and gargoyles that seem mere ornament, and the grotesques that seem rude absurdities, all do work either for the arch or for the eye; and every inch of material, up and down, from crypt to vault, from man to God, from the universe to the atom, had its task, giving support where support was needed, or

[3] London, 1952 (p. 23).

weight where concentration was felt, but always with the condition of showing conspicuously to the eye the great lines which led to unity and the curves which controlled divergence; so that, from the cross on the flèche and the keystone of the vault, down through the ribbed nervures, the columns, the windows, to the foundation of the flying buttresses far beyond the walls, one idea controlled every line; and this is true of St. Thomas's Church, as it is of Amiens Cathedral. . . .

"Granted a Church, St. Thomas's Church was the most expressive that man has made, and the great Gothic cathedrals were its most complete expression. Perhaps the best proof of it is their apparent instability. Of all the elaborate symbolism which has been suggested for the Gothic cathedral, the most vital and most perfect may be that the slender nervure, the springing motion of the broken arch, the leap downwards of the flying buttress—the visible effort to throw off a visible strain—never let us forget that Faith alone supports it, and that, if Faith fails, Heaven is lost. The equilibrium is visibly delicate beyond the line of safety; danger lurks in every stone."[4]

Now in the fourteenth century the strain became too great to be borne. The centrifugal thrust of royal power and national ambition became too strong to be mastered by the centripetal aspiration of Western culture towards the center of Christian unity. The arch was broken and the vault collapsed. Out of the ruins men began to build again, with lower aims and more divided purposes. Yet the inheritance of the great age of medieval culture was never completely lost. All the new elements which that age had created were taken over and incorporated into the new national cultures —the universities and their philosophies, the cities and their liberties, knighthood and chivalry, the new forms of Christian art and architecture—above all, the quest for spiritual perfection and the reform of the Church. And all these elements are fully represented in the poem of William Langland which gives us a wonderfully

[4] *Mont-Saint-Michel and Chartres* (Boston, Houghton), pp. 376–377.

true and profound vision of the conflicting forces at work in this later medieval world.

In this respect he had no rival among fourteenth-century writers. For Dante still looks back to the ideal unity of the central period, though he is tragically aware of its failure, while Chaucer has already cheerfully accepted the conditions of the new age and takes the world as he finds it without moral indignation or lamentations over what has been lost. These differences of attitude are not purely personal, since they have their roots in three different social traditions. Dante belongs to the world of the universities and the Italian city-states, and he was deeply involved in the last forlorn hope of the Empire to reassert its universal claims in Italy. Chaucer, on the other hand, was a courtier of the new national kingdom, and he adapted the old courtly traditions of the feudal world to the new vernacular culture which united the courtier and the wealthy citizen in a common national society. But Langland was the spokesman of the people as the ultimate social reality. In spite of his harsh criticism of the Friars, his mind was formed by their vernacular preaching and his ideals are those which the Franciscans had popularized during the previous century. His work shows how the movement of spiritual reform which had inspired the great age of medieval unity had now become assimilated by the vernacular culture and had become part of the Western tradition, although it had ceased to exercise an effective influence on the international and ecclesiastical organization of Christendom.

One cause for this decline of the wider social influence of the reforming movement lay within the Franciscan Order itself, the left wing of which, the so-called "Spirituals," developed revolutionary tendencies which brought them into conflict with orthodox Catholic tradition and the authority of the Holy See. This weakened the reforming movement as a whole, and especially that alliance between the spiritual reformers and the Papacy which had been the basis of the whole religious movement from the eleventh to the thirteenth centuries. At the same time the growth of nationalism destroyed the international unity of medieval culture and prepared the way for that great schism between Northern and Southern Europe which came to a head at the Reformation. The last two centuries of the Middle Ages saw the gradual disintegration of the unity built up in the previous age. The spiritual vitality of medieval religion was still strong, but it had lost its center of unity and its constructive power.

For the political leadership of the medieval Papacy could not survive in the changed political atmosphere produced by the constitutional development of medieval society and the formation of the new national monarchies. The State became conscious of its independent aims and functions, and this process was facilitated by the Neo-Aristotelianism of St. Thomas, which gave the State an independent basis in nature and reason. Thus the later centuries of the Middle Ages saw the liquidation of the unitary conception of Christian society and of the theocratic ideals which had accompanied it. The defeat of the theocratic Empire by the Papacy was followed by the defeat of the theocratic Papacy by the national monarchies. These latter, however, still preserved a great deal of the older tradition.

The Church historians and the reformers, whether Catholic or Protestant, hardly do justice to the motives and characters of the ecclesiastics who concerned themselves with political interests. The State bishops were, many of them, men of the highest character without whom the work of the State and of the State-Church or Church-State could not have been carried on. They include saints like St. Bruno the Great, the brother of Otto I, who was a scholar as well as a statesman and a leader of the Church; and in the early Middle Ages this type was quite common. Now, however, when the cleavage had begun between the international society of Western Christendom and the national society, a dilemma arose. It was the product of two potentially hostile forces operative already in the earlier centuries.

Many other forms of social organization had transcended na-

tional boundaries and produced a common Western society. There
were first the monastic orders which united communities of different nationality under the same rule. And in the eleventh and
twelfth centuries the expansion of the Cluniacs and the Cistercians
produced new forms of international corporate organization which
associated the individual units much more closely than in the older
Benedictine monasticism. Secondly, there was the order of chivalry,
which imposed common standards and common ideals on the warrior class which had hitherto been a source of dissension and barbaric lawlessness. Thirdly, there was the order of scholars, which
developed later than the others and found its principle of organization in the thirteenth-century university; though even in the
twelfth century it was already one of the most important elements
making for a common Western European culture.

On the other hand, in the Western monarchies which developed
during the same period there was an alternative system of social
or political organization which was in competition or conflict with
the first. The kings, first in England after 1066, then in Sicily and
in France, tended to organize their kingdoms as units under lay
authority. But they were forced to rely on the clergy to do this
work. For as yet there was no lay educated class from which they
could draw their officials. The bishops, in particular, had to fulfil
a double role, as ministers of the universal Church and as leaders
and administrators under the crown. Throughout the whole Middle Ages in England, and in the earlier period in France, the
bishops were the king's chief ministers and chancellors. This had
a secularizing influence on the Church. Nevertheless these bishops
were not only men of the world. Many were fully conscious of
their responsibilities towards the Church and they did much more
than the layman to promote culture. Witness the services rendered
for English education by Edward III's great minister, William of
Wykeham. They provided a democratic element in the state. For
some of the greatest of them, like Wykeham himself, were of
humble origin, men who had risen through the Church.

The development of the Estates system at the end of the thirteenth century did much to nationalize the Church. For the bishops and the great abbots were treated as one of the Estates of the Realm, and though this may have had evil consequences for the Church, the Estates system, which was the beginning of representative government, could not have existed without it.

At the same period, however, in France under Philip the Fair (1285-1314), there are the beginnings of laicization in the class of the King's Knights—Marigny, Pierre Flote and William of Nogaret—who carried out the attack on the international order of Christendom as represented by Boniface VIII and the Order of the Temple. In England also there was a definite movement in favor of lay ministers, first in 1341 and then in 1371. The results were not permanent, and the clergy continued to hold the chief posts down to the Reformation. Of this Wolsey is an outstanding example. It was in Italy that the lay state first developed, in the Republics of Florence, Venice and Genoa, and it was there that an educated lay class first appeared. This was due primarily to the predominance of the cities in Italy and to the fact that the Italian universities like Bologna had specialized in the study of law—not only canon law but civil law also. This provided the social basis of the Renaissance. Indeed the lay secretaries of the Republic, especially at Florence, were the initiators of the movement as early as the fourteenth century. These men were not therefore anti-clerical. Dante himself was one of the new lay educated class, and Salutati, the first great humanist of Florence, was an extremely religious man. But there was an anti-clerical tendency shown by the growing hostility of these lay scholars to the Church, culminating in Machiavelli in the early sixteenth century.

On the other hand, the laicization of the State in Italy (outside the Papal States) did go far to solve the problem of Church and State, and the reform of the Church was not complicated by the difficulty of disentangling their relations. It is no accident that the Reformation took place in Germany where Church and State were most inextricably entangled and the Counter-Reformation developed in Italy where conditions were relatively modern—where Church and State were clearly distinguishable and each could follow its own line of development, as for instance in Venice, where the State did not tolerate interference by the Church, but the Church was left quite free in matters of religion.

The last great attempt to reform the Church and to restore the unity of Christendom—the Conciliar movement—was a failure because it based its action on a kind of ecclesiastical constitutionalism inconsistent with the divine authority of the Holy See. Thus the Papacy, deserted by the reformers and opposed by a strong Gallicanizing movement, was forced to make its own terms with the new secular powers, and became itself increasingly absorbed in the secular politics and humanist culture of Renaissance Italy.

It was, however, only in Renaissance Italy that new notions concerning the non-moral character of the State were applied logically and consistently to political and ecclesiastical problems. Elsewhere the State retained a semitheocratic character which found expression in novel Gallican theories and in that doctrine of the Divine Right of Kings which played so large a part at the Reformation and in post-Reformation times. Not content with depriving the Papacy of the quasi-political functions it had possessed in the unitary society of the medieval Church-State, it attacked its apostolic authority as the divinely-ordained head of the Church, and set up instead the new ideal of a State-Church under the control of the secular power. Unfortunately, during this period the Papacy was weakened, first by its removal from Rome to Avignon, then by the Great Schism, and finally by the secularizing influence of the Renaissance.

It was indeed at Rome that the Middle Ages first came to an end. Already in the first half of the fifteenth century, the age of St. Joan, the Curia was thronged with bright young men who regarded the whole medieval development as an unfortunate episode that was best forgotten, and who looked back to pagan antiquity with romantic enthusiasm. More than a century was to pass before the old alliance of the Papacy and the spiritual reformers was renewed by St. Ignatius and the heroes of the Counter-Reformation. In the meantime the great revolt had taken place and Northern Europe had ceased to be Catholic. Consequently, it was not until the age of the Counter-Reformation and the Council of Trent that the Papacy was able fully to reassert its authority as the ruler of an autonomous spiritual society, distinct both in its end and its functions from the secular society of the State.

III.

To sum up the medieval development, we may say that its essential characteristic is to be found in the transmission to the young peoples of Northern and Western Europe of the Catholic tradition, as formed by the patristic age and the late Roman culture, and in the gradual process of assimilation that followed. In every manifestation of medieval religion we can trace the interaction of these two factors. Thus medieval religion is not simply Catholicism, it is Catholicism as expressed through a particular medium, a stubborn and resistant medium which often refuses to be moulded into Christian forms. There is, therefore, much in medieval religion which belongs not so much to the Catholic tradition as to the other element, native and barbaric, that underlies medieval culture, just as there is also much in it which is not specifically medieval but simply Catholic. Hence that revolt against medieval culture which is the Renaissance is by no means to be identified with that revolt against medieval Catholicism which is the Reformation. Wycliffe is a thoroughly medieval man, but he is already more than half a Protestant, while his contemporary Colluccio Salutati was Catholic without being medieval. When the religious revolt came, it came from the Gothic North, not from the classical South. Luther himself was hardly less medieval than Wycliffe, whereas the Rome against which he revolted had been saturated by the influence of the Renaissance for a century, and was now the citadel of the new culture.

Nevertheless, while recognizing that what is Catholic is not necessarily medieval, and what is medieval is not necessarily Catholic, we must at the same time admit that there has never been an age in which European culture was more penetrated by the Catholic tradition, or in which Catholic ideals found a fuller expression in almost every field of human activity. The age of St. Bernard and St. Francis, of St. Thomas and St. Bonaventure, of St. Louis and Dante, is perhaps the one age in which all that was strongest and most living in European thought and society accepted Catholic principles and consecrated itself to the service of God and his Church. Hence the positive achievements of medieval religion have been incorporated into the Catholic tradition and have become part of the Church's spiritual patrimony. This is evident in every aspect of Catholic life; in theology and philosophy, in organization and canon law, in liturgy and worship.

The culture of the later Middle Ages was only one of the five or six successive ages of Christian culture, each of which had its own mission and vocation and deserves to be studied for its own sake. Each of them provides an equally good field for study—not because they are equal from the point of view of material and intellectual culture—but because in each we see how Christianity has entered into vital relations with some particular social world and has changed it by creating a new pattern of Christian life according to the conditions of this particular age and society. Each has its own record of achievement and failure and each has played its part in the world mission of the Church, the progressive transformation of humanity by the new principle of divine life which was brought into the world by the Incarnation and which will continue its work through the whole course of human history until the end of time.

Epilogue

XIX. THE CATHOLIC IDEA OF
A UNIVERSAL SPIRITUAL SOCIETY

Two essential characteristics distinguish the Christian faith and the Catholic Church: uniqueness and universality. Each of these can be extended by a number of associated features. The uniqueness of Christianity is related to its divine origin, its historic revelation and its sacred or supernatural character. Its universality is related to its unity, its character as a visible society and its sacramental nature. These characteristics are summed up in the traditional doctrine of the four notes of the Church—unity, sanctity, catholicity and apostolicity—as we find in the statement of the creeds, "I believe in one Holy, Catholic, and Apostolic Church," and this definition underlies all the later developments of theological doctrine.

Against this Catholic conception of the Church as the universal spiritual society, there have always been two opposing views—so far opposed to one another that Catholicism stands midway between them. These are Sectarianism and Humanitarianism.

Sectarianism represents a rigorist or puritan tendency which has always been strong among Christians from the days of Tertullian to the Jansenists. It exalts the note of *holiness* above that of universality. The Church was seen as the society of the elect, the saints, to the exclusion of sinners. This was the cause of a whole series of early schisms—the Montanists and Tertullianists, the Novatians and the Donatists—all of whom held that there could be no forgiveness for those who had once fallen away from the Church, especially in times of persecution. Again with the Reformation, many Reformers, and especially the Calvinists, emphasized the idea of the Church as the society of the elect—an invisible Church to which the different visible or local churches belong in varying degrees. So too, Calvin's emphasis on the doctrine of predestination tended to limit the Church to a relatively small number of Christians who possess an assurance of their salvation. Thus the Church is not so much a universal society as a select society, and its mission is not to save the world but to separate a chosen remnant from the condemned mass of mankind.

There has, however, been an opposite tendency, which I have termed Humanitarianism, to criticize the Catholic conception of the Church as too narrow and to go beyond it towards the ideal of a universal Christian or natural religion—not limited to any particular form of belief or system of organization—an all-inclusive spiritual society of all men of good will. According to this view the Churches are simply voluntary associations of men for religious worship, and the less they claim to be exclusive, the better. This liberal, humanist or relativist view of the Church became very prevalent from the eighteenth century onwards, and it has contributed no less than the Puritan view to form the religious pattern of the modern world. It is, however, political as well as religious. For since the French Revolution the concept of the Church as the universal society has been replaced by Rousseau's ideal of the democratic state as a spiritual community, or the religion of humanity, which has taken many different forms and has been a powerful force in modern times.

Here it is clear that Catholicism stands or falls with the belief in a universal visible spiritual community. It is a very simple idea at first sight, and one which is neither mysterious nor hard to understand; yet everything depends on it, and every aspect of Catholicism illustrates it in one way or another. No doubt all Christians agree in affirming the importance of the Church as a universal spiritual society and even agree in the specific terms in which they profess the doctrine. But this agreement is obviously deceptive, since in modern times it has not precluded the belief in a variety of different existing spiritual societies which all have a share in the universal community without being identified with it. As the Westminster Confession explains, they are partial and transitory representatives of the Catholic Church, in which they participate according to the manner in which they preach their doctrine and maintain apostolic order and evangelical worship.

But when once this relativist view of Catholicity had been introduced, the idea of the Church was inevitably devalued. There was a tendency to base religion upon the experience of the individual believer and to regard the Church, as Daniel Jenkins has written, "as little more than a convenient form of religious association." It culminated in the Latitudinarianism of the eighteenth century in England and the Unitarianism of the nineteenth. Yet the word *Catholic* first became current in the early days of Christianity to express just the opposite conception; that is to say, the objective fact of the Church as a universal visible society. That very influential writer St. Cyril of Jerusalem defines this in the fourth century in terms which could not be clearer: "The Church is called Catholic then because it extends through the world from one end of the earth to the other; and because it teaches universally and completely one and all the doctrines that men ought to know concerning things both visible and invisible, heavenly and earthly; and because it brings into subjection to godliness the whole race of mankind, governors and governed, learned and unlearned; and because it treats and heals every class of sins that are committed in soul and body, and possesses in itself every form of virtue which is named both in deed and word and in every kind of spiritual gift. . . .

"And so if you are staying in a town, do not ask simply where is the Lord's house, nor even where is the Church, but where is the *Catholic Church*. For this is the peculiar name of this Holy Body, the Mother of us all, which is the Bride of our Lord Jesus Christ the Only Begotten Son of God. . . . And while the kings of particular nations have bounds set to their dominions, the Holy Catholic Church alone extends her illimitable sovereignty over the whole world."[1]

Very much the same thing had been said by Irenaeus much earlier, though he does not use the term Catholic, since he is more concerned with the Unity of the Faith than the Unity of the Church. His argument against the Gnostics is that the heretics are all different in their doctrines and all relatively modern, whereas the Church has always been there, has always taught the same faith and has been the bearer of the same apostolic tradition. "This preaching," he writes, "and this faith, the Church diligently observes, as though it occupied one house, and believes as though it had one mind, and preaches and teaches as though it had one mouth. And although there are many languages in the world, the meaning of the tradition is one and the same. For the one faith is held and handed down by the Churches established in the Germanies, the Spains, among the Celtic tribes, in Libya and in the central parts of the world. But as the sun, the creation of God, is one and the same in all the world, so is the light of the preaching of the truth which shines on all that desire to come to the knowledge of the truth. Not even the ablest of the teachers in the Churches will say anything different from this. Nor will the feeblest say less. For the faith is one and the same, and it can neither be increased nor diminished by the mind of the teacher.[2]

Thus the Church is Catholic because the truth is universal, and since the word is one, the Church must be one, and she is the bearer and guardian of the Apostolic tradition, which has been handed on from generation to generation by the Apostolic Churches, and above all pre-eminently by the Apostolic See—"the greatest, most ancient and well-known Church founded by the two most glorious Apostles Peter and Paul at Rome."[3]

---

[1] *Catechetical Discourses* xviii, 23, 26.
[2] *Contra Haereses* i.x.
[3] *Ibid.*, iii.iii.

This insistence on the unity and universality of the Church goes back before the beginning of Christianity. For the Church was the New Israel and had inherited the promises and the vocation of that very distinct and unique society. The fact that it had been transformed by the coming of the Messiah and extended by the vocation of the Gentiles did not destroy its sense of corporate identity. On the contrary it strengthened it by raising it to a higher plane of cosmic significance. For the Church is the organ of human salvation, through which the redemptive work of Christ is transmitted to mankind. As Christ is the New Adam, the Church, which is the body of Christ, is to be the new humanity in which the broken fragments of fallen humanity are brought back to unity and restored to the life of God. Thus the Church must be one, because Christ is one, and it must be universal, because it extends to the whole of the human race: indeed, it is the whole human race, in so far as humanity recovers its spiritual nature and returns to the divine fellowship.

Thus the Incarnation and the Church form one whole. They are the two aspects of a single process, and they are bound together not only by faith but also by the sacraments which provide the organic link between the Head and the Body—between the life of Christ and the life of the Church. The Church therefore is not a voluntary religious association formed by the coming together of individual believers, but a supernatural divine organism which transmits the gift of eternal life to mankind.

These truths have always been accepted in some sense by all Christians everywhere in so far as they have accepted the teachings of the New Testament. But we know only too well that there have been differences and discussions among Christians as to the interpretation of these principles. The thousand sects of Christendom, present and past, bear a very discordant witness to the one body. Some of them have staked everything on a particular interpretation of a particular doctrine, while others have gone into the wilderness in pursuit of a mirage of perfection which separated them from their fellow Christians. But the mark of the Catholic Church has always been its undeviating insistence on its universal mission. As Matthew Arnold wrote in one of his critical essays, it differs from all other religious bodies because it does not represent any particular type of man or school of thought, but is as wide as humanity. If the Christian Church was predestined from its foundation to be a universal society, it was necessary for it to be an international society, and this the Catholic Church has achieved on a scale of time and space wider than that of any other Christian body. The remarkable thing is that it has transcended national frontiers without destroying or weakening national individuality and sentiment, so that the most nationalistic peoples—Irish, Poles, Spaniards—are often the most ardent Catholics.

Even more important is the way in which Catholicism has succeeded in reconciling its universality with the claims of the individual soul. Dr. Arnold Toynbee has recently written that the ultimate inescapable issue is the tug of war between individual souls and the universal society. He is no doubt thinking primarily in terms of secular society—of the welfare state or even a totalitarian state. But the same problem exists for the spiritual society also—indeed what makes the claims of the totalitarian state so formidable is that it makes almost unlimited claims on the spiritual as well as the natural aspects of life. But even if this were not the case, if the universal society were represented by some non-totalitarian organization, some democratic world state organized on federal lines, a difficulty remains. The larger the unit, the more impersonal it becomes, so that the personal link with the individual man disappears. The Stoics had already conceived the ideal of a universal world society, so that Marcus Aurelius could contrast the "dear City of God" with the human city. But it was a very abstract and remote ideal—a kind of ivory tower into which the philosopher-emperor could withdraw from the bloody reality of empire on the Danube frontier. And the same thing is true in some degree of the ideal of Christian unity itself when it becomes sublimated as an invisible heavenly reality and divorced from the human realities of our existent religious community.

But the Catholic Church, in spite of its elaborate hierarchical organization, its world-wide extension and its authoritarian claims, has never lost contact with its individual members. The men of power and the men of learning have quarrelled with the Church, but the little men and women of all ages have made it their home. For the relationship of the individual Christian to the Church is never external or legalistic: every Christian has a direct access to the heart of the mystery, and his importance does not depend on his social or ecclesiastical position but on his personal participation in the life of the spirit by which the Church is animated. Thus we see how an uneducated peasant girl like Bernadette Soubirous played an important part in the religious life, not only of her country, but of the whole Catholic world, so that today she is far more widely known than contemporary ecclesiastical politicians like Cardinal Antonelli, or theologians like Cardinal Franzelin. In this way Catholicism depends, and has always depended, on the spiritual contributions of its individual members. It is a charismatic as well as a hierarchical society, and its universal mission is carried on not only by the organizing work of the great religious orders and congregations but by the unpredictable intervention of saints like Bernadette of Lourdes or Jean-Baptiste Vianney of Ars who are the representatives of the common Christian people—the *Plebs Christi.*

These are the two poles of the Church's life, and the closer the communion between them, the more flourishing is its condition, whereas if they become in any way disconnected or dislocated, everything tends to go wrong, as in the fifteenth century when the hierarchical Church condemned and burned St. Joan of Arc and Savonarola. The Catholic recovery in the following century was due not merely to the ecclesiastical and disciplinary reforms of the Council of Trent but no less to the appearance of so many great spiritual figures—like St. Ignatius Loyola, St. Philip Neri, St.

Francis Xavier, St. Teresa, and St. John of the Cross, who reopened the paths of Christian perfection, restored the ideals of Christian life, and renewed the patterns of Christian sanctity.

The view has become widespread in modern times that the essential difference between Catholicism and Protestantism is due to the former being predominantly priestly or sacerdotal and the latter mainly prophetic. In the fourteenth century, however, when the sacerdotalism of Catholicism was more highly developed than ever before by the Avignon Papacy, the prophetic element was at the same moment most strongly asserted, as by the two great women mystics, SS. Bridget of Sweden and Catherine of Siena. In this case the connection between the mystical and the prophetic seems clear. But can we extend this to mysticism in general? Are the mystical and the prophetic element equivalent?

The movement of mysticism was of central importance to the religion of the fourteenth and fifteenth century, e.g. the Friends of God, Eckhart, St. Bridget, St. Catherine, Nicholas of Cusa, Savonarola. The mysticism of the fourteenth century comprised two dominant aspects—the prophetic and the philosophic. There is need for further study of the earlier medieval tradition of mysticism, with its strong Augustinian spirit—of mystics such as John of Fécamp, Anselm, Bernard, Richard of St. Victor and the prophetic strain of the women mystics like St. Hildegard of Bingen. This movement extended to the Netherlands with Bl. John Ruysbroek of Groenendal and the Abbey of Windesheim. From the Netherlands it moved to England in the fourteenth century. The author of the *Cloud of Unknowing*, Walter Hilton and Juliana of Norwich were all influenced by the continental mystics. We lack detailed knowledge of fourteenth-century mysticism in England. In the case of Richard Rolle, there do not seem to have been any foreign influences.

Mysticism, that is to say, was of central importance to medieval Catholicism, and this raises the point of the relation between mysticism (with its prophetic element) and the priestly aspect. More broadly speaking, it is clear that in medieval Catholicism the mystical element is part of the larger notion of the saint. The cult of the saint is most important in Catholic culture. In fact the very idea of a saint as a charismatic individual, definitely belonging to the prophetic type rather than the sacerdotal, has always been characteristic of the Catholic rather than the Protestant tradition.

The idea of the saint comprises three elements: (1) The numinous or supernatural element. (2) The democratic element, since it is always the voice of the people that counts. In distinction from the hierarchical character of the Church, recognition of saints comes from the laity: the popular cult precedes the Church's recognition. (3) The moral or mystical element. The saints are seen as mirrors of the holy, patterns of the perfect Christian life: of this aspect St. Francis is an outstanding example.

Surely we may question the assertion that Protestantism is predominantly prophetic? Can it not be said that the characteristic element of modern Protestantism is intellectual and social? In the past, no doubt, the Puritans, Quakers and Baptists were strongly prophetic. In these cases, however, the prophetic element was related to the mystical, though the Protestant mystic was not the same type as the Catholic. Certainly the strong prophetic character in Protestantism led to the formation of new sects. I am, however, increasingly convinced that the mystical and prophetic elements are *different* aspects of the same thing. And about the relation between them there has been little discussion. Von Hügel, for example, analyzes religion into three categories: (1) the institutional; (2) the intellectual; (3) the mystical. He does not mention the prophetic.

For Protestants the problem presents a special difficulty. For Lutherans, Luther himself was such a unique and outstanding figure. Few others of mystic or prophetic type are known. Luther, moreover, was very hostile to the ideal of sanctity expressed in medieval Catholicism. He regarded these Catholic saints as representative of the doctrine of good works, embodiments of human perfection—both notions which he, of course, rejected.

The seventeenth-century German Pietist movement, which has in the past been regarded as having a mystical character, is now a highly controversial subject. Many modern Lutheran scholars deny that this was the case.

It is easier to study and parallel mysticism in Calvinism and Puritanism. In the Church of England, Anglican piety is well represented by George Herbert, who exercised a lasting influence on Anglican devotion even to the time of John Keble in the nineteenth century.

Today the study of mysticism is overshadowed by the influence of existentialism and the emphasis given to the prophetic. The new religious type of personality, such as Kierkegaard, is not representative of either Catholic or Protestant spirituality.

In Catholicism the mystical tradition (with its prophetic and philosophic elements) is inseparable from the tradition of the saint, the cult of the saint. Too sharp a distinction is therefore unjustified between the sacerdotal and the prophetic, either in themselves or as representing the essential characteristics of Catholicism and Protestantism.

Co-ordination of the common ecclesiastical order and the individual quest for spiritual perfection is, I think, one of the characteristic notes of Catholicism and one of the secrets of its strength. For it is not the case elsewhere. In other religious bodies the two movements rarely coincide, so that each renewal of spiritual life involves the creation of a new sect or denomination. We see a striking example of this in England in the eighteenth century. John Wesley was no rebel. He was a thoroughly loyal son of the Church of England in the traditional sense. Yet the ecclesiastical organization could not find room for him or his work. The new wine burst the old bottles and he was driven into schism against his will and his principles.

If we attempt to look deeper into the causes of this combination of universality and individuality which lies at the heart of Catholicism, I think we shall find it in the economy of the sacraments. It is evident from the history of Catholicism that the development of the ecclesiastical polity, the growth of canon law, and all the other forms of external organization, have been accompanied *pari passu* by a development of the sacramental system which brought the whole ecclesiastical order into immediate contact with the psychological experience of the individual. Thus in the patristic period, the greatest public act of the Church, which still survives in the Paschal liturgy of the Roman rite, was the annual or bi-annual ceremony of the blessing of the Font and the communal baptism of catechumens. Here the Church is seen not as a ruler, lawgiver, or guardian of orthodox tradition but as the mother of a reborn humanity, each member of which is the heir of the divine promises, recipient of the gift of the spirit.

Similarly in modern times the increase in ecclesiastical centralization has been accompanied by an increasing emphasis on the participation of the individual Christian, daily if possible, in the sacrament of unity. For as Peter Damian wrote, "Is it not true that the Church, by reason of the Sacrament of unity, is wholly present wherever there exists a single individual who shares her faith and devotion? . . . Just as man is said to be a microcosm . . . because he is made up of the same four elements as is the Universe, so too each of the faithful is the Church in miniature, when in the mystery of the hidden unity he receives all the sacraments which have been conferred by God on the universal Church."[4] Thus the sacramental system brings home to the believer the psychological dimensions of the changes in human nature involved in the construction of the universal spiritual society. Without the spiritual rebirth of the individual there can be no restoration of humanity, and unless the new man has an immediate access to the source of divine life, he cannot remain a living cell of the new divine organism. All this is explicitly stated in the Fourth Gospel and in the teachings of St. Paul, and it remains the theological and moral and psychological center of Catholicism.

But if Catholicism means a universal spiritual society, so that the

[4] In Migne, *PL* CXLV, pp. 235–236 and 239. Quoted in Henri de Lubac's *Catholicism* (New York, Sheed and Ward), pp. 274–276.

Church is the organ by which mankind as a whole is spiritually transformed and re-created, how comes it that the Catholic Church remains such a limited and incomplete society, so that there are great masses of humanity to which it has barely penetrated, if at all, and then only in the last few centuries? This has always been an obvious difficulty, common to all forms of Christianity. The Scandal of the Church is inseparable from the Scandal of the Cross. If it is difficult to believe that this particular historical society is the form of a new humanity and the organ of the renewal of the universal human race, it is also difficult to believe that this individual Person is the Incarnate Word of God and that his ignominious death is the source of the redemption of humanity.

However we look at it, there is no avoiding this scandal or paradox which is central to the Christian faith, and which St. Paul insisted must always be unacceptable to the wisdom of the world and its princes. For it is only accessible to Revelation, that is to say, the knowledge that God has chosen particular means, which human reason could not have discovered, to realize his purposes for man which equally transcend the limits of human knowledge and reasoning. But if we once accept the principle of a divine intervention in history, so that particular events, personalities and social traditions may be used as the vehicles of divine purpose, the idea of a universal spiritual society, which is the medium for the realization of these purposes, is not only conceivable but necessary and inevitable. For then the Church can be accepted as an integral part of the supernatural economy of salvation—that economy which St. Paul calls "the Mystery" *par excellence*.

The difficulties of which I have just spoken were very much in evidence during the first centuries of Christianity. They have never perhaps been more fully stated than by Celsus in the second century, who focuses his attack—the most formidable attack the Christian apologist had to meet—on this very issue, the implausibility and absurdity of the unique claim of the Christian Church and of the whole Judeo-Christian system of revelation. What could be more ridiculous, he says, than that God should have made a unique revelation to one little corner of the world, to a set of barbarian shepherds and herdsmen, that he should have chosen this barbarous race among which to become man; while the Christian Church has made matters still worse by deliberately appealing to sinners and social outcasts to join it, as though it were recruiting a gang of robbers instead of men of wisdom and virtue, as the philosophers had done. Above all Celsus condemns the Christians, in language that Voltaire might have used, for their presumption in believing that man can have a unique spiritual destiny which distinguishes him from other creatures. It is as though, writes Celsus, "a swarm of ants coming out of their nest or worms crawling together in the corner of a dunghill should quarrel with one another as to which were the greatest sinners, and should assert that God reveals to them everything beforehand; and that abandoning the whole world and the heavens and this great earth, He becomes a citizen among us alone and to us alone makes His intimations known."[5]

In this criticism of Judeo-Christian national or ecclesiastical exclusivism Celsus goes even further than the modern critic inasmuch as he attacks anthropomorphism also, putting man firmly in his place among the other forms of animal life. The world was not made for man, and God is no more concerned with the doings of man than he is with monkeys or flies. In all this Celsus was perfectly consistent, but against him Origen was able to appeal to the humanist tradition in Hellenism in support of the Christian doctrine of man.

Nor is Celsus exceptional. Throughout history we are always finding similar situations, in which the enemies of Christianity or Catholicism are also the enemies of humanism: not least today when the main attack on Christianity comes from Communism and other forms of secular totalitarianism, all of which protest their devotion to the cause of humanity, but which in practice treat human beings ruthlessly as expendable material in their plans for social engineering.

[5] In Origen, *Contra Celsum* iv.xxiii.

To return, however, to Origen: in his reply to the attacks of Celsus he always comes back to two points which are complementary aspects of one truth. Christianity proves its divine mission, first by its regenerative power, its power to take the rejected and forgotten men—the poor, the sinners, and the ignorant—and to transform them into a spiritual society; and secondly, by its universal mission, for if the Church were not divine, how is it possible that an obscure group of outsiders from Galilee should have been able to conquer the world-wide Roman Empire and create a new society that already extended throughout the known world?

No doubt the Church was a minority in Origen's age and it is still a minority today. Nevertheless, it is more universal than any other human society and it is still in the process of growth. Above all it is a real society, not an abstraction like Humanity or an ideal like that of so many religious and political sects. It is a true society with its own visible institutions and objective laws and an intense consciousness of its social identity. So it was in the beginning and so it is today. This objectivity, of course, necessarily involves certain limitations and exclusions, and it is this limitation and exclusiveness which is the main source of criticism at the present day as it was in the time of Celsus and Origen.

Even a writer who accepts wholeheartedly the ideal of a universal spiritual society as the goal of history, Dr. Toynbee, cannot bring himself to admit that the hope of the world should be committed to a spiritual tradition and prefers to put his faith in a consensus of the great world religions, East and West. Catholicism, however, does not rest on a consensus of human wisdom—even on its highest and most spiritual plane—but upon a divine revelation which is also an act of creation. And since creation in itself transcends human reason, how much more must this be so with the act of spiritual creation or regeneration which brings the human animal into immediate relation and communion with the divine nature. It is, however, a rational presupposition to suppose that this cannot be brought about by the cumulative labors of human reason—by adding philosophy to philosophy and religion to religion. It must come *a parte Dei* not *a parte hominis,* from God not man. And this is what all Christians confess by their faith in the Incarnation and the work of Christ—a particular person who lived in a remote corner of the Roman Empire at a particular moment of history. It is therefore entirely consistent that this work should be carried on and fulfilled in a particular society which develops throughout the whole course of human history bearing the seed of a new world and a new humanity.

Thus apart from the continuity of Catholic tradition there are ample historical reasons for insisting on the dogma of the visible unity of the Catholic Church. We must, however, bear in mind that this doctrine has a dual aspect. In the past much has been written about the distinction between the soul and the body of the Church. Most modern theologians reject this terminology because it suggests a duality in the membership of the Church and a distinction between those Catholics who belong to the body of the Church and those who belong to its soul. If, however, the distinction is referred to the two aspects of the one visible Catholic Church, such objections do not arise and there is much to be said in its favor. Thus if we are asked, "What is the Catholic Church?" the obvious answer is, There it is before your eyes: an enormous visible social institution which is as much a part of our daily experience as our own country. We all, or most of us, know something of its organization—pope, cardinals, bishops, priests, religious orders and so on—and of the influence it exerts over its members by its hierarchical authority and its code of ecclesiastical law. But all this is only the *body* of the Church, and anyone who knows this alone knows very little about Catholicism. For the Church is also a society founded on faith and animated by the Spirit. This is the *soul* of the Church without which it could not exist and upon which the spiritual life of the individual Catholic depends. Both these aspects, however, are necessary to one another—the body cannot exist without the soul that animates it; the soul cannot *be* a soul without the body it animates.

To understand the Catholic idea of a universal spiritual society, it is above all necessary to understand this unity of the two elements that comprise the spiritual organism, for this is the entire Catholic system. At every stage and in every activity these two elements coexist and interpenetrate. As humanity is one, the Church must be one, because the Church is humanity restored to Christ. The principle of unity is the person of Christ, but there must also be an external organization of unity and of institutions in which this internal unity finds its contemporary forms. Otherwise the unity of the spiritual society would be lost among the multiplicity of sects, in the same way as the unity of humanity has been lost in the Babel of mutually incomprehensible languages and cultures. The *raison d'être* of the Church is to heal this division by bringing back the nations—the *gentes* or Gentiles—into spiritual unity. For, as St. Thomas has said, the union of men with God is the union of men with one another—*conjunctio hominum cum Deo est conjunctio hominum inter sese*. On the other hand, if Christianity were to lead the nations still further apart from one another into spiritual disunity, it would defeat the central purpose of the Church's institution.

INDEX

Abaka (Mongol khan), 267
Abelard, 234, 236f.
Abgar IX, King of Edessa, 113
Abraham, 69f., 81, 89, 91
Abrahams, I., 102
Acacian Schism, 253
Acts of the Apostles, 88f.
Adalbert, St. (archbishop), 199
Adalhard, 186
Adam, Karl, 28
Adam Parvipontanus, 233
Adamnan, 175
Adams, Henry, 218, 272
Adelaide (empress), 199
Adelard of Bath, 236
Aethelhere (king), 171, 172 and note
Agnes, St., 99
Agobard, 185, 223
Aidan, St., 174
Aistulf, K. (Lombard), 180
Aix-la-Chapelle, Council of, 171
Albert of Saxony, 250
Albertus Magnus, St., 231, 240ff.
Alberic, 199
Albigenses, 221; see also Catharism
Alcuin, 175, 181, 184f.
Alexander III (pope), 263
Alfred the Great, 191f.
Amalgest, 235
Ambrose, St., 127, 141, 142, 158
Anastasius (patriarch), 254
Andronicus (emperor), 264
Angilbert, St. (abbot), 186

Anglo-Saxon Chronicle, 192
Anna (king), 172 and note
Anselm, St., 25, 212, 233f., 290
Anselm the Peripatician, 233
Antinomian Protestant sects, 151
Antipas (martyr), 96
Antonelli, Cardinal, 289
Antoninus, St., Bishop of Florence, 213
Anthony, St. (of Egypt), 132
Aphraates, St., 99
Apocalypse, 95-96
Apocalyptic, 79
Apologists, 102, 108, 145
Apostolic Succession, 93f., 108
Argyrus, 260
Arianism, 110, 145
Arika (rabbi), 102
Aristotle, Aristotelianism, 32f., 40, 232, 233-239, 242-247, 249, 275
Arnold, Matthew, 288
Arnulf (emperor), 197
Art, Christian, 98, 136f., 160, 216-218, 272f.
    Indian, 217
    Islamic, 217
    Paleolithic, 45
Aspar the Alan, 157
Athenagoras, 108
Augustine, St., and Augustinianism, 15, 22, 25, 81f., 112n., 127-147, 155, 192, 233, 238

Augustine of Canterbury, St. (archbishop), 170, 174
Aurelian (emperor), 123
Australia, indigenous culture of, 41f., 45, 54
Avakkum (founder of Russian Old Believers), 150
Avars, conquest and baptism of, 182
Averroes, 59
Averroism, 239, 244, 267
Avitus, St., Bishop of Vienne, 159
Avitus (emperor), 159

Bacon, Sir Francis, 236, 247
Bacon, Roger, 240, 244, 247-250
Baganda, 50
Balduin (Charles the Bald's son-in-law), 193
Bardesanes, 140
Barth, Karl, Barthians, 22
Basil, St., 102, 111, 121, 127, 133, 150
Basil I (emperor), 258
Beauvais Cathedral, 218
Bede the Venerable (and his *Ecclesiastical History*), 161, 171, 174, 184, 192
Benedict, St., 134, 169, 170f., 174, 189
Rule of, 169, 170f., 176f., 192
Benedict of Aniane, St., 171, 187, 195
Benedict Biscop, St., 170f.
Benedict, Ruth, 31
Berengar, 199
Berengarian controversy, 233
Bernadette Soubirous, St., 289
Bernard of Chartres, 232
Bernard of Clairvaux, St., 206ff., 218, 221, 234, 280, 290
Bernard of Hildesheim, St. (bishop), 199
Bernard of Verdun, 249
Bernardino of Siena, 213
Berno, St. (abbot), 195
Bgoul, 150

Bible, Protestant and Catholic use of, 80f.
Bishops, functions of, 158f., 275f.
Black Death, the, 269
Boccaccio, Giovanni, 269
Boethius, 169, 192, 198, 232
Boethius of Dacia, 267
Bogomils, 220
Boileau (Despreaux), Nicolas, 229
Bonaventure, St., 212, 238n., 241, 247, 280
Boniface, St., 171, 175, 178-180, 185, 201, 257
Boniface VIII (pope), 204f., 241, 277
Brahmanism, 48, 62f., 105
Bridget of Sweden, St., 290
Brownson, Orestes, 10
Buddhism, Chinese, 47, 53, 152
  Indian and Far East, 62f., 104f.
  Japanese, 53
Bureaucratic government of later Empire, 122f.
Buridan, John, 250
Burke, Edmund, 46
Butler, Cuthbert (abbot), 147
Byzantine influences on Western culture, 152f.

Cadoc, St., 166, 168
Caedmon, 172
Caesarius of Arles, St., 134, 159, 165
Caesaropapism, 131, 254-265
Cajetan, Thomas de Vio, 241
Calvin, John, and Calvinism, 284
Canon law, 211, 214, 280, 293
Cappadocian Fathers, 149f.
Cappadocian monasticism, 133f.
Capuchonnes, 224
Carloman, 179
Carolingian Empire (culture and structure), 182, 184f.
Caspar, E., 256
Cassian, 132, 134
Cassiodorus, 134, 169, 174, 232

Catharine of Siena, St., 213, 290
Catharism, 220, 221
Catholic Church
  body and soul of the, 297f.
  charismatic and hierarchical, 289f.
  the new humanity, 287
  unique and universal, 283
Cato the Elder, 118
Cerularius, Michael, 260ff.
Celsus, 120, 295f.
Ceolfrid, St., 170, 175
Chalcedon, Council of, 143, 154, 251ff.
Channing, William Ellery, 3
Chansons de Geste, 162, 195, 209
Charlemagne (emperor), 175, 181, 186, 192, 197, 200, 201, 204f., 223
Charles of Anjou, 267
Charles II (the Bald), 186f., 193
Charles Martel, 178, 186
Charles III (the Simple), 193
Charter of Abbeville, 224
Chartres, art of, 218
  school of, 232
Chaucer, Geoffrey, 269f.
  ploughman of, 226
China, Chinese (Buddhism), 53
  Buddhist effect on culture, 152
  Confucian, 41, 47f., 62f.
  culture compared with Hellenistic, 119
Church, Primitive; *see* Primitive Church
Cicero, 230
Cistercians, 207
Civilization and culture, 32, 38, 47f.
Cleanthes, 145
Clement of Alexandria, 107ff., 147
Clement of Rome, St., 93f.
Clement IV (pope), 248
Clermont, Council of, 207, 215
Cloud of Unknowing, The, 290
Clovis, 159
Cluny, 195f., 199, 206

Codex Hadriana, 183
Codex Regularum, 171
Coffin, Charles, 143
Columba, St., 134, 168, 171, 174
Columban, St., 161, 171, 175
Communes in medieval cities, 210, 233-238
Comnena, Anna, 262
Comnenus, Alexius (emperor), 261ff.
Comnenus, Isaac (patriarch), 261
Comnenus, Manuel (emperor), 261ff.
Congar, Yves, 28
Conrad of Marburg, 222
Constantine the Great, 118, 121, 124, 128, 130, 156f.
Constantine II, 130
Constantine IV, 130
Constantine VII (Porphyrogenitus), 138
Constantine the African, 235
Constantinople, foundation of, 121, 128
  fall of, 251
Constantinople, Second Council of, 253
  two ninth-century Councils of, 258
Constantius Chlorus, 123
Constitutum, 253
Conversion of Magyars, Poles and Vikings, 214
Converts from Anglicanism to Catholicism, 8f.
Copernicus, 236, 250
Cosmas and Damian, SS., 98
Covenant, the New, 88
Covenant, the Old at Sinai, 70f., 78f., 85
Covenant, Sons of the, 99
Crusades, 207ff., 215, 221, 225, 248, 261ff., 266ff.
  the Fourth Crusade, 264
  pseudo-, 267
Culture, four factors of, 40, 42-47
Cuthbert, St., 175

Cyprian, St., 99, 112f.
Cyril of Alexandria, St., 131
Cyril of Jerusalem, St., 136, 285
Cyrus, 81

Damian, Peter; *see* Peter Damian
Daniel-Rops, H., 87
Dante Alighieri, 205, 269ff., 274, 280
Dark Age a missionary age, 173ff.
David, St., 166
De Causis, 239
De Intelligentiis, 246
Decius (emperor), 123
Delhi, Turkish kingdom of, 59
Descartes, René, 236
Dictatus Papae, 204
Diffusion, cultural, 50-61
Diggers, 151
Diocletian (emperor), 123f.
Diognetus, Epistle to, 99
Dionysius the Areopagite, 22, 143, 186
Dominic, St., 213
Dominicans, 246-250
Domitian (emperor), 95
Donation of Constantine, 181
Donation of Pepin, 180, 201
Donatists, 283
Dostoievsky, Feodor Mikhailovitch, 150
Duchesne, Mgr. Louis, 254
Duhem, Pierre, 249
Duns Scotus, 240
Dunstan, St., 196

Ebionites, 89
Eckhart, 290
Economic theories, medieval, 224-228
Ecthesis, 130
Ecumenism, prospect for, 15f.
Edessa, 140
    conversion of, 113
Edward III, 276
Egbert (archbishop), 184

Egypt (ancient religion-culture), 55f.
Egyptian monasticism, 132f., 150
Einhard, 185
Elijah (Elias), 72, 81
Eliot, President of Harvard, 3f.
Elkesaites, 89
Ephesus, Council of, 154
Ephrem Syrus, St., 140, 144, 152, 155
Epictetus, 103
Erasmus Desiderius, 229
Eskimo culture, 42f.
Essenes (Qumran), 76f., 84
Etablissements de St. Quentin, 224
Euric, 159
Eusebius of Caesaria, 96, 111, 129, 146f., 174
Eusebius of Vercelli, St., 134

Faber, Frederick William, 8
Family, the, 40ff.
Families, English, religious divisions of, 9
Fathers of the Church, theology of, 143-151, 160
Faustus of Riez, St., 165
Finan, St., 175
Florence, Council of, 251, 264
Flote, Pierre, 277
Fourth Gospel, the, 293
Francis, St., 211ff., 280, 291
Franciscans, 82, 223, 245f., 269, 274
Franciscan "Spirituals," 274
Frederick II (emperor), 221, 222
Friars, 210ff., 213, 223, 274
Fulbert, St. (bishop), 232
Fulda Abbey, 185
Fulrad (abbot), 180, 184

Gainas the Goth, 157
Galerius (emperor), 123
George, St., 98
Gerard of Brogne, St. (abbot), 196
Gerbert of Aurillac (Sylvester II), 200

Gerhoh of Reichersberg, 221
Germanus of Auxerre, St., 159, 165,
    166 and note
Ghellinck, de, 211
Gibbon, Edward (*Decline and Fall*),
    121, 172
Gildas, St., 166, 168
Giles of Rome, 240, 244, 267
Gilson, Etienne, 241, 243
Giordano Bruno, 231
Gnosticism, 104ff., 286
God, human conceptions of, 21
    knowledge of, 24f.
    Thomist doctrine of, 243
Gothic architecture, 217ff., 272f.
Gratian (canonist), 211
Gratian (emperor), 118, 157
Greek, study of, 245
Gregory the Great, St. (pope), 170,
    174, 177
    Pastoral Care, 191f.
Gregory II (pope), 178, 256f.
Gregory III (pope), 178, 180
Gregory V (pope), 200
Gregory VII (pope and saint), 203ff.,
    208, 223n.
Gregory IX (pope), 222
Gregory X (pope and blessed), 267
Gregory of Czanad, 233
Gregory Nazianzen, St., 25, 102, 111,
    121, 150
Gregory of Nyssa, 102, 111, 121, 149f.
Gregory of Tours, St., and his *His-
    tory of the Franks*, 160, 161, 174
Grosseteste, Robert (bishop), 240,
    245f., 249
Gui, Bernard (inquisitor), 222
Guibert de Nogent, 210
Guilds, 223
Gundasallinus, 239

Harnack, Adolf, 11f.
Harvard University, religious tradi-
    tion of, 3f., 6, 11

Hebrews (*Apiru*), 69
Hebrews, Epistle to the, 91f., 94
Hegel, Georg Wilhelm Friedrich,
    240
Hellenic Philosophy, 21f., 102f.,
    110f., 119f., 144f., 230f., 237,
    245, 275
Hellenism and Christianity, 102-111,
    119f., 143-153, 244f., 295
Henoticon, 130, 253
Heresy, suppression of, 221ff.
Henry I (emperor), 197
Henry III (emperor), 203
Henry VIII, King of England, 254
Heraclitus, 120, 145
Heraclius (emperor), 130, 255
Herbert, George, 292
Hermas, Shepherd of, 98
Herodotus, 55
Hildegard of Bingen, St., 290
Hilton, Walter, 290
Hinduism, 24, 41; *see also* Brahman-
    ism
Hippolytus, St., 111, 143
History, Christian, 173ff.
    religious understanding of, 80f.
Honoratus, St., 134, 165
Honorius I (pope), 254
Hrotswitha of Gandersheim (play-
    wright), 198
Hugh Capet the Elder, 194
Hugh, St. (Abbot of Cluny), 206
Hugh of Remiremont (abbot), 203
Humanitarianism, 283
Humanity; the new is the Church,
    286f.
Humbert, Cardinal, 260
Humbert, Abbot of Moyenmoutier,
    203
Hurrians, 70
Hymnody, 140f., 151f.

Ibas, 253
Ibn Gebirol, 239

Ibn Khaldun, 59
Icelandic culture, 190f.
Icelandic Sagas, 162, 256f.
Iconoclasm, 178, 256f.
Idrimi, King of Alalakh, 69
Ignatius, St. (patriarch), 258
Ignatius Loyola, St., 279, 289
Illtyd, St., 166, 168
India, 57
Indian art, 217; *see also* Brahmanism
    and Buddhism
    and Christianity, 114f.
    defective knowledge of, 30
    and religion, 104f.
Indians of the Plains, 54
Innocent III (pope), 205, 208, 221,
    240
Inquisition, 220, 223, 224
Investitures Conflict, 203f.
Irenaeus, St., 107, 111, 149, 286
Isaiah the Second, 75
Isaurian Emperors, 121, 256f.
Isidore, St. (archbishop), 134
Isidore Agricola, St., 226
Islam, 24, 57, 60, 151, 154f., 209f.,
    231, 235, 236, 237, 251, 259, 261,
    268
Islamic art, influence of, 217
Israel; see Judaism
James, St., 117
Jansenists, 283
Jainism, 104
Japan, Buddhism in, 53
Jenkins, Daniel, 285
Jeremiah, 73, 81
Jerome, St., 80, 112, 127, 128, 141,
    147, 192
Jesuits, 213
Jesus, devotion to humanity of, 212
    messianic teaching of, 84f.
    parable of the marriage feast, 91f.
Jewish Christianity, 86f., 104
Jewish revolts against Rome, 83ff.
Jezebel, 72

Joachim of Flora, 269
Joan, St., 278, 289
John, St., 81f., 96
John VI (emperor), 264
John VIII (pope), 199
John XI (pope), 199
John XII (pope), 199
John XVI (pope), 200
John Chrysostom, St., 126, 148
John of the Cross, St., 290
John of Damascus (Damascene), St.,
    256
John of Fécamp, 290
John of Salisbury, 232
John Scotus Erigena, 186, 233f.
John of Sicily, 249
John of Vandières, St. (abbot), 196
Judaism, Old Testament, 68-82
    Babylonian, 101
    Jewish sources of Christian liturgy,
        139f.
    Palestinian contrasted with Hel-
        lenic in Diaspora, 86f.
    transition to New Testament, 79f.,
        83-87
    (*See also* 208, 236, 237)
Juliana of Norwich, 290
Justin Martyr, 108f., 145
Justinian I (emperor), 118, 130, 131,
    177, 252f.
Justinian II (emperor), 256
Juvenal, 112
Juvencus, 147

Kant, Immanuel, 240
Keble, John, 292
Khomiakoff, 150
Kierkegaard, Sören, 292
Kiriakos of Kantzag, 61
Knighthood, medieval, 227
Knowles, David, 243
Kroeber, A. L., 61
Lactantius, 123
Laicization, 277

Langland, William, 226, 269f.
Language, social function of, 32f., 40, 49, 68
Lateran Council, Fourth, 221
Latitudinarianism, 285
Lausus, 126
Lea, H. C., 222
Leo III (pope), 181
Leo III (emperor), 180, 256f.
Leo VI (emperor), 259
Leo IX, St. (pope), 196, 203, 206, 260
Leonardo da Vinci, 236
Lérins, school of monastic theology at, 165, 168
Lessing, Gotthold Ephraim (*Education of Humanity*), 81n.
Light, Grosseteste's theory of, 246f.
Liturgy, Catholic, 136-143, 160, 175, 184f., 189, 198, 280, 293
Liutprand of Cremona, 259
Logos, doctrine of, 22, 102, 109f., 120, 145-146
Lorraine, importance of, 196, 203
Lothair, 187f.
Louis I (the Pious), 171, 183, 187f.
Louis IX, St. (king), 209, 223, 267 280
Louis, son of Louis I, 187f.
Louis (Lewis) the Child, 197
Lubac, Henri de, 28
Lucian, 120
Lucretius, 112
Luke, St., gospel of, 90, 140
Lupus, St., 159, 166
Luther, Martin, 229, 279, 291f.
Lyons, Second Council of, 264, 266

Maccabees, 75, 87
Machiavelli, Niccolo, 277
Macrobius, 232
Magdeburg Centuriators, 173
Magyars, 189, 197, 214
Maimonides, Moses, 236

Maistre, Joseph de, 82
Mandaeism, 104
Mani, 104
Manicheism, 81, 104ff., 151, 221
Marcellinus, Count, 126
Marcion, 81, 104, 148
Marcus Aurelius, 103, 107, 120, 288
Marigny, 277
Mark, St., gospel of, 90
Marozia, 199
Marsh, Adam, 246f.
Martianus Capella, 198, 232
Martin, St., 134, 165f.
Martin, St. (pope and martyr), 255
Martin IV (pope), 267
Martyrs, early Christian cult of, 96ff.
Maximian (emperor), 123
Maximus, St., 255
Mayeul, St., Abbot of Cluny, 199
Medieval society Christian but barbarous, 160ff., 171ff., 279
Melania, St., 127
Memluk Sultanate, 59
Mesopotamia, civilization of, 53
Messianic King and Kingdom, 74ff., 83-86
Michael III (emperor), 258
Michael VII, Palaeologus (emperor), 264, 267
Michael of Anchialus (patriarch), 263
Middle Ages earlier and later contrasted, 271f.
Missi Dominici, 183, 185
Moehler, J. Adam, 29
Mohammed, 58f., 154
Moissac, 217
Monasticism, 132-135, 150, 165f., 168-171, 174, 177, 184ff., 194-198, 202, 206f., 215, 232, 276
    Celtic, 166-168, 174f., 197, 232
    Egyptian, 132f., 150
Mongols destroy Bagdad, 61
Monologion, 234

Monophysitism, 5, 151, 154, 212, 253f.
Monothelitism, 130, 154, 255
Montanism, 283; *see also* Tertullian and Tertullianists
Moses, 70, 72, 81, 243
Motekalim, 235
Munster Revolutionaries, 151
Mysticism, 290-292

Neo-Platonism, 22, 109f., 120, 146f., 186, 239, 242
Nero, 95, 239
Nestorianism, 253
Newman, John Henry Cardinal, 8f., 82
Nicaea, First Council of, 143
  Second Council of, 257
Nicetas of Remesiana, 142f.
Nicholas I, St. (pope), 202, 222f.
Nicholas of Cusa (cardinal), 290
Nietzsche, Friedrich Wilhelm, 27
Ninian, St., 166
Njul Saga, 162
Nominalism, 249
Normandy, Normans, 193f., 215
Notker Balbulus, 198
Notker Labeo, 198
Notaras, Luke, 263
Novatianism, 283
Novellum, the Fifth, 253
  the *Sixth*, 130, 252

Odilo, St., Abbot of Cluny, 195f., 199
Odo, St., Abbot of Cluny, 195f.
Odovacar (king), 157
Old Testament religion; *see* Judaism
Onesimus, 118
Oresme, Nicholas, 250
Origen, 97, 107ff., 145ff., 295f.
Orosius, 174, 192
Oswald, St. (abbot), 196
Otto I (emperor), 197-199, 202

Otto II (emperor), 199
Otto III (emperor), 200
Ottoman Turks, 263, 268f.
Oxford Movement, 8f.
Oxford University, 237, 245f.

Pachomius, St., 132
Paleolithic art, 45
Paley, William, 26
Palladius, 132
Pammachius, 126
Papacy and Western Empire, conflict between, 203ff.
Papacy enslaved by Roman nobility, 199, 202f.
Papal sees in Byzantine Empire annexed by Constantinople, 257
Paris University, 237, 244
Parsis, 60, 62
Pascal, Blaise, 229
Passant, E. G., 208
Patrick, St., 37, 166ff.
Paul, St., 81-90, 118, 126, 140, 148f., 286, 294
Paula, St., 132
Paulicians, 220
Paulinus of Nola, St., 159
Peace of God, 207
Penda (king), 172
Pepin (king), 175, 178ff., 184, 186, 197, 201
Pepin the Younger, 178
Persecution of Christianity by Roman Empire, 95, 123f.
Peter, St., 85, 90
  First Epistle of, 94
Peter the Great (czar), 51
Peter Damian, St., 206, 233, 293
Peter Lombard, 211, 238
Petrarch, Francesco, 269
Pharisees, 76
Philip IV, King of France, 240, 268f.
Philip Neri, St., 289
Philo, 110

Photius (patriarch), 258
Pierre d'Ailly, 249
Piers Plowman, 226, 269, 273
Pietism, German, 291
Pinianus, 127
Plato, 120
Platonic Dialogues, 103
Platonism, Christian, 238f.; *see also*
    Neo-Platonism
Plotinus, 109, 120
Polybius, 55
Polycarp, St., 107
Polynesians, 50
Pomponazzi, Pietro, 231
Pothinus, St. (bishop), 107
Pretenders to Empire, British and
    Gallic, 157
Primitive Church, 90-100, 107-118
Prophetic Religion a variety of mysti-
    cal, 291
Prophets, Jewish, 72f., 78f.
Protestant and Catholic cultures,
    cleavage and encounters, 5-14
Protestantism, Protestants,
    antinomian sects, 151
    Barthian, 22
    contempt for medieval culture, 173
    liberal and neo-orthodox, 20
    not predominantly prophetic, 290f.
    Ritschlians, 144
Prudentius, 142, 158
Psalter in Christian worship, 139f.
Ptolemy (astronomer), 235
Pythagorus, 145

Qumran, 76f., 84

Rabanus Maurus, 185, 198
Rabashi (rabbi), 102
Rabelais, François, 229
Race and culture, 39f.
Ranke, Leopold von, 15
Regula Magistri, 169n.
Reformers, Protestant, 82

Remigius, St., 159, 166
Revelation, 20-24, 67-82, 242, 247,
    294f.
    limits of, 107
Richard of Middleton, 240
Richard of St. Victor, 290
Ricimer, 157
Ritschlians, 144
Robert Capet (the Strong), 194
Robert le Bougre, 222
Roger, King of Sicily, 235
Rolle, Richard, 212, 290
Roman Empire, Western, collapse of,
    155ff.
Rome the first to reject medievalism,
    278
Roscellin, 233, 237
Rousseau, Jean Jacques, 284
Rudolf of Hapsburg (emperor), 267
Rufinus, 109, 132, 134
Russian Christianity, 150
    culture, 53
Russell, Bertrand, 9, 272f.
Rutebeuf, 267
Rutilius Namatianus, 158
Ruysbroek, Blessed John, 290

Sacraments, 292f.
Sadducees, 76
Saint, the Catholic concept of, 15,
    292f.
Saint Denis, 217
St. Gall Abbey, 198
St. Vedast, chronicler of, 190f.
Salerno medical school, 235
Salutati, Collucio, 277, 279
Samson, St., 168
Santeuil, J. B. de, 143
Sapir, 35
Saracens in the South of France, 194
Sardica Edict of Toleration, 118
Savonarola, Girolamo, 213, 289
Scheeben, M. J., 29
Schenouti, 150

Schism, Acacian, 252
  between Eastern and Western
    Churches, 253-265
  completion of in 1054, 259, 261
Scholars, international, in service of
    Carolingian Empire, 185
Scholasticism, 22, 213, 214, 229, 232-
    250
  in Dante, 269ff.
Schools, episcopal, 232f.
Science, revival of, 209, 230f., 235,
    241, 245-248
Sectarianism, 283ff.
Sedulius Scotus, 186
Seneca, 230
Septuagint, 80, 87
Sergines, Jofroi de, 267f.
Sergius, St., 98
Servatus Lupus, 186
Severinus, St., 166
Severus of Antioch, 143
Sidonius Appolinaris, St., 158f.
Siger of Brabant, 240, 244, 267
Sigismund of Radecki, 137
Sinai, Covenant of, 70-74, 78f., 91
Slavery, 116f., 125f.
States of the Church, foundation of,
    181, 201
Stephen, St., 96
Stephen II (pope), 181, 201, 203
Stephen of Tournai, 204 and note
Stilicho, 157
Stoicism, 22, 102, 288
Suarez, Francisco, 241
Subcultures, 61f.
Suetonius, 95
Suger, Abbot, 217
Suhard (cardinal archbishop), 28
Sumeria, 72
Supercultures, 60, 61
Sutton Hoo ship cenotaph, 172 and
    note
Swahili language, 60

Sylvester II (Gerbert of Aurillac),
    200, 232, 235n.
Symmachus, 158
Syriac Christianity, 89, 99, 114, 140-
    153, 155f.

Talmud, 80, 102
Tasmania, indigenous culture of, 54
Tatian, 145
Technology, danger of, 26f.
Te Deum, 142, 147
Telesio Bernardino, 231
Tempier, Archbishop of Paris, 244;
    see also 267
Templars, 207, 268f., 277
Tenth-century breakdown of tem-
    poral and spiritual authority,
    187
Terence, 198
Teresa of Avila, St., 290
Tertullian, 107, 112-145, 233
Tertullianists, 283
Theodora (empress), 199, 253
Theodore of Mopsuestia, 253
Theodore of Studium, 256
Theodoret of Cyrrhus, 102, 147f., 253
Theodoric the Ostrogoth (king),
    169
Theodosius I (emperor), 118, 123,
    157
Theophano (empress), 199
Theophylact, 199
Thomas à Kempis, 212
Thomas Aquinas, Thomism, 231,
    234, 236, 240-245, 267, 270f., 273,
    280, 298
Thomas of York, 240, 246
Three Chapters, The, 130, 253, 255
  Edict, 253
Torture, judicial, 222
Totemism, Australian, 42-45
Toynbee, Dr. Arnold, 288, 296
Tradition, cultural, 49-54

Trench, R. Chevenix (archbishop), 141, 142
Trent, Council of, 279
Troeltsch, Ernst, 19
Troslé, Synod of, its lamentation, 194
Trullo, Council of, 255, 258

Unitarianism, 285
Universities, medieval, 210f., 213, 216, 232, 237f., 276
Upanishad Maitrayana, 105
Urban II (pope and blessed), 205-208, 215, 262

Valens (emperor), 130
Valerian (emperor), 123
Varro, 230
Veccos, John (patriach), 267
Verdun, partition of, 188
Vianney, Jean-Baptiste, St. (Curé d'Ars), 289
Vigilius (pope), 253, 261
Vikings, 53, 189, 190, 193, 214
Vincent of Lérins, St., 165
Virginity, honored in primitive Church, 99
Vittoria, 241
Vives, Juan Luis, 229
Voltaire, François Marie Arouet de, 219, 295
Von Hügel, Baron Friedrich, 291
Vossler, 269
Vulgate, 80

Walafrid Strabo, 185f.
Wesley, John, 292
Westminster Confession, 285
Whitehead, Alfred North, 26, 230
Wildo the Pole, 246
Wilfred, St. (archbishop), 70
William I, King of Sicily, 235
William of Auvergne, 237
William of Conches, 232
William of Gellone, St. (abbot), 195
William of Moerbeke, 246
William of Nogaret, 277
William of Ockham, 249f.
William the Pious (duke), 195
William of St. Cloud, 249
William of Wykeham, 276
Windesheim Abbey, 290
Wolsey, Thomas Cardinal, 277
Word of God and of man, 68
Word of God, 78
World civilization as yet nonexistent, 63
Writing, invention of, 50
Wycliffe, John, 279

Xystus III (pope), 136

Yoruba, 50

Zachary (pope), 179
Zealots, 76
Zeno (emperor), 130, 253
Zeno (philosopher), 145
Zoroastrianism, 62